FAITH SEEKING UNDERSTANDING:
Learning and the Catholic Tradition

*Selected papers from the Symposium
and Convocation celebrating
the Saint Anselm College Centennial*

Edited by:
GEORGE C. BERTHOLD

SAINT ANSELM COLLEGE
PRESS

© Order of Saint Benedict of New Hampshire, 1991
All rights reserved.
Library of Congress Catalog Card Number: 91-061465
ISBN 0-9629547-0-5

Library of Congress Cataloging-in-Publication Data

Faith seeking understanding: learning and the Catholic tradition:
    selected papers from the symposium and convocation
    celebrating the Saint Anselm College centennial.
        p.   cm.
    Includes bibliographical references.
    ISBN 0-9629547-0-5
    1. Catholic Church – Doctrines – Congresses. 2. Theology,
Doctrinal – Congresses. 3. Catholic Church – Education –
Congresses. 4. Faith and reason – Congresses. 5. Anselm, Saint,
Archbishop of Canterbury, 1033-1109 – Congresses. I. Berthold,
George C. (George Charles) II. Saint Anselm College
(Manchester, N.H.)
BX1751.2.F294   1991   91-61465
230'.2 – dc20   CIP

PUBLISHED: BY
Saint Anselm College Press
87 Saint Anselm Drive
Manchester, New Hampshire 03102-1310
USA

Statue of Saint Anselm of Canterbury sculpted
    by Sylvia Nicolas O'Neill

Photograph of statue of Saint Anselm of Canterbury
©1986, Martha Mae Emerson

CONTRIBUTORS

Dom Jean Leclercq, O.S.B., F.B.A., F.R.H.S., is a monk of Clervaux Abbey, Luxembourg.

Professor Charles Kannengiesser is Catherine Huisking Professor of Theology at the University of Notre Dame, Indiana.

Rev. John J. Connelly is Professor of Systematic Theology at St. John's Seminary, Brighton, Massachusetts.

Rev. Sidney H. Griffith, S.T., is Associate Professor of Semetic Languages at The Catholic University of America, Washington, D.C.

Fredrick Van Fleteren is Professor of Philosophy at La Salle University, Philadelphia, Pennsylvania.

Montague Brown is Associate Professor of Philosophy at Saint Anselm College.

Ulrike Wiethaus is Assistant Professor of Religion at Central Michigan University.

Calvin Stapert is Professor of Music at Calvin College.

Thomas J. Jambeck is Associate Professor of English at the University of Connecticut.

Thomas A. Losoncy is Professor of Philosophy at Villanova University.

James M. O'Toole is Assistant Professor of History at the University of Massachusetts—Boston.

Peter J. Cataldo is on the staff of the Pope John XXIII Medical-Moral Research and Education Center, Braintree, Massachusetts.

Rev. Louis Roy, O.P. is Associate Professor of Theology at Boston College.

Rev. Francis J. Murphy is Associate Professor of History at Boston College.

Robert Nicholas Berard is Associate Professor of Education at Dalhousie University.

Vincent J. Capowski is Professor of History at Saint Anselm College.

Robert L. Fastiggi is Associate Professor of Religious Studies at Saint Edward's University.

Kevin M. Staley is Associate Professor of Philosophy at Saint Anselm College.

Richard Law is Professor of English at Kutztown University, Pennsylvania.

Rev. George C. Berthold is Professor of Theology at Saint Anselm College.

Kevin A. McMahon is Assistant Professor of Theology at Saint Anselm College.

Rev. Stephen F. Torraco is Assistant Professor of Theology at Assumption College.

Anthony M. Matteo is Associate Professor of Philosophy at Elizabethtown College.

Beverly Kienzle is Instructor in Latin Studies at Harvard Divinity School.

CONTENTS

INTRODUCTION

The papers presented in this volume were delivered at a symposium of the same title held in observance of the Saint Anselm
College centennial April 20-23, 1989. They represent a selection of
the seventy-four addresses delivered there on all aspects of Catholic
education. The centennial celebration was climaxed with the
awarding of the first Saint Anselm Medal to Father Jean Leclercq,
O.S.B., renowned scholar of the Abbey of Clervaux, whose address
is printed in this collection.

Learning is at the very heart of the Christian commitment and
challenge. The apostles received from their risen Lord the command to "Go, teach all nations" (Mt. 28:29). In the spirit of St.
Thomas Aquinas' advice *contemplata aliis tradere* (S.T. II-II,
188,6), this volume is offered as a series of reflections on learning
and the Catholic tradition at a signal moment in the history of this
College as it remembers the past, grapples with the present, and
launches hopefully into the future.

A centennial milestone presents a college with a twofold opportunity. First, it invites us to look back with gratitude, pride, and
even nostalgia over the accomplishments of the past one hundred
years. Second, it challenges the institution to redefine itself and to
reshape its goals, to renew its dedication if its purpose is noble. The
founders of Saint Anselm College, Bishop Denis Bradley of Manchester and Abbot Hilary Pfraengle, O.S.B., envisioned the school
as fitting into the centuries-old tradition of Benedictine education.
In full appreciation of the complexity of human striving this tradition has always sought to meet the needs of men and women on
the level of the mind, will, and heart. Thus a pursuit of intellectual
excellence will go hand in hand with a training in character and moral
sensitivity. Moreover, this education will be marked by an awakening
of the heart to the transforming call God has addressed to his people.

1

Learning of the wonders of nature is meant to lead to learning of the wonders of revelation. The dialogue with nature invites us to a living dialectic with the God of nature, who joined himself to it in incarnate love. God has spoken humanly in order that we may speak divinely. The Catholic tradition of learning grounds itself on this bold faith that God "has first loved us" (1 Jn. 4:19). Beyond the realm of human comprehension we seek nevertheless to comprehend this truth of the supernatural order in a faith ever in search of understanding. Or rather, we live it.

At the heart of this College, both architecturally and symbolically, is the Abbey Church where day and night the praises of God are sung and the eucharist celebrated by the monastic and educational community. This dialectic with God is the basis of the Christian challenge to go out and "renew the face of the earth" (Ps. 104:30). A century of alumni have been commissioned to carry out this task. May this College be impelled by Christ's love to continue and deepen its transforming mission.

I wish to express my thanks to the many people whose support has made this volume possible. First, the original symposium committee provided help in selecting and organizing the papers delivered at the conference. Next, Dr. Elona Lucas and Dr. James O'Rourke responded generously and competently to my requests for advice on editorial matters. Brother Malachy McCarthy, O.S.B. and James Morrison were supportive of this project and invaluable in offering practical aid in its realization. The publication of this book has been made possible through a generous gift of Esther Routhier of Amesbury, Mass. as well as one from the Charlpeg Foundation, Inc. Mrs. Jane Daly has been with this undertaking from its inception. I have relied on her for secretarial and other help and she has provided it with unflagging enthusiasm. Finally, I want to thank all those scholars who responded to our appeals for papers, especially those appearing in this volume. They have helped us to celebrate the Saint Anselm College centennial in a worthy and memorable way.

In the division of this volume a separate section could well have been devoted to Saint Anselm, as in the original symposium. But it soon appeared clear that his influence was more pervasive than to be confined within the limits of a single section. After nine centuries the light of his learning and influence still burns brightly. As he touched every age from his own onwards to the present, so does he find a place in each of the sections of this volume. Its title, as we hope its spirit, is his.

G.C.B.

PART ONE

———

Plenary Papers

FAITH SEEKING UNDERSTANDING THROUGH IMAGES

Dom Jean Leclercq, O.S.B.

The choice of this topic results from the convergence of two major concerns: an interest in medieval monastic culture and the ever-increasing attention being given to one of the most outstanding phenomena of present day culture, the influence of the mass media. Both these great cultural trends use a language with common characteristics even though it is often applied to different realities and for purposes which can sometimes be antagonistic.

The language used by mass media, especially audio-visual techniques and others, is above all symbolical: it makes a spectacle of thought. Contrary to conceptual language, it includes the body, sensations, emotions, images. It is narrative. And since there is a mixing of images perceived with the eyes and sounds picked up by the ears, an important part is given to music and the sound quality of words, sentences and slogans.

These facts have an impact on catechesis and pastoral teaching: it is no longer possible to teach religion by holding forth on ideas. We now have to narrate.[1] And any intellectual, abstract expression of thought takes second place behind symbolical expression. There is no need here to follow in the wake of MacLuhan and others and repeat the historical reasons for which in religion conceptual language took the lead over symbolical language. But the fact is that today images and sounds dominate, and this new way of understanding, transmitting facts and getting people to grasp them, opens up new avenues of approach to the things of the mind.[2]

The truth is that for a long time in the religious tradition symbolical, narrative, effective, aesthetic, and sound elements were primary. The Bible is a history book and a book of images. Even the so-called wisdom books include the Parables of Solomon. And in

5

the teaching of Jesus, the parables are as important as his discourses. These too are sprinkled with stories.[3] This tradition of using symbols is a constant in early, patristic, monastic Christian literature. We have examples from the second century collection of the *Parabolai* — in Latin, the *Similitudines* — of the *Shepherd of Hermas*, and other examples up through the centuries to the twelfth with St. Bernard's series of *Parables*, along with those of Galland of Reigny and other writers.[4] Often, all that has been remembered of the writings of the authors in this long stretch of time are the doctrinal works belonging to the category of learned literature. But besides these scholarly writings there were also, especially among the greatest — St. Augustine and St. Bernard, for example — more popular writings which merit greater attention than they have so far enjoyed. I will not here draw up a programme of research work to be done in this field. But in all this patristic and monastic literature an important place is given to three elements which are characteristic of present-day mass media language: language, emotions, the specific musical quality linked with the rhythm of phrases and which are so often smattered with those plays on sound and sense called paranomasia.

Here I shall be using parabolic vocabulary in the sense it has had throughout the profane and the religious literary tradition the essentials of which were summed up by Erasmus in the days of humanism when he wrote in the Prologue of his *Parabolae vel similia* (Ed. Paris 1649, p. 2-3): *Nihil autem aliud est parabole quam Cicero collationem vocat, quam explicata metaphora.* The Parable, which Cicero calls a comparison, is just an explained metaphor. He says: "Reading the philosophers, I understand that metaphors not only give brilliance to language, but account for practically the entire dignity of the discourse. *Et intelligerem non nitorem modo, sed universam prope sermonis dignitatem a metaphoris proficisci....*" Among the writings of Aristotle, Pliny, Plutarch, Cicero, Xenophon, Demosthenes and Theophrastus, Erasmus compiles a volume with a selection of pearls of this kind. Each one has a phrase with two members: "Just as... *ut*..., So..., *sic*..." These are no ordinary gems, he says. It is not surprising that Jesus and Solomon coined some. The use of parables is one of the characteristics common to both profane and sacred literature: "Deprive orators of the decoration of metaphors and all is lost. Take the parables out of the prophetic books and the gospels and you will deprive them of a great part of their charm: *Tolle metaphorae supellectili ex oratoribus, ieiuna erunt omnia. Tolle parabolae a propheticis et evangelicis litteris, magnam gratiae partem detraxeris."* There are parables in the liturgy too, for example in the Collect for the feast of the Presentation of Jesus in the Temple (Feb. 2) where we read *Ut sicut...ita....* The entire ceremony of this feast and the texts which explain it make up one great parable.

Now, what about St. Anselm? Did he use parables? The question is a good one and could furnish subject matter for some quite new studies. Anselm practiced several literary genres: he wrote treatises, dialogues, short or long letters, meditations, prayers. One of the sermons he preached was preserved in different forms before finally being drafted as a treatise, *De beatitudine*.[5] Furthermore, Eadmer, Anselm's disciple, collected a series of spiritual talks which his abbot gave to the monks. The title of the collection is *Liber similitudinum*.[6] This last word translates the Greek *parabola*. Both terms had already been used equivalently in the Latin version of the Gospels, for example in the Vulgate, in Luke 21:29: *Dixit illis similitudinem: videte ficulneam.* In fact, the *Liber similitudinum* is made up of an alternation of sometimes very subtle talks on subjects which are also dealt with in the *Treatises* — for example, the will, free choice, the faculties of the soul — and real parables, moralising fables, stories invented for the purpose of illustrating truths. The subtleness of these tales sometimes goes as far as to propose complex distinctions. For example, there are many kinds of pride: simple, double, triple or quadruple pride. And twenty-eight kinds of curiosity, and so on. From the very first page, after having stated the "three meanings of the word will," the title Anselm gives to Chapter II is "Will compared to a woman: the will, as a power, is set between God and the devil like a woman between her lawful husband and another man...." Then follow dozens of short stories with titles like: the mill, the dog, fire, wind, the knife, freestone, wax, the hare, the little bird. The entire setting of human existence is evoked, and also every social category: the mistress, serving maids, the architect, the doctor, the woodcutter, the soldier and the cellarer of a monastery. It is all very concrete, easy to grasp and often amusing.

One wonders whether Anselm resorts to the imaginary in his treatises. It seems that in these it is mainly the reasonings which have been examined, and they are sometimes very subtle and abstract. In this paper I shall be looking only into the treatises, to the exclusion of Anselm's other works, to see whether the imagination has some part to play. And if so, what is this role? Particularly in the form it takes in the parables and other comparisons. In the treatises the word *similitudo* has three meanings.[7] It is the first applied to the relation of equality between the Son and the Father, and it has even been said that it is the "key word" of Anselm's teaching on the Trinity.[8] It is also used in connection with the ability, even the necessity, which man has to create images as well as words in order to be able to think thoughts. And finally, *similitudo* has the traditional Gospel meaning of parable or comparison. For, though the word itself may not always be used, we find the imaginary in Anselm's treatises in the form of parables and many comparisons which he develops more or less according to the case.

Here, for example, is a typical parable in the *Cur Deus homo* (II, 16, t.II, p.118): "A king against whom the whole population of the city, except for one man, has so greatly sinned...." And about ten lines further on we read: "According to this parable...." Then follows the interpretation in which the different parts of the story are applied to the mystery of the redemption. In this way the imaginary is enlisted in order to illustrate and clarify the idea being expounded, thus making it easier to understand.

The longest analogy used by Anselm is the parable of the river Nile, inspired by a few lines of St. Augustine, after Tertullian.[9] It is used in connection with the Trinity in the treatise *De incarnatione Verbi* (c. 13, t.II, p.31-33) and takes up three pages. Having set out the speculative principle of any impossibility existing in God (31, 3-8), Anselm brings in a series of images, prefacing them with his declared intention: "However, let us see whether we can, to a certain extent, find in creatures what we deny in God." The parable begins with the word *Ponamus...* Let us suppose..., which means let us frame a hypothesis, namely: "Let us suppose there is a source from which rises a stream flowing into a lake, and called the Nile." Then the three elements of the allegory are taken up again and applied to the distinction between the three divine Persons who, though Three, are the one and self-same God. And as though that did not suffice for his demonstration, Anselm makes an important statement: "I also want to say something which, though very dissimilar, has even so some similitude with the Incarnation." Here, the wordplay opposing *dissimilitudinem* and *similitudinem* insinuates that even what seems to be very different can also be a valid parable. And he goes on to bring in another image, that of the channel, *fistula*. Does this manner of speaking seem to be unworthy of such a high mystery? Anselm foresees the objection and staves it off: "Though perhaps some reader might despise this, I am going to say it even so, because if someone else said it, I myself certainly would not despise it. Supposing indeed, that a stream runs through a channel from the source to the Nile...." We see there how great is the esteem which Anselm, so well-versed in metaphysics, has for such concrete comparisons. And in fact, in the treatise *De processione Spiritus Sancti* (9, t.II, p.203-205) he comes back to the analogy offered by the source, stream and lake and adds new variations: "In the fountain welling up from the abyss, the water is seething; in the lake it is collected and still...." The conclusion? "So, just as the lake...so the Holy Spirit."

In one of Anselm's most speculative writings, the *De concordia praescientiae et praedestinationis et gratiae Dei cum libero arbitrio*, (III,9, t.II, p.277-278), we have the parable of a servant who is punished by his master: "If someone had a servant whom he intended to make rich one day with great honors, and had just struck him roughly for a serious fault...." Every element of this parable is then recalled in almost a whole page of text: the prison, wounds and sufferings, correction, the heavy blows which make him ill, then reconciliation. The moral behind the story? "So it is between God and man." First came sin, then forgiveness.

Elsewhere in the same treatise, four pages (III, 6 p.270-273) are given over to the vocabulary of agriculture applied to the activities of the will: the earth, plants, trees, food, labour, culture, seed, germination; all that, applied to spiritual activities is part of what St. Paul calls God's tillage (1 Cor 3:9). Then other words of the same category and in the same context — to plant, water and give increase — are used and applied to the work of evangelization and linked to more images: the nutriment of souls, the food for the body, fertilization of the soil. Then Anselm goes into more detail: "Now let us see by means of examples, how the word is the seed...." And he goes on interpreting agricultural comparisons in connection with what God, by his "agricultures," accomplishes in the earth of our heart.

Quite obviously Anselm took pleasure in using these long parables. He also has some shorter but no less meaningful ones. One such is presented as an "example," in connection with the will and free choice: "Now let us imagine an example in which this is clear."

Here the analogy is taken from psychological activities: "A man has it at heart to say nothing but the truth.... But now he meets another who threatens to kill him if he does not tell a lie.... So we see there...," (*De concordia*, I, 6-7, t.II, p.257). In the treatise *Cur Deus homo* (II, 8, t.II, p.104) Anselm uses the vocabulary of painting: three times he uses the word "Paint...*pinge*". But a painting can only be done on solid material and not on clouds. Boso, the partner in the dialogue, cannot help exclaiming: "These paintings are very beautiful and rational!" Before this (3-4, p.51-52) Anselm shows in what order an argument should be unfolded in order to be credible for unbelievers: first, "show the reliability of the truth" then in order that the main body of truth shine out more brightly, set out the suitability of the reasons which are to be the paintings of the body.

Often, though the words "example" or "painting" may not be used, the very construction of the sentences makes us realize that we are going to read imagined comparisons: "Just as... *quemadmodum* or *sicut*...so, *ita*...." The terms of the comparison are sometimes borrowed from realities belonging to the material order of things, like hot and cold (*De concordia*, III, 13, t.II, p.215,22), white wood (*Ibid.*, I,2, p.249,14), the wind coming through an open window and blowing out a lamp (*Cur Deus homo*, 9, t.II, p.64, 3-6). Other terms are borrowed from realities which are inside us, for example the tongue, sight, or outside us, such as the stylet, the axe (*De concordia*, II, t.II, p.224, 1-6). In other places the image used is one of human behaviour, for example the way a blind man reacts to light (*De processione Spiritus Sancti*, 2, t.II, p.188, 28-30), or the reactions of a man suffering for a good cause (*Cur Deus homo*, I, 10, t.II, p.15, 19-25), or the joy we usually feel when we celebrate the feast of the saints (*Ibid.*, I, 18, t.II, p.80, 2-10), or a promise which we swear to keep on the following day (*Ibid.*, II, 5, t.II, 5-9). There is also the image of a wild animal which has broken loose from its chains, or a sailor who lets go of the rudder in a stormy sea (*De conceptu virginali et de originali peccato*, 5, t.II, p.146, 8-11). Or again, Anselm uses the image of a river to be crossed on horseback or by boat, or the fact of eating nothing before celebrating Mass (*Cur Deus homo*, 9, t.II, p.63, 2-9).

As we see, the scale of comparisons is quite varied. How do these images operate in man's psychology and in the process by which faith seeks understanding? That is a question on which Anselm has a whole theory set out in the *Monologion* (9–12, t.I, p.24–26). The important thing for our purpose here was simply to observe some literary and linguistic facts: they oblige us to note that the imagination has a major part to play in thought and that doctrinal explanations are of a different order of research. It will be enough here to point out that before a rational concept can be formed it is necessarily preceded, so to speak, by an example (*quasi exemplum*) of the thing itself or, more aptly (*sive aptius*) of its form, its similitude or its pattern (24, 12–13). Before we can "say" things, they have to exist inside us, so to speak, "either by our imagination of the bodies, or by our understanding of the reason" (25, 1–3). And it is this similitude (*similitudo*) which is formulated by the thinking mind (25, 20–21). And it can only be communicated by means of a parable, an instrument used by a workman (*faber*) by "word or in painting to embody an animal such as has never been seen before" (26, 5–23). Further on Anselm again mentions these similitudes and images (*similitudines et imagines*, 31, p.48,16) of what is depicted (*in picto*, 49,2). Later he links this vocabulary to the words enigma and mirror (*per aenigmata...*, *in speculo...*, 65,p.76).

* * *

St. Anselm uses a vocabulary connected with the imaginary: he proposes a doctrine of the imagination. Have the analysts of his teaching always given to this aspect of his work all the attention it deserves? It would seem useful at least to ask the question. Certainly, in his works, we find a language and a way of thinking dependent on highly metaphysical reasoning, one which is sometimes so speculative, abstract, subtle and refined that we could go on scrutinizing it forever. But his texts also make it evident that he appealed to the imagination, his own and that of his readers. Now, does this mean that he had two languages, or did he always use the same one? His comparisons and his parables fit perfectly into the fabric of the most speculative treatises. Such a fact can only derive, surely, from a single and deep reality: Anselm was a unified man. There was only one Anselm in whom metaphysical genius allied itself harmoniously with the most authentic legacy of biblical, patristic and monastic culture.

We find in Anselm's writings not only visual images, but sound images too and both categories are moving, transformational. Allusion has already been made to one of the great qualities of Anselm's literary production: beauty. The aesthetic quality of his elocution comes from its musicality. This has already been pointed out.[10] However, his plays on sound and sense — the paronomasia — the rhythm of his phrases merit the same esteem as the writings of St. Augustine and St. Bernard and should be more fully admired and exploited.

NOTES

1. So it is that we are now hearing talk today of a theology and a catechesis which is "narrative," and even a "narrative Church," as in the title of a recent work *Erzahlter Glaube—erzähltende Kirche*, ed. Rolf Zerfass (Herder, 1988): and in the articles of the collective work *La narration, Quand le récit devient communication*, ed. P. Buhler and J. F. Habermacher (Geneva, 988).

2. Pierre Babin, *L'ère de la communication. Réflexion chrétienne* (Paris, 1986).

3. J. F. Habermacher, "Jesus conteur d'histoires. La narration dans les paraboles," in *Semiotique et Bible*, 45 (March 1987) 4-14. Numbers 45-48 of this review contain a series of articles on the parables in the New Testament.

4. This question will be the subject of a publication of which a first draft was printed in *L'Osservatore Romano* (7 May 1988), 3.

5. I have described the first draft of this text, found in a manuscript, under the title "Sur la transmission d'un opuscule anselmien," in *Studi storici*, Fasc. 188-192. *Cultura e societa nell'Italia medievale. Studi per Paolo Brezzi* (Rome, 1988), 449.

6. Ed. P.L., 159, 605-708. French translation: *Entretiens spirituels (De Similitudinibus) de St. Anselme*, by the nuns of the Monastery of Ste Croix de Poitiers, Lille-Paris 1924, with an excellent introduction, i-xxxix. I have described this work in "Les Similitudines anselmiane, testimoni della littera monastica popolare," in *Anselmo di Aosta*, (Milan, 1988). In the most recent edition of the *Life of St. Anselm* by John of Salisbury (*Giovanni di Salisbury, Vita di Anselm d'Aosta*), ed. Inos Biffi, (Milan, 1988), rapprochements are pointed out between this text and the *De similitudinibus*. This work and the collection of letters are the one most frequently used in the *Vita* written in 1163 at the request of Thomas Becket, in view of the canonization of Anselm. Cf. the index of citations, 143 and the chronology, 137.

7. The texts are indicated in *St. Anselmi Opera*, ed. F.S. Schmitt, vol. VI (Edinburgh 1961), 336-338.

8. The expression is used by H. Kohlenberger, "Konsequensen und Inkonsequensen der Trinitätslehre in Anselms Monologion," in *Journées internationales d'étude*. "St. Anselme, ses predecesseurs et ses contemporains," ed. Helmut Kohlenberger (Aosta-Turin, 1973) in *Societé académique, religieuse et scientifique de l'ancien Duché d'Aoste*, 47 (Rome, 1974-1975), 177.

9. Texts in *St. Anselmi Opera*, ed. F. S. Schmitt, vol. II, (Rome, 1940), 32.

10. R. Berlinger, "*Zur Sprachmetaphysik des Anselms von Canterbury. Eine spekulative Explication*," in *Journées internationales* (see note 8 above, 110).

SCRIPTURE INTERPRETED: THE DEFINITION OF CATHOLIC THEOLOGY

Charles Kannengiesser

Our faith seeks understanding today at least as much as in St. Anselm's day, if not in the same culture or the same mind-set. For Anselm, the rational consistency of his Catholic faith was a matter of silent contemplation and logical rigor. The true issue of his mystic quest as a Christian believer was to reach by strict abstraction the best definition possible of his notion of God. A well-established monastic tradition nurtured that notion in him with a daily reading of Scripture and the Fathers. What Anselm needed was to translate adequately the traditional notion of divinity into the rational categories of his time. That he succeeded in such a conversion of the Christian mind is precisely the occasion of our present gathering. I would like to imagine that the best tribute we might be able to pay to St. Anselm's paradigmatic figure would be to share for a few moments our concerns about the conversion of the Christian mind in *our* time.

I

Precisely, our time seems to call on us for a conversion of the *mind*, more than for any other kind of conversion. Our Christian engagements display a striking variety of tasks and purposes, some being more directly educational, others turned to social services, and some keeping us inside our familiar communities, whereas others push us into unknown territories. But, practical or theoretical, individual or collective as they may be today, our Christian engagements impose on us to convert our minds, to seek a new understanding for basic convictions of our faith. When Pope John convoked the council of Vatican II, he stressed the need for rethinking the very foundations of our whole religious tradition. He made a clear distinction between scholastic problems, to be debated by professional theologians in the framework of their theoretical systems, and open questions arising from the church as a living reality in the modern world. The council itself addressed these latter questions. A quarter of a century later, we still find ourselves addressing them. Thus Pope John's intuition continues to regulate the present quest of our faith for a renewed self-understanding as members of the church.

You know well the typically Catholic questions about social justice, peace in the world, women in the church, or about the Catholic responses to current challenges in ethical issues. You know also those broader questions about massive hunger and irresponsible pollution on our planet. Much closer to daily life in our Roman church, how could we ignore all the urgent questions about clerical celibacy, or about the immediate survival of so many forms of religious life, created during the nineteenth century and before that. To such questions you would certainly have more answers than we could collect in the next hour, and the media never tire of reminding us of them. I would rather try to discuss with you another kind of question, also addressed to the church as a whole today, which brings us closer to St. Anselm's paradigmatic initiative. Listening to the contemplative silence behind the Anselmian discourse, one cannot miss hearing the many readings in Scripture and the Fathers which nourished Anselm's thought and which are echoed by each page of his writings. The ultimate goal of this courageous intellectual in the church of the twelfth century was indeed to make Scripture credible with the logical inventiveness of his time. God, as addressed in the *Proslogion*, is undoubtedly the God of Israel's ancient prophets and the God of the psalms. This God is undoubtedly divine Trinity, as revealed in the gospels. Amazingly enough, St. Anselm inaugurated a strictly speculative and systematic kind of theology which seemed to betray the monastic tradition of the *lectio divina* and of its paraphrases. He even introduced such a deep shift in the cultural trends to which he belonged that the history of European thought would be changed forever.

Here then is our question of today, already positioned as decisive for the whole future of Western Christianity: what are we going to do with the Bible in the present state of our changing civilization? In other words: which kind of an interpretive rationality should we apply today in our contemplation of Scripture, if we intend to participate actively in the current history of Christian thought? In Anselm's case, it was a necessity of thoroughly rethinking classical theistic metaphysics. It was sort of a new beginning which had to be conceived in the continuity of an age-long cultural tradition. With a Latin grammar of language and of thought, St. Anselm gives a new voice, which is Christian, to Greek and Roman thinkers from centuries before Christ; and he takes over St. Augustine's theological lyrics into the more sober framework of his own reasoning. Our interpretive rationality near the end of the twentieth century is no longer the same as it was in Europe at the beginning of the twelfth century. Strangely enough, our need of today, in regard to a reassessment of the Biblical message about God, does not seem to focus on the notion of God as such. It has more to do with God's incarnation in history. We are more concerned about Christ in our daily experience than about Trinity contemplated for itself. Our mind-set is less open to theistic and classical metaphysics than it was in St. Anselm's intellectual awareness. Our talk about God, even when taking a more ontological turn, remains permeated by the historical consciousness characteristic of our time. More than that, God, today, can no longer be understood by our faith in need of reason without admitting, be it unwillingly, God's absence, or God's death, in the main trends of modern rationality. Christian faith, seeking today for a consistent understanding, faces a *collapse*, rather than a *continuity*, of the philosophical foundations of Antiquity on which St. Anselm relied in such an inventive way.

Therefore the interpretive task of giving Scripture a new relevance for future generations no longer follows the logic of the Anselmian paradigm. It rather defines itself more empirically in the light of the present situation in the church. For over two hundred years, Protestant and Catholic theologians have opposed the rationalistic aggression of the Enlightenment. With remarkable success, Christian exegesis has faced the challenges of enlightened critics denying the Bible's credibility. Generations of exegetes scrutinized the letter of the Hebrew Bible as well as of its Greek counterpart, the Septuagint. Innumerable methodological insights have been experimented with for interpreting the Old Testament as well as the New. Countless essays line up on the shelves of our libraries, explaining where Holy Writ comes from, or more often where it does *not* come from. Jewish scholars joined their Christian colleagues in the scientific exploration of the Bible, including the New Testament. In short, let us acclaim the enormous amount of critical work done by Biblical scholars since the eighteenth century and let us also recognize that the collective *lectio critica* of Scripture during the past three centuries, as in a new kind of early middle ages, call for its Anselm, just as the earliest centuries of western *lectio divina* call for their systematic interpreter, capable of leading them towards a new theological appropriation of Scripture, unheard of in the church, but nevertheless providential.

We have to appropriate theologically the scientific evidence resulting from centuries of *lectio critica* in Biblical matters. God's message is no longer given over to us through the categories of a Greco-Roman humanism hungry for divine transcendency, as Anselm and all the intellectual leaders in the classical tradition of Christianity enjoyed it. God's message is in fact the Spirit of God addressing the church of today in the actual fulfillment of divine salvation. The Spirit of God always liberates believers, as the apostle Paul states it. The Spirit opens their minds in making them available for a new understanding of their deepest convictions. Today, God's revelation in Scripture is mediated to us through the critical conclusions of a scientific exegesis, more than through anything else. Here is the test through which our generations of believers are going to be authenticated by the liberating Spirit of God.

Which test? Which conclusions? And what consistent theological vision, no longer Anselmian, can we expect from such a critical passage through history in our own future?

II

Before preparing answers to these questions, let me grasp some wisdom from the past experience of the church.

When the Christian communities found themselves united by a same "apostolic tradition," as they called it from the end of the second century, they were engaged in a dangerous struggle against gnostic sectarians. For those Christian communities, the main issue, the test of their vital self-identification, was the Bible. Gnostic theologians, Christian and non-Christian alike, were at that time one in their rejection of the Hebrew Bible. The apostolic churches canonized the Hebrew Bible as their Old Testament, and Irenaeus of Lyons, the anticipator of St. Anselm in that generation of the church, demonstrated convincingly that the same God operates on our behalf through both testaments.

In third century Alexandria the Christian tradition matured enough to assume the full heritage of Plato and Aristotle. That heritage was transmitted through flourishing schools of pagan theology linked with Stoic cosmology and psychology. Origen of Alexandria, who exhibits an Anselmian importance for the third century, succeeded in building up a Christian synthesis out of the classical heritage of Hellenism. Origen conceived a synthesis of Christian doctrines and beliefs, in dedicating the full passion of his intellectual energies to the study of the Bible. Being at once the founder of systematic Christian dogmatics and of a global exegesis of Scripture, Origen, once more, illustrated the fact that only when Scripture as a whole is interpreted in a unified and consistent way can the Spirit of both Testaments speak to the church and engage her in a new creative self-awareness.

Unpredictable as history always is, the fourth century became the century of St. Athanasius. In his life-long duel with the imperial administration to secure the inner freedom of his Alexandrian church in theological matters, Athanasius applied such a powerful strategy that modern historians felt compelled to stamp him as a man essentially hungry for power. Such a prejudice led historiography into a dead-end, so much so that not one single biography of Athanasius has been published for over a century. The truth is, as many critics have observed, that Bishop Athanasius is characterized, in his passionate dedication to the Alexandrian church, as a genuinely original interpreter of Scripture. He did for the new generation of Constantinian Christianity what Anselm did for generations of students: Athanasius concentrated into a few hermeneutical principles the substance of the kind of *lectio divina* traditional in his church, namely, the Origenian interpretation of Scripture. He centered his broad vision of Christian salvation on God's incarnation, and focused on the actuality of that divine incarnation in the daily life of the church community: a vision which opened a new perspective for Christian faith itself, and inaugurated a new self-understanding in the church at large, that was unheard of in the Origenian tradition before Athanasius.

Augustine of Hippo's contribution to the whole of western Christianity was to offer a new interpretive approach to Scripture which created a consensus among believers from the fifth to, at least, the eighteenth century. In calling on his personal experiences Augustine used the human self, with its needs and its deepest expectations, as a key for reaching the true meaning of Holy Writ. At each crucial shift inside that long-lasting tradition, be it with Anselm of Canterbury or with Martin Luther, the Augustinian model of interpretation played a decisive role.

I should also underline the hermeneutical relevance of the councils and of the major magisterial decisions in the church of the Fathers and in medieval Christianity. It would be easy to show that all these institutional events in the history of Christian thought contributed to fix a dogmatic interpretation of Scripture, and that, reciprocally, Scripture was always the touchstone of magisterial orthodoxy. You would not need me to persuade you about that. What we all need as Catholic believers is to become aware of the truly formidable test of a new kind imposed on the church *now*, in the post-modern age, when the essential objections of the Enlightenment have been successfully overcome by the scientific study of the Bible, and when the whole people of God in the church call for a new theological appropriation of the Bible, responding to the real spiritual needs of humankind today.

Having learned from our Christian past that the active reception of Scripture has always been the keystone of a consistent doctrine and that the cultural, mystical and rational assimilation of the biblical revelation has been, from century to century, at the core of any creative stage in the Catholic tradition, it is quite plausible that, in our days also, what the church needs, more than anything else, is what I would define as a new theological appropriation of the Bible.

Let us just position ourselves more explicitly in the church and the world of today, to come closer to the very challenging future opened for Christian believers by that new and much needed scriptural awareness.

In the church and the world we are positioned four centuries after the time of the Reformation and the start of western Modernity. St. Anselm lived four centuries after the Carolingian restoration. The collapse of the Roman empire created a cultural discontinuity in Anselm's past, just as the rupture of Christian unity and the confessional warfare have created a cultural discontinuity in our own tradition. But the form of scholarship sponsored by Alcuin, who was one of Charlemagne's advisors, fructified through the centuries until Anselm brought it to its decisive blossoming. Equally, the founding initiatives of Luther and Loyola, at the time when modernity was born, developed their mystic potentialities in the most spectacular way through four centuries, each of these initiatives claiming to bring the whole church back to the gospel. Had Luther and Loyola worked hand-in-hand, instead of polarizing two antagonistic understandings of the church, history would have taken another course, and being today a Christian in western Christianity would mean something quite different. But as Christians, though belonging to separate bodies of believers, we are together turned toward the same kingdom of God to come, and the gospel is our central reference for any of our self-definitions as believers.

Modern theological scholarshp in the church was made possible thanks to the new institutions based on the creative insights of Luther and Loyola. The extraordinary amount of scriptural studies, to which I alluded earlier, is precisely an outgrowth of both of their allegiances to the spirit of Modernity. As always in such processes of acculturation, a double effect was inevitable. In engaging their effort into the secular structures of modern science, Protestant and Catholic theologians adopted new criteria and new methods; they fixed for themselves a new rational quest. In doing so they shared the common standards of secular culture in Modernity. At the same time, as the new western society was heading toward democracy, the new western awareness of history, as belonging to the very nature of human societies, began to impinge upon theological issues. The church itself was more and more understood in theological categories embedded in that process. Theology as such became a theology of history, of God's acting in history, of the church as the actual witness of God's acting in history. Secular historical criticism, becoming theological, determined increasingly the course of biblical studies, and gave up old-fashioned apologetics and antiquated forms of a priori supernaturalism.

At the same time there was a spectacular awakening in the western churches. After the many revivals and devotional innovations of the nineteenth century came the militant movements of the twentieth against social and racial segregations, in favor of peace, or against the nuclear madness. In the Roman Catholic church in particular, the so-called institutionalized Catholic Action from the thirties on, combined with renewed biblical studies and with a dynamic liturgical movement, culminated in the celebration of the Second Vatican Council from 1962 to 1965. Catholic theology became more and more a discussion of God's incarnation in history as made visible and proclaimed in the church of today.

There is our test. There is the ultimate challenge, taking the proportions of a crisis deeper in our current debates than it ever was in Luther's tormented consciousness: what are we really speaking about when we refer to God's incarnation in history? What has Christian faith to do with history? As Karl Barth stated loudly in the twenties, history is at most a predicate of the divine incarnation, but the incarnation of God can never be regulated by history. That statement gave Barth enough space for a few thousand pages of his *Church Dogmatics*. Rather for us it illustrates the need to learn how to interpret in a non-a priori way the essential links between history and divine incarnation.

If I am correct, there is only one way to fulfill that task, which would not be a priori or dogmatic: it is to contemplate the gospel. All the paradigmatic leaders in the history of Christian thought did it. They were pastoral and social, they were true to their traditions, creative in their contemporary culture, filled with a vision of their fellow-believers' future, be they the canonical gospel writers, or Irenaeus and Origen, Athanasius and Augustine, Anselm and Luther. All of them contemplated the gospel narratives, and reached a genuine understanding of the gospel event, before they engaged in any paradigmatic initiative for the benefit of their churches. They are vivid landmarks for the ongoing journey of Christian believers.

But why then should our present contemplation of the gospel become such an awesome task? Why couldn't we add just some variations to the symphonic performances of so many outstanding contemplators of the gospels in our past traditions? My answer may sound strange: because, at last, we know who Jesus was. Never has any Christian generation, before ours, absorbed such a mass of information in biblical matters. Therefore, we can no longer content ourselves with paraphrases of Scripture, or with moral allegories applying scripture to our own situations. We no longer belong to a school of thought in which Christian beliefs rest on scriptural statements as literally divine. We have to explain any book or sentence of the Bible in its own context, as produced in a given language, and we must determine the peculiar setting of the local culture out of which it originated. That was already the solemn prescription of Pius XII in his encyclical *Divino Afflante Spiritu* on Catholic exegesis. The central message of the gospel about God incarnate is now really received as what it claimed to be, a message in which anonymous believers, far behind our oldest written sources, speak to other believers. Their message is mediated through the literary legacy of the gospel narratives. The first believers had not the slightest idea of such a mediation. Therefore their message needs to be carefully decoded, because of a surprising amount of older beliefs and of traditional sayings, still known to the gospel-writers, or transmitted to them by popular traditions. It also contains many allusions to experiences and realities of their contemporaries. Thus we hear in Scripture a multitude of authentically human voices. Throughout the ages the Spirit of God addresses the church through them, but they themselves remain rooted in the world in which they were produced, just as we are a product of our time.

The challenge then for us, as Catholic theologians and believers, is to face the full evidence of our whole religious tradition as deriving from an episode in the general religious history of humankind, which is well documented and which we should never tire of scrutinizing. The challenge is to refuse, in the light of that evidence, any rationalistic reduction of the gospel-event, as if God's revelation, properly linked with it, could be replaced by our scientific analysis of it. The challenge is to admit that, as God is revealed to us in no other way but through the contingencies of our present world, so does God deliver for us the gospel message in nothing else but in a contingent human experience and in an unpredictable circumstance. Finally, the challenge is to discover, through the conversion of our mind in faith, what Christian faith, born out of the gospel-event, really means.

Should I be bold enough, and tell you now what Christian faith really means? Is it not the first duty of any Christian theologian to explicate the meaning of his or her faith? Christian faith means a personal re-enactment of the gospel-event. What I call an "event" is really a whole sequence of events. Numerous people are included in it, with Jesus remaining the central figure. Complex as it was in its physical happening, the gospel-event keeps a unique and simple relevance: it is an interpretive event. Its divine nature is quintessentially hermeneutical. Nothing belongs to the event that was not understood as happening "according to the scriptures," *secundum scripturas.* Above all, the death and the resurrection of Jesus were witnessed, from the start on, by believers eager to proclaim the actual reality of events announced in their ancient sacred Scriptures. The gospel-event is precisely a *gospel* event, because Scripture is interpreted in it once and for ever. Scripture fulfilled in the light of the gospel-event means Scripture interpreted in such a way that it stops being the kind of Scripture it was before the event. It becomes a new kind of Scripture, namely as interpreted in what was to be called the New Testament. We are believers born out of a radically hermeneutical event, and therefore our faith remains by definition open to radical interpretations of ourselves.

In reference to the gospel-event the evangelists, Matthew and Mark, Luke and John, conceived their original theological visions of Jesus and the church. Irenaeus and Origen integrated the central values of classical Hellenism into their own vision of the gospel-event. Augustine, Anselm and Luther developed a synthesis of their own, each of them in the framework of his own culture, but all three being entirely motivated by their understanding of the gospel-event. The same happens to us now. In taking for granted verifiable evidence, worked out through centuries of critical studies in the Bible, we are called to the needed hermeneutical conversion in order to articulate our Christian self-understanding made possible by our contemporary approach to the gospel-event. Once more, the touchstone of an authentic Catholic theology, creating for itself the possibility of a new future, is and will be scripture interpreted.

Let me conclude this address as honestly as possible. If we must consider today a conversion of our minds as Christian believers, it can only mean for us a new discovery of the gospel-event out of which our whole religious tradition derives. The essential truth of the gospel-event is of a hermeneutical nature. We are called to re-enact for ourselves today the gospel-event in applying to our own tradition the interpretive relevance of that event.

We can only be true to the gospel and honest to God in our present church if the interpretive power of the gospel, which means the Spirit of God acting in history, leads us to a new understanding of our faith.

The basic doctrines, on which we rely as Christians, need faith seeking for such a new self-understanding. Three centuries of *lectio critica* have freed Scripture for us from its dogmatically canonized, some would say fossilized, understanding. To refuse such a conclusion is to prefer one form or another of fundamentalism. To accept it, means to face the urgent task of a *theological* appropriation by the whole church community of the *critically* studied Scripture.

Such a *theological* appropriation will be the achievement of future generations in the church. It will no longer presuppose the self-understanding of western Christianity, as it was transmitted to St. Anselm and developed after him. It will no longer conceive theology itself as we are used to conceiving it. But it will certainly call the whole church to a new discovery of God's revelation and God's salvific incarnation through the gospel-event.

Maybe you find these final remarks too cryptic. If an apology is needed, I would only suggest a comparison. Look at what happened to music and to painting in the twentieth century. Instead of classical music, be it medieval, or Renaissance music, baroque, or romantic music, we have, the so-called second school of Vienna, with composers like Arnold Schönberg, Alban Berg and Anton Webern. It is a completely different kind of music, without the traditional tonalities, a music which is called dodecaphonic. There is no doubt that such a contemporary music is less popular than rock-n-roll, and it remains apparently a marginal phenomenon in our society; nevertheless it has galvanized the whole musical creativity of the century.

The same happened in the history of western painting since the first decade of the twentieth century. The most influential painters of our time are abstract, or non-figurative painters. Again, we may neglect them as a short-lived phenomenon; but they opened a completely new horizon of colors and forms, they established entirely new cultural links between the western tradition of painting and non-western traditions. They signified an end and a new beginning in the art of painting.

Today, Scripture, theologically interpreted out of several centuries of its *lectio critica*, leads us to admit the end of a certain classical self-definition, canonized in the church for many centuries; and it engages us in the hermeneutical conversion of our Christian mind, in need of a *new* self-definition still to come. This *lectio critica* still has a tonality and a look which is alien or marginal to the Christian profession of faith today. As long as it remains on the periphery of faith, and as long as we remain critically unreflective about Christian identity, this potentially creative moment in Christian history will be lost. No Anselmian redefinition and appropriation will revitalize the tradition. We may yet be uncertain how this new Christian self-understanding will sound; we may even be somewhat diffident, somewhat uneasy about the forms and colors to appear on the new canvas. Nevertheless, Scripture, critically interpreted, and the gospel-event theologically re-enacted in regard to the whole classical tradition, will, once more, secure the definition of an authentically Catholic community of faith.

A RESPONSE TO
CHARLES KANNENGIESSER
Reverend John J. Connelly

It is a delight to have a modest share in this exciting symposium and convocation celebrating the Saint Anselm College Centennial. I am happy to join Professor Kannengiesser at this particular session. He has given us a thoughtful, provocative paper which could keep us in discussion well into the night. Though I will be expressing a number of disagreements with the paper, I want to join the author in complete agreement with his opening observation, "Our faith seeks understanding today at least as much as in Saint Anselm's day, if not in the same culture or mind-set." I would like to say by way of introduction that over the course of many years a good number of the Benedictines have come to Saint John's Seminary in Boston for their theological studies. As a result, I have developed enormous affection and admiration for the work and accomplishments of Saint Anselm College. The Benedictine monks and their collaborators in education have taken seriously their significant objectives. They successfully set as their goal a small-in-size, liberal arts, Catholic Benedictine College. It is exciting to speculate on what the next one hundred years will bring.

The theological question most likely to promote widespread disunity among theologians is the question that asks about the unity proper to theologians. The situation seems to be such today that the best way to dissolve a gathering of theologians is to raise the question, "What is theology?" I happen to belong to an ecumenical theological society which we call The Boston Theological Society. Our interests range far and wide. Our success in staying together as a society for the past twenty years lies in our uncanny ability to avoid direct discussion on the nature of the discipline that brought us together in the first place. Fortunately or unfortunately, as the case may be, the issue of the nature of theology is one that cannot be avoided this evening. The title of Professor Kannengiesser's address tells us that he intends not only to discuss but to define the very nature of theology. He considers, we must presume, that the phrase "Scripture Interpreted" modified to mean "in terms of *lectio critica*" is definitive of Catholic theology. In a personal note to me, Professor Kannengiesser has written, "I have tried in my paper to find a constructive and peaceful way to deal with highly controverted issues." I very much appreciate that sentiment. While my remarks will be critical of the paper, I trust that I will do my task also in a constructive and peaceful way.

To begin with, I must admit that I found the text difficult to follow. No doubt, my students would attribute this difficulty to personal opaqueness. However, were that totally true, that would reflect badly on Father Berthold who invited me to come this evening. As I ponder my own question, "Why am I having difficulty following the argument of the text?" I found a clue in a remark the author makes towards the end of his paper. He says to the reader, "Maybe you find these final remarks too cryptic." My problem is that I found the entire paper too cryptic. So, I had recourse to the dictionary which described a crypt as a vault wholly or partially underground, so that "cryptic" means hidden, secret, obscure; and of course — this in my addition — what is hidden and obscure could be by design or by chance. This, then, is my problem. There are all sorts of interesting things in the text, but I suspect that there are other interesting things in the crypt — and the things in the crypt are the very things that would clarify what is in the text. To begin with, let me comment on the situation and present tasks of theology.

Professor Kannengiesser tells us that what the Church needs more than anything else is "a new, theological appropriation of the Bible." St. Anselm sought to make the Scriptures credible in his day with the logical inventiveness of his times. This is our task today, the author says, in the ongoing, always necessary search for intellectual conversion. And so we are to ask, "What are we going to do with the Bible in the present state of our changing civilization? What kind of interpretative rationality should we apply today to our contemplation of Scripture, if we intend to participate in the current history of Christian thought?" *Lectio divina* sought and found its systematic interpreter in Anselm. *Lectio critica* seeks (I think we must ask, *whose lectio critica?*) and has yet to find its systematic interpreters for our times. When found, these systematic interpreters will lead us to a new theological appropriation of Scripture, hitherto unheard of in the Church, but indeed providential. This is not the way I would describe the theological task today. Rather, I would say, *lectio divina* needed its Anselm as monastic theology gave way to scholastic theology. Scholastic theology was a remarkable achievement. As a matter of fact, the Church gave its allegiance to scholastic theology's classical culture even into the early decades of our present century, and in such a way as to keep itself effectively out of the modern world, as far as intellectual conversion is concerned. All of us here this evening know something of the history between "the Church *and* the nineteenth century" and "the church *in* the world of this time." For the past century and a half there have been developed highly refined methods for doing history and hermeneutics, and also new modes for studying the Scriptures, the Fathers, the Scholastics, the Renaissance, the Reformation. We have but to think of the cultural factors impinging on the work of contemporary theology: new methods of historical study, a variety of turns in philosophy, developments in the field of religious studies, explosive developments in the area of communications. To delimit the task of theology to the interpretation of the *lectio critica* of the Scriptures is just not an adequate explanation of theology's present task. Is there and where is there, novelty in the present situation? There is no new revelation and no new faith and no new Scriptures and no new Church. The novelty resides in theology's cultural context. As Bernard Lonergan reminds us,

> Theology is the product not only of the faith it seeks to investigate and expound but also of the cultural ideals and norms that set its problems and direct its solutions. Just as theology in the thirteenth century followed its age by assimilating Aristotle — just as theology in the seventeenth century resisted its age by retiring into a dogmatic corner, so theology today is locked in an encounter with its age. Whether it will grow and triumph or whether it will wither to insignificance depends in no small measure on the clarity and accuracy of its grasp of the external cultural factors that undermine its past achievements and challenge it to new endeavors.[1]

Does this not force us to ask how does the theologian deal with the interpretative rationality of its age? It does what Thomas Aquinas did with Aristotle, it adopts and adapts. Thomas was not an Aristotelian. He was Christian. When the logical inventiveness of his day helped Thomas to explain intelligibly the Catholic faith he made good use of it. When Aristotle stood in the way as he did so frequently, Thomas would say: off with his head! So it is with modern day interpretative rationality. If we are modern men and women, we must make use of the logical inventiveness of our day to present, defend, and illustrate the truths of faith with concepts and words that are more comprehensible to minds trained in present-day philosophical and scientific culture. But we must not confuse ends and means. The *lectio critica* does not determine the faith. The faith is the master; modern rationality must serve.

Professor Kannengiesser has taken us on a whirlwind, selective tour of history. He deals with what he considers "creative stages" in that history — involving Irenaeus, Origen, Athanasius, Augustine, Anselm, Ignatius of Loyola and Martin Luther. The leap from Anselm to Loyola and Luther was for me mind-boggling and breathtaking, bypassing as it does the central figures of the thirteenth century who are the primary analogues for the word "theologian" in any Catholic sense. What Loyola and Luther are doing in a text which aims to define Catholic theology is somewhat of a puzzlement. I hope that Luther is not included because of his raging, ill-informed disdain for the Scholastics. At any rate, I will not comment on the history lesson but will move to some systematic concerns which call for a measure of clarification. They are three in number: 1) The adjective *Catholic*; 2) The location of the truth-question in faith-profession; 3) The role and limits of hermeneutics in theology.

1) If Professor Kannengiesser is going to give the reader a definition of Catholic theology, the reader, in turn, will have to ask the author to clarify his understanding of the noun "theology" and the adjective "Catholic." What is it that makes theology theological? What happens to theology when the adjective Catholic is employed? Many today think of theology in a wide sense as including a whole range of disciplines, enormously important, which are not really theology at all, such as Old Testament history, literary, form, and redaction criticism of the Bible, liturgiology, and many others. The work of theology — in keeping with Augustine, Anselm and Aquinas — is to seek understanding of the truths of faith so as to mediate, interpret, and commend the faith to all in the culture. Interpreting Scripture, even working from the *lectio critica*, is an

essential though partial contribution to the task. The adjective Catholic in the paper figures only as sociological indicator devoid of any theological content. The basic question is, "How does the invisible God, dwelling in inaccessible light communicate with us in such a way that we can experience God?" This is the God question, God at work in Jesus Christ, God at work in the Risen Christ through the Spirit at work in the Church. Terms like theology and Christian theology are abstractions. Theology is always ecclesial, obviously within the context of Pneumatology.

2) This comment on the adjective Catholic suggests another point in need of clarification. It concerns the location of the truth-question in faith-profession, prior to philosophical theology, biblical theology, systematic theology. This is why I would like to take a look into the crypt. Would I find an old copy of Schleiermacher, telling us that the theses of faith become the hypotheses of theology? I raise this possibility because the author tells us that God's revelation in Scripture is mediated to us through the critical conclusions of scientific exegesis. What does this imply? It suggests to me that secular faith is normative for Catholic faith, that the theologian's allegiance to the academy overshadows allegiance to the Church. To define Catholic theology means to situate the theological enterprise within the intentionality of faith. Faith here means God's inner word given by the Spirit in transcendental revelation and God's outer word expressed in history in and through the tradition and Scripture of the Church. Theology studies God revealed in Jesus Christ as that revelation is mediated in the faith of the believing community. The theologian can work only from within that body which is the Church. Here Professor Kannengiesser mentions the ecumenical problem. Christians, though belonging to separate bodies of believers, are all turned in the direction of the same kingdom of God to come, and find in the Gospels their central reference for self-definition. Together, we are to appropriate theologically the scientific evidence resulting from centuries of *lectio critica* in biblical matters. I do hope down in the crypt there is no dusty, discarded bumper sticker which says "Sola Scriptura" which in this case means *lectio critica* to be interpreted in a way that is neither a priori nor dogmatic. Once again, whose *lectio critica*, that of Raymond Brown or Elizabeth Schüssler-Fiorenza? We at last, the author tells us, know who Jesus is. If the Jesus we know is the Jesus of the *lectio critica*, we are in deep trouble! But the Jesus we know is

the Jesus preached by the Apostles, celebrated liturgically in the Eucharist, expressed in praxis by Christ-like charity and whom we have come to know as faith became reflective down the centuries and continues to be reflective in the systematic theologies of today. Obviously, the reading of *lectio critica* has its important but modest contribution to make.

3) Anyone who has wrestled with question thirteen of the *pars prima* of Thomas' *Summa* realizes the difficulty of talking humanly about God. The analogical process, the key to question thirteen, expresses the principle that theological statements are not only meaningful but true. The student of theology seeks modestly to make adequate statements about God. Adequacy of theological statements mean "appropriateness" and "understandability." Appropriateness means "in continuity of the tradition" and understandability refers to contemporary meaningfulness. Theology is concerned with truth and meaning. The important work of hermeneutics seeks intelligibility, that is, the development of insights, insights into the truths of faith expressed in the Creed — obviously the non-negotiable expressions of the apostolic preaching which was given literary objectification in the New Testament canon. Insights prove that a person is bright. They do not prove that a person is right. Once again, we see the enormous importance of where one places the truth-question in the theological enterprise. Theology does not lead to the truth of faith. Theology leads from the truth of faith. There are profound problems embedded in hermeneutics which will not disappear whether one elects a wholesale acceptance of modernity or a wholesale rejection of modernity. What are the creedal, liturgical and theological parameters within which hermeneutics can do its valued work of presenting the meaningfulness of faith without destruction of its truth? I suggest that we need some instrument like Lonergan's *Method* which will help us to distinguish problems of hermeneutics from those of history, dialectics, foundations, doctrines, systems, and communications — all functional specialities in theology where no one specialty enjoys totalitarian control. As Lonergan remarks, "The most striking feature of much contemporary discussion of hermeneutics is that it attempts to treat all these issues as though they were hermeneutical. They are not."[2]

Professor Kannengiesser, you have given us a paper that deals with controverted issues. I trust that my remarks are pertinent to any ongoing discussion. Because faith is never changing and theology is ever changing, I do not wish to be locked into some classical definition which may have enjoyed ecclesial canonization for centuries. Important though it is to say that Scripture must be interpreted in terms of the *lectio critica* of the past several centuries, this is a fraction of what must enter into a contemporary definition of Catholic theology. If you are going to press your argument, you will have to let us see what is really in the crypt.

NOTES

1. B. Lonergan, "Theology in its New Context," in *A Second Collection*, ed. Ryan and Tyrrell (Philadelphia: Westminster Press), 58.
2. B. Lonergan, *Method in Theology* (London: Darton, Longman and Todd, 1972), 155.

PART TWO

———

Early and Medieval

'FAITH SEEKING UNDERSTANDING' IN THE THOUGHT OF ST. EPHRAEM THE SYRIAN

Sidney H. Griffith, S.T.

It is a commonplace of scholarship to acknowledge the fact that St. Anselm's characterization of the theological enterprise as *fides quaerens intellectum* owes a debt to the thought of St. Augustine. At a number of crucial points in his own work St. Augustine cited a phrase from the Latin version of the Septuagint text of Isaiah 7:9, *crede ut intellegas*, to underscore the point.[1] Faith comes first, these saints taught, and the human effort to understand a truth of the divine revelation must therefore begin with the prior acknowledgement of the veracity of the revelation, precisely because it is a divine revelation. This premise was to become almost a first principle of theology in the west, right up to the time of the Enlightenment. In modern times it was John Henry Newman who gave it a classic formulation, in his rejection of what he called "liberalism." Newman said,

> Liberalism is the mistake of subjecting to human judgment those revealed doctrines which are in their nature beyond and independent of it, and of claiming to determine on intrinsic grounds the truth and value of propositions which rest for their reception simply on the external authority of the Divine Word.[2]

In the east in the fourth century, during the years that elapsed between the first council of Nicea (325) and the first council of Constantinople (381), St. Ephraem the Syrian (306-373) commended a similar approach to intellectual inquiry on the part of believers about the truths of the faith as did St. Augustine, St.

Anselm, and John Henry Newman. St. Ephraem wrote in Syriac, in the wake of controversies aroused in the church in response to the Arian crisis. It is the objective of the present essay to call attention to St. Ephraem's work, to outline his thought on the nature of religious belief, and very briefly to suggest the relevance of St. Ephraem's ideas to present-day concerns about the intellectual implications of the act of faith.

I

St. Ephraem the Teacher

The one certain date in the biography of St. Ephraem the Syrian is the day of his death, June 9, 373.[3] We know it because the date was recorded in the *Edessene Chronicle* and the document was pre-served in the archives of the city of Edessa, where St. Ephraem lived for the last ten years of his life. Previously, until the year 363, Ephraem lived in Nisibis, a strategically important city on the borders of the Roman and Persian empires. In the peace negotia-tions that followed the death of the emperor Julian (363), the new emperor Jovian ceded Nisibis to the Persians, a move that provoked an exodus of Christians from the city, St. Ephraem among them. These Syriac-speaking Christians accepted it as axiomatic that because of the providential relationship between the church and the Roman empire, to be Christian was to be Roman.[4] Conse-quently, it was unacceptable to them to live under Persian rule.

In Nisibis, and later in Edessa, St. Ephraem served the successive bishops of the cities in a ministerial capacity that in all probability ranked him among the deacons in the church. He lived an ascetical style of life in that celibacy, prayer, and fasting were important religious observances for him. But it would be anachronistic to call him a monk. And it would be simply wrong to think of him as a hermit or an anchorite in the Evagrian style, as the later iconog-raphers of Byzantium persisted in portraying him. In fact, St. Eph-raem was a bishop's man all his life.[5] He was a single man, who offered his life and services to the church together with other single men and women who altogether thought of themselves as taking on in this special way something of the singularity of Jesus the Messiah — the single Son of God the Father, who was also of one mind and heart with Him. In the Syriac-speaking churches such devoted people enjoyed a status in the community that others recognized by calling them "Sons and Daughters of the Covenant," or simply "Covenanters," as their title is customarily translated into western languages.[6]

St. Ephraem's personal vocation was that of a teacher, perhaps in an earlier form of what was to become a famous catechetical and exegetical school at Edessa in the early fifth century, before its relocation to Nisibis later in the century, as a consequence of the Christological controversies.[7] In the traditions of the Syriac-speaking churches, St. Ephraem is always remembered simply as "the Teacher (*malpānâ*)," as if this sobriquet alone would be a sufficient testimony to his patristic significance for later generations. And even Greek writers such as Sozomen attest to Ephraem's effectiveness as a religious thinker, albeit with a note of surprise that such a distinction could attach to someone not educated in Greek![8]

St. Ephraem was a prolific writer and there survives from his pen a long list of biblical commentaries, metrically constructed sermons, doctrinal, moral, and commemorative hymns, as well as more prosaic texts in heresiography and devotional writing. The overwhelming majority of the works authentically attributed to St. Ephraem are in Syriac. But there is a large corpus of material in Greek that is also attributed to him, about which there can be no confidence at all as to authenticity. Only a few lines of *Ephraem Graecus* can be shown to have genuine Syriac texts behind them. Nevertheless, the popularity of St. Ephraem in the Greek-speaking communities of the church, in spite of the inauthenticity of the Greek writings attributed to him, attests to his religious authority in the Christian world beyond the borders of his native Syria.[9]

St. Ephraem's writings were not academic in the sense in which we have come to use this word. Rather, one has the impression that like many of the works of St. Augustine, and most of the works of Cardinal Newman, the majority of St. Ephraem's compositions were occasional pieces, in the sense that he wrote them for specific occasions, to meet particular pastoral requirements in the churches he served. Such was certainly the case with the doctrinal hymns that bulk so large among his works, as well as for the leisurely reflective and metrical homilies which, like the hymns, probably had a liturgical setting for their first appearance. Many of them may still be found in longer or shorter passages in the several liturgical rites of the Syrians.[10] As for the biblical commentaries and other prose compositions, they often carry a conventional ded-

ication to someone who has requested enlightenment on the subjects they discuss, thereby suggesting that St. Ephraem composed
them in answer to a personal query, but with the understanding
that a larger public will read them.[11]

St. Ephraem's religious writing is in a different key from the
style of theological expression one thinks is typical of fourth century
writers in Greek or Latin. And this different key has prompted
scholars to discern a distinctive theological method at work in his
compositions when one compares them to the works of thinkers
such as the Cappadocian Fathers, Basil and the two Gregorys, who
were his contemporaries, and who addressed a number of the same
problems as did St. Ephraem. The distinctive key is a poetic style in
Syriac diction, coupled with a narrative technique that is allusive in
character and elliptical in expression. It alludes to various aspects of
an issue under discussion, presuming an audience's familiarity with
it, and it alludes to scriptural stories and motifs in terms St. Ephraem
thinks will bring clarity to a discussion. But he presumes the reader
knows the Bible, and that an allusion to a scriptural passage or to
an incident in a biblical story will suffice to call a whole pericope to
mind. So quotations from the Scriptures in his works are often
elliptical, with the expectation that several key words will suffice
for the total recall of a passage. Furthermore, St. Ephraem's writing
is full of rich visual imagery both from the world of nature and
from the Bible stories. And in his writing he often visualizes the
narrative action from either source, the Bible or the natural world,
in scenes that are almost cinematic in their dynamism. In this
imaginative form the scenes function typologically in St. Ephraem's
thinking, so that the reader is best prepared to interpret them who
is ready to think of them as a series of verbal icons.[12]

The iconographic character of the thinking behind much of St.
Ephraem's writing has led commentators on his works to describe
his religious thought as "symbolic theology."[13] In this way the suggestion is made that the logical rigor one expects in more discursive
doctrinal treatises of the sort that St. Athanasius or the Cappadocian
fathers wrote, is not to be expected from St. Ephraem. And in fact
commentators often do spend much of their time showing that St.
Ephraem's Syriac lexicon of theological terms lacks the precision of
definition and the consistency of usage that one has come to expect
in Greek works of theology from the fourth century —especially
when one compares the Syriac terms St. Ephraem uses to their

putative Greek equivalents. But the problem here is the supposition that St. Ephraem meant simply to reflect in Syriac what Greek speakers were saying on a given topic, in Syriac terms exactly equivalent to the Greek terms the Greek writers were using. As a matter of fact, St. Ephraem had his own theological purposes, and they were not simply to reflect in Syriac a discussion that others were conducting in the Greek language. Rather, St. Ephraem meant to explore in a Syriac idiom issues in Christian doctrine that were by their very nature before the minds of all fourth-century churchmen.

A short-hand way to refer to one of the doctrinal issues that all fourth century thinkers addressed in one way or another is to mention the term "Arianism." The name of the heresy has come to serve as a code-word for the whole host of theological topics. One of them is the role of intellectual inquiry in determining the articles of Christian faith. St. Ephraem addressed this issue in his hymns and homilies, "On Faith." And it is clear that for him the threat posed by the followers of Arius and Aetius was not only the unorthodox doctrine they espoused in regard to the divinity of the Son of God, but also, and perhaps even more so, the methods they adopted to discover the truth about God. According to St. Ephraem, the mistake these people made was to prefer "the poison of the wisdom of the Greeks," to "the simplicity of the apostles."[14]

II
Homilies and Hymns "On Faith"

St. Ephraem faced two sets of adversaries in his efforts to commend the Nicene faith of the Roman empire to the Syriac-speaking churches of Nisibis and Edessa. On the one side were the indigenous groups who always exercised an influence on the thinking of people at the borders of Persia and Rome: the Marcionites, the Manichaeans, and the followers of Bar Dayṣān, the native of Edessa, whose thought had a special attraction for his fellow citizens. On the other side there were in the Roman world the theological adversaries of the Great church at large: followers of Paul of Samosata, Sabellians, Novatianists, Arians and Aetians, to name only the most significant few of them in Ephraem's day, whom he actually mentions.[15] He took all of them into account because it was his purpose at least in part to promote the church of the empire in the Syriac-speaking communities, and these were the two groups of dissenters from that point of view whose ideas Ephraem had to counter with clear doctrinal positions. The Arians and the Aetians were the adversaries whose doctrines St. Ephraem was particularly concerned to undermine in the two sets of compositions we have from him under the general title, "On Faith." The common opinion is that he wrote the "Homilies on Faith" in Nisibis, prior to his exile in 363, while the "Hymns on Faith" are products of both periods in Ephraem's life, the time in Nisibis, and the last decade in Edessa.[16] However, it is not clear that St. Ephraem himself was the person who gathered these homilies and hymns into the two distinct compilations we now have. There is a considerable amount of evidence to show that later compilers assembled the separate pieces into collections of homilies or hymns that the manuscript tradition attributed to St. Ephraem. He did not usually sign his work. The compilers simply accepted the traditional ascription of the pieces to St. Ephraem and put them together on the basis of formal considerations such as literary genre (*mêmrâ* or *madrāshâ*) and prosody (metre-melody), and with some attention paid to the congruity of the subject matter in each piece with the other compositions in each collection.[17] This feature of the publication of St. Ephraem's work calls the reader's attention to the occasional character of his writing. He wrote in response to actual crises in the communities he served. His work was not abstractly academic. The genres he employed were the popular literary genres of religious piety, and congregations of worshipers were his audience. His purpose was to commend right doctrine to his congregants, and to highlight the shortcomings in the thinking of the adversaries.

While the Arians and neo-Arians and "Anomoeans" such as Aetius and Eunomius, were St. Ephraem's adversaries, he does not name them as such in the homilies and hymns "On Faith." One recognizes them and their characteristic positions in the ideas Ephraem rejects. Nor is Ephraem interested in counter-arguments against the adversaries in any dialectical sense of the word 'argument.' Rather, he concentrates his efforts on the cultivation of what he regards as the proper attitude of the believer toward the Scriptures and the limits of human knowing. And he excoriates any attempt to derive the truths of divine revelation by way of the logical manipulations of doctrinal formulae. In all of this one sees that for St. Ephraem there is a deeper issue under the doctrinal problem of Arianism. And it is the position of the act of faith in the conscience of the believer. Put another way, one might even say that Ephraem puts his finger on the tension between belief and theology, and exhibits a strong distrust of the latter.

There are many lines in the homilies and hymns "On Faith" that echo phrases one might read in works by St. Basil or by St. Gregory Nazianzenus, who wrote against the teachings of the same adversaries as did St. Ephraem. Indeed, St. Ephraem goes to great lengths to show from Scripture and from analogies in nature that it is appropriate to confess one divinity, one God, in three divine persons (*qnômê, hypostases*) and that the Son of God is co-equal and co-eternal with God the Father and God the Holy Spirit. He rejects any Arian or semi-Arian notion that would in any way lessen the full acceptance of what one might call the Athanasian or Cappadocian Trinitarian formula. But as we shall see, St. Ephraem is not really satisfied with just the elaboration and defense of doctrinal formulae, although he fully reflects the Cappadocian Trinitarian formula in his works "On Faith."[18]

One will search almost in vain in histories of doctrine for any mention of St. Ephraem as one who made a contribution to the solution of the Arian problem. And in reading the history of this crisis of Christian thinking in the fourth century one is often left with the impression that it was all merely over the effort to find a fitting doctrinal formula in which to state the church's Trinitarian beliefs. St. Ephraem's homilies and hymns "On Faith" point to another dimension of the issue —the nature of faith itself, and its relationship to the normal ways of human intellectual inquiry.

III
On Believing

The Syriac word for faith is *haymānûtâ*, and in the present context is makes most sense to translate it actively by the verb 'to believe.' St. Ephraem means by it exactly what the tenth century Syriac lexicographer Bar Bahlūl meant when he defined *haymānûtâ* as "conviction about those things which are in the Gospel, as what happened in fact."[19] The definition puts the accent on the action of believing; and it specifies what the Gospel says, or what God says, as the object of belief. Put personally, faith is believing God. And for St. Ephraem this means believing what God says in the Bible, as we shall see.

As for the place of faith in the life of the believer, St. Ephraem puts the matter succinctly in the following quotation from the "Hymns on Faith,"

> Faith is the second soul.
> Just as the body subsists by means of the soul,
> So the soul's life is dependent
> On faith.
> If it denies, or doubts,
> It becomes a corpse.
> . . .
> The soul depends on faith,
> Faith in turn depends on God.
> From the Father and the Son
> There flows the truth that
> Enlivens all in the Spirit.[20]

The last lines of the quotation recall the Trinitarian controversies that were the occasion for St. Ephraem's composition of the "Hymns on Faith." In these controversies it was his position that the act of faith was primary, and he rejected the idea that the articles of faith could be determined by academic research, or by intellectual scrutiny of the sort that put dialectic ahead of believing. It was this position that put Ephraem on a collision course with some of the more academically inclined theologians of his day, especially in the Greek-speaking world. And he actually said such things as, "Blessed is the one who has never tasted the poison of the wisdom of the Greeks," and he went on to speak of the more academic methods of theology in his day as, "accursed dialectic, the hidden rottenness from the Greeks."[21]

Readers have often taken these quotations to mean that Ephraem disdained all things Greek, and that he preferred the pure Semitic usages of the Syriac-speaking community to the propositional logic of Hellenism. In fact, what concerned Ephraem was pretty much the same thing that had concerned Tertullian in his famous question, "Quid ergo Athenis et Hierosolymis? quid academiae et ecclesiae? quid haereticis et christianis?[22] Tertullian went on to explain,

> Nobis curiositate opus non est post Christum Iesum nec inquisitione post euangelium. Cum credimus, nihil desideramus ultra credere. Hoc enim prius credimus non esse quod ultra credere debeamus.[23]

Ephraem's *Hymns on Faith* return again and again to this same theme. he reminds his readers that the apostle Paul had gone to Athens to confound the academics.

> The apostle was more clever
>> than those presumptuous men.
> He went right into the city,
>> the mother of the Greeks.
> He spoke to them in their own idiom,
>> to let them know he knew how to do so.
> And when it was vanquished
>> he discarded that defense of theirs.
> He propounded truth to them;
>> they had let the medicine of life slip away.
> Too long had they been ill,
>> with the disease of inquisitiveness.[24]

What concerned Ephraem concretely were the controversies over the deployment of Greek philosophical and logical terms in the statement of the church's beliefs about Jesus Christ as Son of God and his relationship to God the Father. One the one hand the Scriptures are the measure of Christian faith, but the Trinitarian controversies of the fourth century had largely to do with how creedal statements may be framed in an accurate and intelligible Greek idiom. St. Ephraem's complaint was then that their measure was taken not by the scriptures primarily, but by grammarians and logicians bent on applying the rules of their disciplines to any such statements. One has only to mention words and phrases such as *mia physis, mia ousia, treis hypostaseis*, or *gennetos/agenetos* to summon up the memory of these controversies. Ephraem thought that the application of the academic methodology of his day, the deductive, or syllogistic method as we might call it, was a methodological mistake if one expected to derive information about God or the divine generation from it. Rather, for Ephraem the behavior of the three Magi should be normative for believers. They travelled from afar to worship Christ, and in the *Hymns on Faith* Ephraem invited Christians to consider the Magi's conduct as normative:

Come, let us marvel at the men
who saw the King here below.
They did not conduct an inquisition (ʿaqqebw)
nor did they engage in research (bʿaw);
no one of them made a disputation (drāŝ).
There shone there in silence
a pure act of faith (haymānûtă)
When He was here below, the Magi
were not so insolent to examine Him (bṣaʾuhy)
How can we then be so insolent as to examine Him,
now that He has ascended and taken His seat
at the right hand on high?[25]

Most of Ephraem's negative words are in this passage: "inquisition" (ʿuqqābâ), "research" (bʿātâ), "disputation" (drāŝâ), and "examination" (bṣātâ). He misses only one of his more common academic words, "rationalization," (hemŝâ). Ephraem often used this word, "rationalization," in the *Hymns on Faith* to score the academic activities of which he disapproved. For example, at one place he prays to the Son with the words, "Your birth is under the seal of silence. What mouth would be so insolent as to rationalize it?"[26]

All of these "academic" words constituted a vocabulary of insolence as far as Ephraem was concerned, if God is to be subjected to the processes which they imply. They describe the activities of Sophists, whose speech is governed by mere classroom logic. For Ephraem, human inquiry should not put on such airs when the talk is of God. Rather, human discourse should aim to reflect the teaching of the Scriptures.

On a more positive note, Ephraem could muster a modicum of praise for a scholar, if he was one, "who has polished his research (bʿātâ) like a mirror, for the sake of those wanting in faith (haymānûtă), so that in it they might wipe away their blemishes."[27] And there is even room for a faithful dialectician in Ephraem's world, provided that in the practice of disputation, "his rebuttal is like the medicine of life, enlivening the moribund talkers (mallālê) who behave arrogantly against the Enlivener of All."[28]

The "talkers," of course, are those who hope to learn about God by following the rules of talk, what Syriac speakers call *mallilûtâ* or "logic," as we should say. For Ephraem the rules of talk are still not equal to the task of defining God even when such methods are deployed in His service. It is quite clear in his works that for Ephraem, when all is said and done, human speech about God should rather be in the genre of a song of praise. At one point he offers the following prayer:

> You, O Lord, have written:
> "Open your mouth and I will fill it" (Ps. 81:11).
> Behold, your servant's mouth is open for you,
>   and his mind too.
> Fill it, my Lord, with your gift,
>   that according to your will,
>   I might sing your praise.[29]

One could go on in this vein to quote many passages from Ephraem's hymns and homilies in which he disparages the methods of academics, their "questions" (šu'ālayhôn), as he calls them.[30] But the message would always be the same: "The mouth that wants to speak about that is ineffable, reduces to paltriness the greatness for which it is unfit."[31]

Ephraem was well aware of the fact that even on the human level the most mannered speech falls far short of the thought which the speaker hopes to communicate. At one point in the *Hymns on Faith* he says to God:

> It is easier for us to think,
>   than to speak a word.
> Thinking is capable
>   of stretching out everywhere.
> But when it comes to travel
>   in Your direction, to search You out,
> Its path disappears in front of it;
>   it is confused, forestalled.
> If thinking is thus overcome,
>   how much more so speech,
>   whose path is an abode of contention?[32]

Contention, as far as Ephraem was concerned, was the bane of the church, where peace and quiet should reign before the face of the incomprehensible God. The simple fact for Ephraem then was, as he sang in another prayer to God,

> My mouth is not adequate to You,
> and I rejoice that I am not adequate.
> For if somehow I should be adequate,
> it would be a double-edged blasphemy.
> Human nature would be more exalted than God.
> This is too stupid![33]

Concretely, in terms of the Trinitarian controversies which elicited Ephraem's hymns and homilies *On Faith* in the first place, he had this to say:

> If you ask, "Is there a Son,"
> you may learn the answer in an instant.
> If you ask "How,"
> the question will remain until He comes again.[34]

As for faith itself, that is to say "believing," Ephraem's attitude could not be clearer:

> Between God and man,
> believing is what is required.
> If you believe Him, you honor Him;
> if you investigate Him, you belittle Him.
> Between man and God then,
> there is to be but believing and prayer.[35]

It was not Ephraem's view that human inquiry had no proper role at all to play in one's religous life. Rather, it must respect its limits. And it is error (*tuᶜyay*), Ephraem explains, that "has put believing where investigation would be useful, and has introduced investigation where believing is required."[36]

Ephraem left no doubt about his view that the scriptures are the basis of belief in God. In his *Hymns on Faith* he wrote:

> Someone might say to me,
> whence have you learned of
> the nature of the Lord of All?
>   . . .

> I have left behind what is not in Scripture,
>   and gone with what is in Scripture,
> Lest on the pretext of
>   what is not in Scripture,
>   I should have brought the Scripture to nought.
>   . . .
> If men cross the boundary
>   of what is in the Scriptures,
>   their own inquisitiveness will be their death.[37]

True to his own principles, Ephraem entered the Trinitarian controversies of his day pointing to the names of God one finds in the Scriptures. He did not engage in debate about the definitions and the implications of the several Greek philosophical and/or logical terms which his Greek-speaking contemporaries were using to clarify the relationship between God the Father and God the Son. Rather, he went straightaway to the Syriac text of the Scriptures. In the *Homilies on Faith* he said:

> Sufficient for our infirmity
>   is the reality (*šrārâ*) that has come in
>   revelation.
> Acknowledge that there is the Father and the Son,
>   in reality (*bašrārâ*) as in the names (*bašmāhê*).
> The root of the name is the thing itself (*qnômâ*),
>   to it names are attached.
> For who would give a name
>   to something which itself (*qnômêh*) did not
>   exist?[38]

Again, in another place in the *Homilies*, Ephraem wrote:

> You have heard, Father, Son, and Spirit;
>   in the names get the things themselves
>   (*qnômê*).[39]

Passages such as these draw one's attention to two considerations which were crucial for Ephraem. First are the names of the persons of the Trinity and their verification in Scripture, and second are the "things themselves" to which the names inevitably point according to Ephraem.

In evidence of the names "Father," "Son," and "Spirit," as proper names of God, Ephraem customarily points to such widely quoted gospel passages as the baptism formula, "In the name of the Father, and of the Son, and of the Holy Spirit" (Mt. 28:19); Peter's confession, "You are the Messiah, the Son of the living God," with Jesus' reply, "No mere man has revealed this to you, but my heavenly Father" (Mt. 16:16-17); Jesus' transfiguration, with the divine testimony, "This is my beloved Son on whom my favor rests" (Mt. 17:5), which confirms the report at Jesus' own baptism, "He saw the Spirit of God descend like a dove and hover over him. With that, a voice from the heavens said, 'This is my beloved Son. My favor rests on him'" (Mt. 3:16-17).

Ephraem puts these New Testament names for God on a par with the names of God one finds in the Old Testament. His method is clear in what he has to say in *Hymn* XLIV:

> His names will instruct you,
>   how and whom you should call Him.
> One teaches you He is the 'Eternal One,'
>   another that He is the 'Creator.'
> One shows you He is the 'Good One,'
>   another informs you He is the 'Just One.'
> He is also named and called
>   Father.
> The scriptures are the test;
>   why does the fool gainsay it?
> Try by His own test,
>   His names and His distinctions.[40]

St. Ephraem has a good deal to say about the names of God one finds in the Scriptures. He distinguishes between what he describes as true names and borrowed names. The latter say nothing essential about God, according to Ephraem, but they are God's way of communicating with human beings. For example, when the Scriptures speak of God's 'ears' or 'eyes,' Ephraem says,

> The ears He ascribes by name to Himself
>   are to teach us He hears us.
> The eyes He attributes by name to Himself
>   are to inform us He sees us.
> He takes on the names of these things
>   for the sake of our weakness.[41]

It is a different matter with the names St. Ephraem considers to be "real," or proper names, as one might say. They bespeak reality. St. Ephraem says,

> The root of the name is the thing itself (*qnômâ*),
> to it names are attached.
> For who would give a name
> to something which itself (*qnômeh*) does not
> exist?[42]

The Syriac equivalent for the English noun "self" is *qnômâ*. As in English, the noun is used in conjunction with the personal pronoun in Syriac to serve as a reflexive pronoun. And in this way one might say that the noun *qnômâ*/"self" means an independently existing, individual thing: the technical equivalent for all practical purposes of the Greek term *hypostasis*, as the Cappadocian fathers were using it to designate one of the persons of the Trinity.[43]

What attracted Syriac writers such as St. Ephraem to the term *qnômâ* as a fitting word to express what westerners would call the 'persons' or the *hypostaseis* of the Trinity is surely its appearance in the Peshitta and in the Syriac *Diatessaron* to render the reflexive pronoun *heauto* in a Gospel passage such as John 5:26, "For just as the Father has life in himself, so has he granted the Son also to have life in himself." In fact, Ephraem commented on this verse in its Syriac *Diatessaron* version, relying on the appearance of *qnômâ* for *heauto* in both of its instances here to allow him to interpret the passage to refer to the *qnômâ* of the Father, and the *qnômâ* of the Son, virtually in the Greek sense of two divine *hypostaseis*.[44] Nothing could express St. Ephraem's thought better than to show that the whole Trinitarian formula is literally in the Scriptures in Syriac, one God in three *qnômê*, Father, Son, and Holy Spirit. And since even the word *qnômâ* is in the Gospel in association with the names of the Father and the Son, Ephraem can say,

> If you acknowledge their names,
> but you do not acknowledge their *qnômê*,
> You are a worshiper in name,
> but in fact you are an infidel.[45]

The word *qnômâ* did become a technical term for Syriac theological writers, who used it as an equivalent for the Greek term *hypostasis*. It seems clear that writers such as St. Ephraem intended to teach in

Syriac the same Trinitarian doctrine that Sts. Basil and Gregory Nazianzenus taught in a logically and philosophically correct Greek idiom. There is every reason to think that St. Ephraem was knowledgeably *au courant* with theological developments in Cappadocia, Egypt, and elsewhere in the Roman empire. But it would be a mistake to think that St. Ephraem wanted simply to reflect Greek doctrinal language in Syriac. Rather, Syriac-speaking Christians had their own genres of religious discourse. Like the Latin speakers at the other end of the empire, they also had the Bible in their own language. And they sought to express their understanding of the faith of the church of the empire in literary forms most congenial to Syriac.[46]

IV
Fides Quaerens Intellectum
In the landmark book, *Symbols of Church and Kingdom; a Study in Early Syriac Tradition,* Robert Murray, S.J., wrote the following:

> Ephraem refuses to answer the Arians by developing speculative theology on the orthodox side, as both Athanasius and the Cappadocians did; he sticks to his symbolism and demands that the mystery remain veiled. Not *fides quaerens intellectum* but *fides adorans mysterium!*[47]

While this statement is not untrue, it is nevertheless misleading in that it suggests that St. Ephraem was not really seeking any understanding of the mysteries of the faith in the "symbolic thelogy" that was his *métier* according to Robert Murray. But it does not follow that just because his thinking is not speculative, or rationalistic in the Greek mode, St. Ephraem did not seek an understanding of the truths he believed on the authority of the Scriptures. In fact he sought to have the mysteries enlighten one another by making them the subjects of an extended meditation in verse and song, in a contemplative style that was the preferred mode of intellectual life for Syriac-speaking persons, the genius of whose language found its most natural expression in literary genres that prized wonder over prosaic analysis. As Ephraem himself said of the human desire to look upon God,

> Because we have not an eye which is able to look upon His splendour,
> a mind was given us which is able to contemplate His beauty.[48]

From the foregoing observations it will readily appear that Ephraem was opposed to deciding matters of faith or belief simply on the basis of the rules of academic logic. It was his conviction in fact that in response to the revealed truth which one might find in the Bible, one should, as he put it, "abide in silence (šetqâ)."[49] For God "has given the Law, in place of investigation; and in the place of research, believing."[50] But the silence which Ephraem commends to believers is not absolute. It is the silence of the angels who cry out "Holy, Holy, Holy" before the divine throne in heaven.

The appropriate form of human discourse in the church is first of all the hymn of praise to God, according to Ephraem's way of thinking. But it is immediately clear to anyone who reads his numerous hymns and homilies that praise and acclamation are not their sole purpose. Ephraem certainly had lessons to teach his congregations, just as surely as did the academic Hellenophile theologians whose methods Ephraem was convinced were responsible for the bickering, contention, and false, non-scriptural doctrines at large in the church in his day. So what is the difference between Ephraem's discourse and that of the academy?

Put simply, but hopefully not over-simply, it seems that the literary genres most at home in the Aramaic world of the speakers of Syriac, the mêmrê and madrāšê, fostered a very different approach to the messages of the Scriptures than did the rhetorical practices of public life in the Greek-speaking world. The latter were governed principally by syllogism. From this perspective, the Scriptures were writings to be clarified and explicated, so that their real doctrines might in this way be brought to light. Syriac writers, by way of contrast, came to the scriptures with a very different cast of mind. They took the text at face value, convinced that its words were like paints, to use one of St. Ephraem's favorite images. With them God figured the mysteries in which he communicated his truths to human beings. And as in any such artistic enterprise concreteness is then the essence of the image. So the words must evoke the concrete realities of the persons, the talk, and the events which sketch the mystery. The interpreter, accordingly, never delimits, defines and excludes words according to extra-biblical canons, or rules of human talk. Rather, the words must suggest a whole scenario, which may then function as a paradigm not only for the mysterious truth to be conveyed in any given instance, but to serve as a similitude which may then be taken together with other similitudes to suggest a Biblical approach to all reality.[51]

St. Ephraem did, therefore, seek understanding on the basis of the act of faith he made in what the Scriptures teach. He did not commend an anti-intellectual attitude to the faithful. But he did teach that academic inquiry alone has too short a reach ever to grasp God. Only faith, love and prayer, says St. Ephraem, extend so far — but they do not comprehend. He puts it this way,

> You are too utterly a Wonder,
>   on every side, for us ever
>   to probe into You.
> You are near and you are far.
> Who can come right up to you?
> It is impossible for an investigation's
>   reach to come so far as you.
> When it reaches out to arrive,
>   it is cut off and falls back;
>   it is too short for your distance.
> Faith arrives,
>   and so does love, along with prayer.[52]

So Murray is right to say that for St. Ephraem it is a case of *fides adorans mysterium*. But it is also right to say that in the thousands of lines of contemplative and even didactic poetry he wrote, St. Ephraem's thought may be said to be *fides quaerens intellectum*. The two are not incompatible. Nor is St. Ephraem's attitude foreign to Greek-speaking Christians, as anyone will recognize who reads St. John Chrysostom's homilies on the incomprehensibility of God.[53] What St. Ephraem disapproved was the academic pose that would put its own scrutinies ahead of the scriptures as a source of the truth about God. And on this subject one might give St. Ephraem himself the final word. In the *Hymns on Faith* he wrote:

> Let the church of the True One
>   not become a lodge of disputes,
>   a sect of factions.
> He has painted a manifest portrait
>   of himself as he is.
> He is the one who is suited
>   to give us information.

He is the only one to whom,
the search into how he is, is clear.
He has given out tasteful hints of it,
in his own words for anyone who is true.[54]

NOTES

1. See, for example, the discussion in G. R. Evans, *Anselm and Talking about God* (Oxford, 1978), 59-66, 121-125.
2. Quoted from V. F. Blehl, *The Essential Newman* (New York: NAL, 1963), 45.
3. On the life and thought of St. Ephraem; see A. De Halleux, "Saint Ephrem le Syrien," *Révue théologique de Louvain* 14 (1983), 328-355; Sebastian Brock, *The Luminous Eye; the Spiritual World Vision of St. Ephrem*, Placid Lectures (Rome, 1985). See also S. Brock, *The Harp of the Spirit; Eighteen Poems of St. Ephrem*, studies supplementary to *Sobornost*, no. 4 (London, 1983). On the traditional Life of St. Ephraem that circulates in the Syriac-speaking communities, see Joseph P. Amar, "The Syriac *Vita* of Ephrem, the Poet-Theologian; a Critical Edition" (Ph.D. Diss., Catholic University of America, Washington, D.C., 1988).
4. See Sidney H. Griffith, "Ephraem, the Deacon of Edessa, and the Church of the Empire," in *Diakonia; Studies in Honor of Robert T. Meyer*, ed. T.P. Halton and J. Williaman (Washington, 1986), 22-52; *idem*, "Ephraem the Syrian's Hymns 'Against Julian,' Meditations on History and Imperial Power," *Vigiliae Christianae* 41 (1987), 238-266.
5. See Sidney H. Griffith, "Images of Ephraem: the Syrian Holy Man and his Church," *Traditio*, forthcoming.
6. See Sidney H. Griffith, "'Singles' in God's Service; Celibacy in Early Syrian Asceticism," forthcoming.
7. See Arthur Vööbus, *History of the School of Nisibis*, CSCO, vol. 266 (Louvain, 1965).
8. See J. Bidez and G. H. Hansen, eds., *Sozomenus Kirchengeschichte*, G.C.S. (Berlin, 1960), 127-130.
9. See J. Melki, "S. Ephrem le Syrien, un bilan de l'edition critique," *Parole de l'Orient* 11 (1983), 3-88; M. Geerard, *Clavis Patrum Graecorum* vol. II (Turnhout, 1974), 366-468.
10. André de Halleux, "Une clé pour les hymnes de'Ephrem dans le MS. Sinai Syr. 10," *Le Muséon* 85 (1972): 171-199; *idem*, "La Transmission des hymnes d'Ephrem d'après le MS. Sinai Syr. 10, f. 165-178," in *Symposium Syriacum 1972*, Orientalia Christiana Analecta, 197 (Rome, 1974), 21-63.
11. In late antiquity seemingly personal letters were public epistles, and this literary form came to be the standard preface to many a work in Syriac. See the interesting study of Eva Riad, *Studies in the Syriac Preface* (Uppsala, 1988).
12. See Sidney H. Griffith, "The Image of the Image-Maker in the Poetry of Ephraem the Syrian," forthcoming; see also Verna E.F. Harrison, "Word as Icon in Greek Patristic Theology," *Sobornost* 10 (1988):38-49.
13. See R. Murray, "The Theory of Symbolism in St. Ephrem's Theology," *Parole de l'Orient* 6 and 7 (1975-1976):1-20; S. Brock, "The Poet as Theologian," *Sobornost* 7 (1977):243-250; P. Tanios Bou Mansour, *La pensée symbolique de saint Ephrem le syrien* (Kaslik, Lebanon, 1988).
14. E. Beck, *Des heiligen Ephraem des Syrers Hymnen de Fide*, CSCO, vol. 154 (Louvain, 1955), II, 24:7.

15. Cf. Ephraem's mention of the two groups in E. Beck, *Des heiligen Ephraem des Syrers Hymnen Contra Haereses*, CSCO, vol. 169 (Louvain, 1957), XXII, 2 and 4:78,79. On Bar Daysan see H. J. W. Drijvers, *Bardaisan of Edessa* (Assen, 1966).

16. Both texts have appeared in critical editions with German translations by Dom Edmund Beck, O.S.B., *Des heiligen Ephraem des Syrers Hymnen de Fide*, CSCO, vol. 154 and 155; (Louvain, 1955); *idem*, *Des heiligen Ephraem des Syrers Sermones de Fide*, CSCO, vols. 212 and 213; (Louvain, 1961).

17. See De Halleux' articles cited in n. 10 above.

18. See E. Beck, "Die Theologie des hl. Ephraem in seinen Hymnen Ober den Glauben," *Studia Anselmiana*, 21 (Vatican City, 1949); *idem*, "Ephraems Reden Ober den Glauben; Ihr theologischer Lehrgehalt und Ihr geschichtlichen Rahmen" (Studia Anselmiana, 33 (Rome, 1953).

19. See R. Duval, ed., *Lexicon Syriacum auctore Hassano bar Bahlule* 3 vols. (Paris, 1890-1901), vol. 1, s.v.

20. Beck, *Hymnen de Fide*, vol. 154, LXXX, 1 and 2:246.

21. *Ibid.*, II, 24:7; LXXXVII, 4:268.

22. R. F. Refoulé and P. De Labriolle, *Tertullien: traité de la préscription contre les hérétiques*, SC, 46 (Paris, 1957), VII, 9:98.

23. *Ibid.*, VII, 12-13:98-99.

24. Beck, *Hymnen de Fide*, vol. 154, XLVII, 11:151.

25. *Ibid.*, VII, 6:33.

26. *Ibid.*, X, 2:49. On the "negative words," see T. Jansma, "Narsai and Ephraem; some Observations on Narsai's Homilies on Creation and Ephraem's Hymns on Faith," *Parole de l'Orient* 1 (1970):49-68. See also P. Yousef, "Foi et raison dans l'apologetique de saint Ephrem de Nisibe," *Parole de l'Orient* 12 (1984-1985):133-151.

27. Beck, *Hymnen de Fide*, II, 18:7.

28. *Ibid.*, II, 19:7.

29. *Ibid.*, X, 1:49.

30. Cf. Beck, *Hymnen de Fide*, II, 4:5.

31. *Ibid.*, I, 17:5.

32. *Ibid.*, IV, 12:13.

33. Beck, *Hymnen de Fide*, XI, 17:55.

34. Beck, *Sermones de Fide*, VI, 279-280:48.

35. *Ibid.*, II, 487-491:18.

36. *Ibid.*, II, 537-540:19.

37. Beck, *Hymnen de Fide*, LXIV, 10-12:200.

38. Beck, *Sermones de Fide*, II, 581-588:20.

39. *Ibid.*, IV, 45-46:33.

40. Beck, *Hymnen de Fide*, XLIV, 1:141.

41. *Ibid.*, XXXI, 1:105.

42. Beck, *Sermones de Fide*, II, 587-588:20.

43. See G. L. Prestige, *God in Patristic Thought*, 2d ed., (London, 1952), 157-178. See also A. De Halleux, "Hypostase et personne dans la formation du dogme trinitaire," *Revue d'histoire ecclesiastique* 79 (1984):313-369, 625-670.

44. See L. Leloir, *Saint Ephrem, commentaire de l'évangile concordant, texte syriaque (manuscrit Chester Beatty 709)* (Dublin, 1963), 106-109; *idem*, *Ephrem de Nisibe, commentaire de l'évanconcordant ou Diatessaron*, SC, 121: (Paris, 1966), 236-237. A later Christian Arab writer made the same point arguing with Muslims. See M. Hayek, ed., *Ammar al-Basri, apologie et controverses* (Beyrouth, 1977), 52,163.

45. Beck, *Sermones de Fide*, IV, 49-52:33.

46. E. Beck, *Ephrams Trinitätslehre im Bild von Sonne/Feuer, Licht und Warme*, CSCO, vol. 425 (Louvain, 1981).

47. R. Murray, *Symbols of Church and Kingdom; a Study in Early Syriac Tradition* (Cambridge, 1975), 89.
48. J.J. Overbeck, *Sancti Ephrem Syri, Rabbulae, Balaei aliorumque opera selecta* (Oxford, 1865), 25; C.W. Mitchell, *S. Ephraims Prose Refutations*, vol. I (London, 1912), iv.
49. Beck, *Hymnen de Fide*, LXX, 7:215.
50. *Ibid.*, LXX, 13:216.
51. See Griffith and Harrison, n. 12 above.
52. Beck, *Hymnen de Fide*, IV, 11:13.
53. See F. Graffin and A.-M. Malingrey, "La tradition syriaque des homeliés de Jean Chrysostome sur l'incomprehnsibilité de Dieu," in *Epektasis, mélanges patristiques offerts au cardinal Jean Daniélou* ed. J. Fontaine and C. Kannengeisser (Paris, 1972), 603-609.
54. Beck, *Hymnen de Fide*, XLIII, 5, 139-140. See also E. Beck, "Glaube and Gebet bei Ephram," *Oriens Christianus* 66 (1982), 15-50.

AUGUSTINE AND ANSELM: FAITH AND REASON

Frederick Van Fleteren

It would be but an elaboration of the obvious to prove that the thought of Anselm was greatly influenced by Augustine. Anselm's own description of his thought, *fides quaerens intellectum*, owes much to the *credo ut intelligam* of Augustine and indeed is an excellent description of Augustine's project in the *De trinitate*. The similarities between Augustine and Anselm are partially explainable by the fact that, from Augustine's own time to Anselm's and in large part until the present day, Augustine has defined the mainstream of Christian, and indeed Catholic, thinking. Augustine was not *in* the mainstream; he defined the mainstream.[1] Further, a fund of philosophical *cum* theological teaching, common to all thinkers, existed. This common fund stemmed ultimately from Pythagoras and was enhanced greatly through the Academy of Plato. Augustine, and others, made significant contributions to it until the time of Anselm. Many of the teachings found in both Anselm and Augustine are part of this common fund. That Augustine influenced Anselm at least in these ways is beyond dispute.

Contemporary scholars would, however, like to go beyond a mere noting of common theme. Ideally, they would like to establish a direct literary dependence of Anselm upon Augustine and determine what works of Augustine Anselm had read. And it is precisely here that difficulties begin to arise. Anselm, like many other authors of late antiquity and the early medieval period, only infrequently acknowledges direct positive dependence on an earlier author. The use of other authors was deemed a compliment both to the earlier author and to the reader. Acknowledgement was not necessary.[2] Further, Anselm did not directly borrow entire literary passages from Augustine or other authors whereby direct philological parallelism could be established. Rather, he had imbibed the thought of his master, interpreted it, and made it his own. What then is the contemporary scholar, enamored of nineteenth-century historical principles, to do?

One recent attempt to show the influence of the Augustinian corpus on Anselm has concentrated on thematic development. Professor Klaus Kienzler has shown the similarity in themes in the *Confessiones* and the *Soliloquia*, on the one hand, and the *Proslogion* on the other.[3] It is likely that the same could be done for other works. Another avenue of approach has been to establish the list of Augustinian works which were present in the monastic library in Bec.[4] Such independent evidence would be at least confirmatory of what internal evidence would lead us to suspect. Nevertheless, the results of these investigations have been relatively meager.

Direct references to Augustine in Anselm's corpus are sparse but instructive in establishing dependence. Augustine's name appears eight times in six passages in the works of Anselm. All of the references are to the *De trinitate* and concern the *Monologion* or *Proslogion*. In the prologue to the former, Anselm writes:

> Reviewing this work often, I could not find that I said anything in it which was not in harmony with the writings of the catholic fathers and especially St. Augustine. Wherefore, if it seems to anyone that I have published anything in this small work which either is too new or is not true, I ask that he not immediately cry out that I am a presumer of novelties or an asserter of falsehood, but that he first read diligently the books of the famous teacher Augustine *De trinitate*, and then judge my small work according to them.[5]

This is not the only time that Anselm refers to Augustine in connection with the *Monologion*. Indeed, Anselm seems to have viewed the work as a brief summation of some arguments found in the *De trinitate*. Often Anselm turns to Augustine to support his use of Trinitarian terminology or to show the differences between the Greeks and Latins on this matter. Augustine's name would of course have been enough to end any dispute.

How closely Anselm's intellectual project in the *Monologion* and *Proslogion*, *fides quaerens intellectum*, follows Augustine's *credo ut intelligam* needs little demonstration. Anselm's remark that he was attempting to follow the thought of Augustine in his intellectual project is by and large justifiable.[6] Both Augustine and Anselm are trying to achieve an understanding of the mysteries of faith through philosophy. Both use the philosophical *cum* theological tradition as it has come down to them to achieve this understanding. In several passages, both Augustine and Anselm use the identical text from the book of Isaiah, *Nisi credideritis, non intelligetis* as the scriptural basis for their project.[7] In particular, it is the *De trinitate* which provides the background against which we should judge Anselm's views on faith and reason. Anselm's descriptive title of the *Monologion* as *Exemplum meditandi de ratione fidei* and the *Proslogion* as *Fides quaerens intellectum* would both be apt descriptive titles for the *De trinitate*.

Augustine's over-all project does not change that much over the years. From the beginning in Cassiciacum, it was the role of philosophy to give understanding to the Christian mysteries. A much studied passage from the *Contra Academicos* points this out:

> No one doubts that we are led to learning by the twin weight of authority and reason. I am certain never to depart from the authority of Christ for I do not find a stronger. What must be pursued by the most subtle reasoning — I have been so affected that I desire with impatience to grasp what is true not only by belief but also by understanding—I am confident provisionally that I shall find it with the Platonists, a project that is not repugnant to our sacred writings.[8]

Augustine is but a Christian neophyte at this time. Yet his project is clear. He wishes to understand the mysteries of faith, a project which is in accord with the scriptures. Faith was to provide the subject matter, philosophy the understanding. This project remains fundamentally the same in the *De trinitate*. A classic statement of it occurs in *De trinitate IX*:

> An intention of one seeking is most prudent until that is apprehended toward which we tend and are extended. But that intention is right which sets out from faith. A certain faith in some way is the beginning of knowledge; a certain knowledge is only perfected after this life when we shall see face to face (1 Cor. 12:12). Therefore, let us be so wise that we may know that the disposition to seek the truth is safer than to presume unknown things as if they were known. Therefore let us seek as one who will find; and thus let us find as one who will seek. For when man has been consummated, then he begins (Sir. 18:6). Concerning things to be believed let us not doubt with infidelity; concerning things to be understood, let us

not affirm with rashness; in the former authority is to be held; in the latter truth is to be sought.[9]

The scriptural foundation for this project, as in many other fathers of the church, is Matthew 7:7: *Quaerite et invenietis.*[10] Faith provides the matter of the search; reason provides the understanding. *Fides quaerit; intellectus invenit.*

If these were the only similarities of methodology between Augustine and Anselm, there would be little point in establishing a relationship. Although Augustine may have been the first to attempt on a large scale an understanding of the faith, any Christian intellectual could be said to be attempting an *intellectus fidei.* Augustine's synthesis, if such it might be called, stands out since it was the outstanding attempt at an understanding of the faith through the use of philosophy until the thirteenth century. However, there is much more to the relationship between Augustine and Anselm. An important text for understanding the methodology of Anselm and its relation to that of Augustine occurs in the *Epistola de incarnatione verbi*:

> That God is one, unique, individual, and simple nature and three persons has been argued by the unshakeable reasons of the holy fathers and especially St. Augustine after the apostles and the evangelists. If anyone would deign to read my two small works, namely the *Monologion* and *Proslogion,* which were done especially for this purpose, that what we hold by faith concerning the divine nature and its persons outside of the incarnation, is able to be proved by necessary reasons without the authority of scripture; if anyone, I say, wishes to read these works, I think that he will find there concerning this matter what he can not disapprove or wish to condemn. If in these works I have placed something which either I have not read somewhere else or I have not remembered that I have read —not as if by teaching what our teachers did not know or correcting what they did not say well, but perhaps by saying what they were silent about, which nevertheless is not out of harmony with it or is comfortable to it—in order to respond in behalf of our faith against those who, unwilling to believe what they do not understand ridicule those who believe, or to help the religious desire of those who humbly seek to understand what they firmly believe, I do not think that I ought to be reproved for this.[11]

In this passage, two aspects of Anselm's *intellectus fidei* are relevant to a discussion of his relationship to Augustine. The first is that

Anselm views his work in the *Monologion* and *Proslogion* as providing an understanding of the nature and persons of God outside of the incarnation by necessary reasons without the authority of Scripture. Olivier duRoy has maintained that such methodology is peculiarly Augustinian.[12] In the *Confessiones VII*, when Augustine describes his intellectual conversion after the reading the *libri Platonicorum*, he tells us that he found there a teaching on the Trinity, but no teaching on the incarnation.[13] Augustine understood God becoming man against the Neoplatonic, and especially Porphyrian, background of a way of salvation. Nevertheless, an understanding of the Trinitarian Godhead he was to take from Neoplatonism, the understanding of the incarnation as a way of salvation from the scriptures. And, in duRoy's view, this methodological point of Augustine's intellectual conversion was to have a major effect on his early works and was to remain with him the remainder of his life, so that even in the *De trinitate*, the incarnation does not provide an understanding of the Trinity. And, in duRoy's view, this methodology has had an enormous impact on later theology so that in Anselm and Aquinas, for example, the incarnation does not provide a means to the understanding of the Trinity. And, again in duRoy's view, this influence was not necessarily for the good.

I am not so sure that duRoy's view is entirely correct. First of all, I believe that Augustine read the Neo-platonists through the prism of Christianity. Certainly the preaching of Ambrose, the ambiance of the so-called Milanese Circle, and perhaps the religious teaching of Monica brought Augustine a perspective from which he viewed the Platonists. And I am sure that duRoy would agree with this. It is certainly true that in the *Confessiones* and Augustine's early works, his triadic, if not to say Trinitarian, thought is based upon ancient philosophy, primarily Neo-platonism, understood through the prism of Christianity. It is further true that he viewed the incarnation as a way of salvation and at times tends to see Christianity as Platonism for the masses. Nevertheless, I do not think that it is wholly accurate to say that in the *De trinitate* Augustine's understanding of the Trinity is entirely devoid of scriptural and incarnational understanding. Indeed, the *locus classicus* for finding Augustine's teaching on the incarnation is in fact the *De trinitate*. It is true, however, that in his search for images of the Trinity in creation Augustine is more dependent on ancient philosophy than on the Scriptures. It is even possible that this is as it should be. In any event there is no doubt that this tendency in Augustine becomes a methodology in Anselm.

The second point of this passage in the *Epistola de incarnatione verbi* which I should like to discuss is Anselm's search for "necessary reasons." This is not the only time this or a like phrase is used in his works.[14] *Rationes necessariae* and other like phrases are also found in his treatment of the incarnation. Anselm tried to prove the necessity of the incarnation on the part of God for man's salvation, *remoto Christo* as Anselm himself puts it.[15] But, in the *Epistola de incarnatione verbi* the phrase is connected with the *Monologion* and the *Proslogion* and the discussions of the existence and nature of God found there. Here the words "necessary reasons" seem equivalent to "without the authority of Scripture." In those works, both the unity and the trinity of the Godhead are mentioned.[16]

Anselm is much more optimistic than his mentor in the *De trinitate* about man's ability to reach knowledge of God in this life. In this work — and Anselm is aware of it — Augustine maintains repeatedly that knowledge of God is available to man in this life only *per speculum et in aenigmate*. Augustine explains this Pauline phrase in terms of the figures of speech of classical Latin with which he, as a rhetor, was familiar.

> This is one entire phrase which is said: *Videmus nunc per speculum et in aenigmate*. Next, insofar as it seems to me, just as he wished image to be understood by the word mirror, so he wished by the word aenigma a similitude, albeit an obscure one, difficult to perceive, to be understood . . . . Therefore by the words mirror and aenigma some similitudes signified by the Apostle can be understood which are accommodated to understanding God in the way that he can be . . . ."[17]

Augustine came to be rather pessimistic concerning man's ability to reach any knowledge of the triune God in this life, though, of course, he did not reject the human possibility of such knowledge entirely. This pessimism is perhaps the principal reason why the writing of the *De trinitate* took some twenty years.

Such pessimism was not always the case with Augustine. From the time of his conversion in 386 until well into the next decade, Augustine maintained that man could attain, with the help of God, a direct vision of God in this life.[18] Augustine was influenced in this direction by his reading of Plotinus' *Ennead on Beauty* and Porphyry's *De regressu animae*. And when man would attain this vision, he would also attain a full understanding of the Christian mysteries.[19] At this time, although Augustine saw major differences between Platonism and Christianity on the possibility of the incarnation, he was optimistic concerning their similarities. During the middle of the last decade of the fourth century, Augustine was called upon to examine and explain Paul's *Epistle to the Romans* and *Epistle to the Galatians* in detail. The themes of salvation through grace attainable fully only in the next life are of paramount importance in each of these Epistles. During this period Augustine came decisively to realize that man could attain the vision of God only in the next life and that salvation was attainable only through the grace of God. Of course, Augustine was still interested in the degree of knowledge that man could attain concerning God in this life. Augustine's — and might we say man's — final answer to this question is contained in the *De trinitate*.

The use of the term "necessary reasons" by Anselm still bothers us. The term has been traced back to Marius Victorinus. Anselm's optimism concerning finding these "necessary reasons" is more reminiscent of the early Augustine than the older bishop. If I am correct that the *De trinitate*, and not the earlier works, forms the Augustinian background to Anselm's thought, then Anselm's project bespeaks a greater optimism than that of his master. It is even possible that Anselm did not realize the difference between the early and late Augustine on this point.

In the *Cur deus homo* and elsewhere, Anselm argues to the necessity of the incarnation from its suitability. He argues many times that, because the incarnation was the most suitable means for God to justify man, it was necessary that it happen. Not that Anselm is unaware of the problem which necessity works on the Godhead. He is well aware that necessity would place a limitation on God and this he does not want to do. In the course of the *Cur deus homo* Anselm distinguishes an absolute necessity from a conditioned necessity and tries to show that it is under this second type of necessity that God is necessitated.[21] A complete discussion of necessity in Anselm's works would take us too far afield. Yet, enough has been said to show in what area a problem exists.

Anselm's mindset in the *Cur Deus homo* concerning necessary reasons is not so far different from the *Proslogion* argument for the existence of God. In the latter, Anselm argues from the idea of God to his real existence. While this argument obviously owes something to the argument from eternal truth in *De libero arbitrio* II, iii, 7-xv, 40, it is significantly different from it. Whereas Augustine argues for an immutable ground for eternal truths, Anselm argues from the idea of God to his real existence. Nevertheless, Anselm's reasoning from suitability to real existence is not far removed from a kind of ontological argument for the truths of faith. This mindset almost bespeaks a kind of meliorism by which a good God would be necessitated to act in the most fitting manner. Although Augustine argues the suitability of the incarnation for man's salvation in *De trinitate* XIII, such reasoning is not Augustine's. It would take another two centuries of thought after Anselm to distinguish more clearly between *debet* and *decet*. And it would take the reaction to the *Aufklärung* to show us more clearly that optimism introduced an unwelcome necessity into the Godhead.

What can account for the differences between Anselm and Augustine in these matters? We can speculate about the Dark Ages and the lack of genuine theological genius until Anselm during that period. We can further speculate concerning the monastic life of reflection and meditation to which Augustine had aspired most of his life, and had realized for various short periods, but which Anselm possessed for over thirty years. Augustine's speculations came out of a rugged experience in his own life and the life around him. Anselm's came out of monastic reflection, the life of the spirit. The rise of the monastic school also played a part in this difference. Theology, if it could be distinguished from philosophy, was beginning to be treated as a formalized scientific pursuit in the time of Anselm. While Augustine laid down the first program for the Christian use of the liberal arts and the *De doctrina christiana* remains the charter for the Christian intellectual, his thought, steeped in the ancient tradition of rhetoric and occasioned by contemporary problems in the African Church, was a far cry from the contemplative atmosphere of a monastic school. However, *his dictis*, we must also allow for the difference of individual genius. A thinker is not the mere product of his influences. If *Quellenforschung* has taught us one thing, it is that the thought of a man is not the sum total of the influences upon him. And so it is with Augustine and Anselm. Though they are in the same stream and one has exerted a powerful influence on the other, their thought remains different.

Both of these intellectual giants offer us food for thought on the matter of faith and reason for the contemporary world. In a world which is so highly specialized that one science finds it difficult to speak to another, that even two scientists within the same field find communication difficult, Augustine and Anselm speak to us concerning the unity of truth. In a time when a kind of Cartesian split between philosophy and theology, between faith and reason, has occurred even on Catholic campuses, Augustine and Anselm speak to us concerning the ultimate unity of the theological and philosophical enterprise. In a world grown increasingly interested in the quantitative and the rational, Augustine and Anselm speak to us of the spiritual and the intuitive. And finally in a world which has become increasingly embarrassed in speaking of God, Augustine and Anselm point out that God — and not man — is at the center of the universe. On this, the hundredth anniversary of a school under the aegis of Anselm and his followers, it is well for us to reflect on these truths.

NOTES

1. For this reason, the Catholic Church has been reluctant to condemn even the more extreme predestinationist views of Augustine, given their final formulation in the heat of the Pelagian controversy.

2. Even the scriptures are many times alluded to without direct citation. Both the scriptures and the tradition were so much a part of many writers that direct citation was neither necessary nor indeed possible.

3. K. Kienzler, "Zur philosophisch-theologischen Denkform bei Augustinus und bei Anselm von Canterbury," *Anselm Studies 2*, ed. J. Schnaubelt and F. Van Fleteren (New York: Kraus International Publications, 1988):353-387.

4. The existence of such a list was suggested to me by my colleague Professor Thomas Losoncy, of Villanova University and the Augustinian Historical Institute.

5. *Monologion*, prologue: Schmitt 1,8: Quam ego saepe retractans nihil potui invenire me in ea dixisse, quod non catholicorum patrum et maxime beati AUGUSTINI scriptis cohaereat. Quapropter si cui videbitur, quod in eodem opusculo aliquid protulerim, quod aut nimis novum sit aut a veritate dissentiat: rogo, ne statim me aut praesumptorem novitatum aut falsitatis assertorem exclamet, sed prius libros praefati doctoris AUGUSTINI De trinitate diligenter perspiciat, deinde secundum eos opusculum meum diiudicet.

6. See note above.

7. Isaiah 7:9. Both Augustine and Anselm use an old Latin form of this text not found in the Vulgate.

8. *Contra Academicos* III,xx,43: Green 71: Nulli autem dubium est gemino pondere nos impelli ad discendum, auctoritatis atque rationis. Mihi autem certum est nusquam prorsus a Christi auctoritate: non enim reperio ualentiorem. Quod autem subtilissima ratione persequendum est, ita enim jam sum affectus, ut quid sit verum, non credendo solum, sed etiam intelligendo apprehendere impatienter desiderem, apud Platonicos me interim quod sacris nostris non repugnet reperturum esse confido.

9. *De trinitate* IX,i,1: PL XLII, 961: Tutissima est enim quaerentis intentio, donec apprehendere illud quo tendimus et quo extendimur. Sed ea recta intentio est, quae profiscitur a fide. Certa enim fides utcumque inchoat cognitonem: cognitio vero certa non perficietur, nisi post hanc vitam, cum videbimus facie ad faciem. Hoc ergo sapiamus, ut noverimus tutiorem esse affectum vera quaerendi, quam incognita pro cognitis praesumendi. Sic ergo quaeramus tamquam invenituri: et sic inveniamus tamquam quaesituri. Cum enim consummaverit homo, tunc incipit (Si 18:6). De credendis nulla infidelitate dubitemus, de intelligendis nulla temeritate affirmemus: In illis auctoritas tenenda est, in his veritas exquirenda.

10. J. Daniélou, *"Recherche et Tradition chez les Peres", Studia Patristica*, XII, 1:3-13.

11. *Epistula de incarnatione verbi* VI: Schmitt II, 20-21: Quod utique deus una et sola et individua et simplex sit natura et tres personae, sanctorum patrum et maxime beati AUGUSTINI post apostolos et evangelistas inexpugnabilibus rationibus disputatum est. Sed et si quis legere dignabitur duo parva mea opuscula, Monologion scilicet et Proslogion, quae ad hoc maxime facta sunt, ut quod fide tenemus de divina natura et eius personis praeter incarnationem, necessariis rationibus sine scripturae auctoritate probar: possit; si inquam aliquis ea legere voluerit, puto quia et ibi de hoc inveniet quod nec improbare poterit nec contemnere volet. In quibus si aliquid quod alibi aut non legi aut memini me legisse — non quasi docendo quod doctores nostri nescierunt aut corrigendo quod non bene dixerunt, sed dicendo forsitan quod tacuerunt, quod tamen ab illorum dictis non discordet sed illis cohaereat — posui ad respondendum pro fide nostra contra eos, qui nolentes credere quod non intelligunt derident credentes, sive ad adiuvandum religiosum studium eorum qui humiliter quaerunt intelligere quod firmissime credunt: nequaquam ab hoc me redarguendum existimo.

12. duRoy, *L'intelligence de la foi en la trinité selon saint Augustin* (Paris: Etudes Augustiniennes, 1966), 458ff.; see also his article in the *New Catholic Encyclopedia*, "Augustine", vol 2, s.v.

13. *Confessiones* VII,ix,13: BA 13,608; xxi,27: BA 13, 638-42.

14. Many similar phrases are found, such as *oportet esse* and *necesse est*, throughout the works of Anselm.

15. See *Cur deus homo, praefatio*: Schmitt 1, 42. The proof of the reasonableness of the incarnation is the theme of the entire *Cur deus homo*.

16. For the existence of one God see *Monologion* I-VI, *Proslogion* I-IV. For the existence of a triune God, see *Monologion* XXXVIII-LXI, *Proslogion* XXIII.

17. *De trinitate* XV,ix,16: PL XLII,1069: Una est enim cum tota sic dicitur, Videmus nunc per speculum et in aenigmate; Proinde, quantum mihi videtur, sicut nomine speculi imagine voluit intelligi; ita nomine aenigmatis quamvis similitudinem, tamen obscurum, et ad perspiciendum difficilem .... igitur speculi et aenigmatis nomine quaecumque similitudines ab Apostolo significatae intelligi possint, quae accommodatae sunt ad intelligendum Deum, eo modo quo potest.

18. The texts in Augustine are numerous on this point. See for example, *Contra Academicos* II,ii,4; III, xix,42; *De ordine* I,viii,23ff., II,v,15; xix,51; *Retractationes* I,iii,2-4; *De moribus ecclesiae catholicae* XXXI,66; *De quantitate aniae* XXXII,76; *De vera religione* XII,24; *De sermone domini in monte* I,4,12; *Contra Adimantum Manichaeum* IX,1. See F. Van Fleteren, "Augustine and the Possibility of the Vision of God in this life", *Studies in Medieval Culture*, XI, 9-16.

19. See *De ordine* II, v, 15; ix, 27; xix, 51.

20. See *Cur deus homo, passim,* but especially 1, 25; II, 6.

21. See *Cur deus homo* II, 17.

SAINT THOMAS AQUINAS
AND THE ROAD TO TRUTH
Montague Brown

Saint Thomas Aquinas possessed a deep confidence in reason's ability to get to the truth. Although he knew, as a Christian, that there were some truths which natural reason could never discover on its own — such as the truths that God is a Trinity, and that Christ is human and divine — he was sure that reason could understand the truth about the structure and order of the universe and what it means to be a human being. St. Thomas discovered, however, that these truths are rather more mysterious than anyone had thought. For the answers to the questions which arise concerning the universe and human nature do not appear to be reducible to single, neat formulations of meaning, suitable for placing within a deductive system of truth. This paper will examine St. Thomas' road to truth in three ways. First of all, the general outlines of St. Thomas' method of inquiry will be discussed. Secondly, four central philosophical issues will be briefly examined in the light of this method. And finally, the moral and spiritual context of St. Thomas' quest for meaning will be addressed.

Let us begin by sketching out the problem which St. Thomas faced. When he applied himself to the great philosophical questions, such as "What is the nature of reality?" or "What is it to be a human being?" or "How does the ultimate source of reality interact with human nature?" St. Thomas found himself in each case with irreducibly multiple truths. For example, he found that reason's attempts to explain the universe completely yield, on the one hand, comprehensive laws of physics operating within the universe and, on the other, a cause of the very existence of the universe. No amount of understanding about how the universe conforms to basic physical laws can explain why there is a universe in the first place; and the understanding that there is a creator of the universe tells us nothing about the way the universe itself operates. He also found that reason's attempts to explain human nature uncover the oddity that we are at once material and immaterial. When we examine what it is to be human, we find ourselves to be both sensing and thinking beings. This implies that we are material and immaterial, for one cannot sense without a body, and what is purely material cannot think. We naturally want to know exactly how these irreducibly multiple truths fit together, but our actual understanding falls short of reconciling all meaningful evidence. We seek a perfectly unified explanation, but find truths in tension.

Faced with such a problem, what is one to do? The quickest and most obvious way of reaching unity is to deny one truth or the other. Thus, some claim that there cannot be a God because God could not be verified by scientific method. Others claim that, since there is a God, science is not really certain knowledge; science is superseded by God's Revelation. As for the puzzle of human nature, some claim that we are purely material, and that even thinking is a merely mechanical process; others claim that we are purely immaterial with sensing and all material reality deriving somehow from thought.

In this quickest way of handling truths in tension, one truth is virtually ignored. The attempt is made to handle the evidence covered by the other truth in terms of the one truth chosen. When this happens, an obvious and commonsensical explanation is replaced by one obscure and esoteric. It is absurd for science to adopt the unproven axiom that God does not exist (which is implied by the scientific method, which holds that all that is real is material) and then assume that it has proven that God does not exist. It is equally absurd for the romantic fundamentalist to assume that because God created the universe, there really is no universe — no internally ordered natural world with its own real structure — but only God. As to the issue of human nature, it is ridiculous to explain a stubbed toe in terms of immaterial causes alone, or to explain something that transcends time and place (i.e., thought) merely in terms of what is measured by time and place (i.e., material processes). Thus, the problem with this quickest and most obvious way of dealing with two truths in tension is that it succeeds in achieving unity only at the expense of truth. One truth learned by reason is abandoned in favor of another. In short, it provides an explanation by denying reason. Reason is sacrificed to reason, and we end in absurdity.

The question must always be: what is the evidence which shows that a claim to truth is legitimate or illicit? Unless there is good evidence that science rules out the existence of God, or that God rules out the possibility of science, then we are not in a position to deny one or the other. Unless there is good evidence that our materiality rules out our immateriality or vice versa, we are in no position to deny either aspect of our nature. The inability to formulate perfectly how two truths are one in reality is no grounds for denying either truth. Only obvious contradiction, based on evidence, can justify rejection.

This, then, is St. Thomas' method: keep all truth. Never exclude from consideration any meaningful evidence. This method reveals reality as more mysterious than we might have thought. The commitment to hard thinking discovers the truths about the relation between God and the universe and about the nature of the human being to be, not static achievements of comprehensive knowledge, but dynamic quests for deeper meaning. In the static achievement of knowledge, the intellectual life must die the death of triviality. It does not matter whether one has achieved a closed system if the system does not respond to reality. And, in fact, no system can perfectly respond to reality, for the meaning of reality lies ultimately in this mystery of deepening meaning. Our thinking is a reaching for reality, not its rule.

What is needed to reconcile truths in tension is a higher viewpoint which can allow for what is true on both sides. A case where such a higher viewpoint has not been reached we call a mystery. A mystery is not a contradiction, although it may appear to be so. It is not the destroyer of reason's life, but its spur. The presence of mystery is the invasion of a question, of a wonder which awakens reason to life. This is the normal way scientific knowledge progresses, as, in response to the unexpected, it moves to explanations of reality which are more and more comprehensive. But when one reaches the ultimate questions of reality, to which the answers are these truths in tension, then the higher viewpoint which shows precisely how the truths fit together escapes our grasp. At the frontier of reason, we have a reach into mystery for meaning. However, since mystery is not the enemy of meaning but its source and protector, the discovery that reason lives on the edge of wonder should not be cause for alarm, but for affirmation and celebration of the surprise that is the world and our life. Reason shows itself to be alive in wonder.

Let us now consider some of the actual philosophical problems with which St. Thomas grappled. For the purpose of this paper, I would like to consider four: the relationship between science and the creating God; the mysterious nature of the human being; the relationship between human freedom and God's providence; and the manner in which moral obligation and the final end of man are related to divinity. Of course, treatment of these issues must be brief here, but I hope to show the depth of St. Thomas' philosophical contribution.

The center of St. Thomas' originality in dealing with these perennial problems lies in the revolutionary answers he gives to the two great questions of philosophy. To the question "Why?" he answers with the radical notion of God as creator. To the question "What am I?" he answers with the uncompromised vision of the unity of the human being.

The world raises a question for us that the world cannot answer: "Why is there a world at all?" This is a non-scientific question in the sense that its answer cannot be verified by the scientific method, for there is no possibility of measuring or detecting through experiment the cause of all being. But in another sense, it is the ultimate scientific question, for it is the taking of the question "Why?" all the way to the root of reality. What is revolutionary about St. Thomas' position is that, unlike his illustrious Greek predecessors Plato and Aristotle, St. Thomas does not hold God to be the highest and most powerful of all beings within any common context, in which case God might be regarded as an alternative explanation to the reality and activity of other things. On the contrary, the God of St. Thomas is outside the context of things: he is the creator of the context — the maker and sustainer of the universe.[1]

Oddly enough, the knowledge of God as creator, which holds God to be a cause unlike other causes discovered by science, guarantees the validity of the scientific quest to understand the world. As creating cause, God makes it false to say that his causality is the only real causality: the created things of the universe, with all their casual relationships, really do exist. Therefore, God's causality is not the only explanation for the way the world is.[2] God the creator is not an alternative to natural explanation: he is the explanation for that explanation. He explains the existence of natural knowledge of the world by explaining the existence of the world.

As for St. Thomas' understanding of the profound unity of the human being, this guarantees the validity of the range of human pursuits from knowledge to free choices to the quest for human happiness. The human being is a thinking animal, the unity of immaterial and material being.[3] The only way science can be justified is by admitting that we have an activity (thinking) which transcends the material world that science studies.[4] Universal statements about the structure of reality could never issue from the particularity of material things, since material things are always isolated from each other by time and space— Rover and Spot are not the same matter, yet they are both dogs. In terms of the power of free choice, the only way freedom and ethical obligation can be warranted is if we transcend our material environment. if we are merely material beings subject to determined laws of matter, then we cannot think, we are not free, we cannot do right or wrong, and we cannot love. Of course, even more basically, if we are merely material beings (and hence restricted to this time and this place), we have no reason to suppose that all runs in accordance with universal laws of matter, or even, in fact, to suppose that we are merely material beings; for both these statements presuppose an ability to think in universal terms, to understand beyond the here and now.

On the other hand, the only way it makes sense for us to be in this body and in this material world is if it is natural for us to be so embodied.[5] If we are really only rational souls, then the only explanation for our being in the world is that this is some great mistake, that the material world is evil and we are somehow entrapped. But this makes a mockery of our recognition of goods, for all our basic values presuppose a valuing of being embodied. We value life, and life is organically transmitted from another body; we value knowledge, and we draw our knowledge initially from the material world through our senses; we value beauty, and beauty is appreciated through the senses as well as the intellect; we value friendship, and friendship depends on communication which depends on bodies.[6]

This recognition that we are beings who communicate meaningfully is crucial to understanding our nature, for communication requires both aspects of our being: our rationality and our materiality. We can share meaning because meaning is something that can be shared—an immaterial reality which can be in two places at the same time and in the same way. And we can share meaning in the ways we do—language, art, music—because we have the ability, through being embodied, to make signs and to see and hear them. Finally, this unity really belongs to each unique individual. Knowing God as creator, St. Thomas knows how it can be that thinking beings, which in their immateriality cannot be generated or corrupted, can come to be at a particular moment of time. He need not say, with Plato, that each individual has been moving from body to body, or, with Aristotle, that each individual is lent reason by some transcendent mind. He can say what coincides much better with common sense, that each individual does his or her own sensing and thinking and began to sense and think at a certain point in time.[7] The rational soul cannot, indeed, be generated from the matter of the parents; it must be created by God.[8] But since creation is not something that happened once long ago, but the constant dependence of all things on God, there is no reason why new thinking animals may not come to be.

These two revolutionary ideas transform other problems as well. Without the notion of God as creator, God's providence must preclude free will; for if God is a nature of a particular king which is just more powerful than others and hence can dominate them, then when God acts in another being, that being's own activity is suspended. God the creator, however, makes the activities of all things. His activity in a thing does not suspend that thing's own proper activity but guarantees that the proper activity operate. Hence, God's presence to me is my freedom.[9] As for St. Thomas' understanding of the human being, it is obvious that, if we are not rational beings but mere animals, then we have no freedom regardless of what one's idea of God may be. And if one's rationality is not really one's own, then again there is no real freedom. Only if one can think and hence deliberate, and only if one's deliberation is really one's own—really belongs to this thinking animal—can one be said to have freedom.[10] Thus, St. Thomas' resolution of the problem of providence and free choice depends on his understanding of God as creator and the human being as an individual unity of rationality and animality.

When we turn to the issue of human obligation and the final end of man, we find these two revolutionary ideas of St. Thomas again clearing the way to new insights. In the first place, only if we are thinking beings free to choose (that is, undetermined by the laws of matter) can we be obligated in any way. In addition, only if it is my choice, and not the choice of universal reason in me, can I be said to be obligated.[11] When the questions arise as to whether ethics is purely a matter of divine fiat, and whether the ultimate fulfillment of the human being is human or divine, the importance of St. Thomas' teachings on God as creator and on the human being as individual embodied rationality become even more pronounced. Since God the creator makes and directs all things, one might indeed say that ethics is what God decides. But what could be the fiat of a creating God for a human being? It must be this: be what you are, be human. God makes us to be human in order that we be human, that we fulfill human nature. His requirements for us are what are naturally good for us.[12] Thus, God does not impose ethics from without, but gives us ethics by giving us existence as human beings.

Is it when we ask about the final fulfillment of the human being, that we finally make the jump between the human and the divine? No, again; for human fulfillment is not the replacement of human nature with divinity, but the perfection of human nature in divinity, that is, in love. The beatific vision is not divinization on the model of Plato or Aristotle in which human nature is forsaken in favor of divinity. Our ultimate happiness on St. Thomas' model is human happiness, not absorption into God. In addition, St. Thomas' insistence on the naturalness of human embodiment underscores this point. A properly human activity is one which involves the whole human being, body and soul. Our pursuit of the basic human goods is the pursuit of embodied reason, for, as we detailed above, all these values have something to do with being embodied. The insistence of St. Thomas on the resurrection of the body as our final state is meaningless if our happiness is to be disembodied contemplation and absorption into God.[13] Human happiness is just that—the fulfillment of all that it is to be human. As a Christian, of course, St. Thomas would believe that it is more, that it is a sharing in the divine life. But this sharing will not displace our humanity, for grace does not replace nature but perfects it.[14]

It is St. Thomas' great devotion to reason that allows him so to deepen the philosophical explanation of God and human being. Some might rise up at this point and say, with the Protestant reformers, that this devotion to reason is St. Thomas' very problem, that he lets reason get in the way of faith. Others might object from the other side, in the name of science and philosophy, that St. Thomas' religious commitment ruins his reason. It should, however, be clear at this point that a devotion to reason is not in any way incompatible with a religious devotion to God. Nor is devotion to God incompatible with devotion to reason. That St. Thomas is completely devoted to reason does not make him a rationalist in the sense of one who rejects all that does not fit in a deductive system. The great truths which we have been discussing are all matters of reaching up to open-ended, living truths which surpass the comprehensiveness characteristic of a closed deductive system. Nor does the fact that St. Thomas is a Christian believer vitiate the claim that he is more reasonable than his illustrious pagan predecessors Plato and Aristotle. Faith in God is faith in love; it is a commitment to the way things are (or, in the case of human nature, the way things ought to be). God makes things be what they are, and the only possible motivation for such a gift is love. God as creator is the guarantor of science, not its demise. Likewise, he is the guarantor that we know of human nature is really true of human nature. He is also the guarantor that human beings are really free, and that there really is such a thing as human responsibility and happiness.

As making things to be is the act of love, so knowing how things are requires an act of love. The context of St. Thomas' quest for truth is a moral commitment inspired and supported by love. St. Thomas understands knowing not on the model of snapshots of reality—static images of one-to-one correspondence of what is real with a picture in the mind—but as a dynamic activity of formulating and reformulating the truth, as new elements of the mystery that is reality raise new questions. He says, in one place, that we do not fully know the essence of even the simplest thing.[15] Knowing is a complex, multi-level affair. it involves the reception of sense data by which we are in continuity with a material world, the formulation of ideas which explain that world, and the judgment as to whether the ideas do correctly express the way the world is.[16] New sense data and new ideas raise new questions for judgment. Did I understand correctly? How can I account for this previously unrecognized bit of information? This procedure advances toward a more complete understanding of the way things are only under the directive of a moral concern. Unless we value knowledge, we shall never attain it. We are not passive receptors recording automatically, like video cameras, the way the world is. We are questioning animals, but questioning is not an automatic process. We must decide if we will hear the question. We can easily shut off the questioning because of impatience, weariness, fear, or prejudice. We can easily kill the life that is knowing. Presupposed to finding the truth is the unwavering commitment to the good of knowledge: that is a moral act without which philosophy, which is the life of natural reason, cannot be.

Finally, and by way of conclusion, let us ask how such an unwavering moral commitment is possible in a world vitiated by sin. Sin is the great unexplainable gap or defect in reality. One only sins if one knows an act is wrong yet nevertheless does it. There is no ignorance that needs correcting here, no additional law to be added to the natural law. We know that many of the things that we do are wrong; yet we do them. Before this mystery of sin we indeed appear helpless. What God offers us, according to St. Thomas, is love to free us from the fears and prejudices which keep us in self-imposed ignorance. Love, of course, cannot be a requirement, since love is a letting be — the freeing of someone to be himself or herself. Thus, the presence of a religious commitment to the creating God of love is not the addition of an alternative to reason, but the underscoring of reason's own requirement: the demand for a moral commitment to finding the truth, which commitment perfects the judgment, which perfects the insight, which grasps reality. The fully perfected human being, the happy human being, is the human being in love — that is, in God.

NOTES

1. See *Summa Theologiae* (hereafter cited as *S.T.*) I, Q. 44; Q. 104; and Q. 2, a. 3.
2. See *S.T.* I, Q. 103, a. 6; and *Summa Contra Gentiles* (hereafter cited as *C.G.*) III, 69.
3. See Preface to St. Thomas's Treatise on Man, S.T. I, Q. 75.
4. On the rational soul's transcendence of matter, see S.T. I, Q. 75, a. 2 and 6.
5. See *S.T.* I, Q. 76, a. 1.
6. For St. Thomas's teaching on the basic goods, see the foundational text *S.T.* I-II, Q. 94, a. 2.
7. On thinking as the operation of the individual, see *S.T.* I, Q. 76, a. 1.
8. See *S.T.* I, Q. 90, a. 1.

9. On God as the cause of free will, see S.T. I, Q. 105, a. 4; and C.G. III, 89 and 90.
10. On free choice as a concomitant of reason, see S.T. I, Q. 83, a. 1.
11. Right and wrong for St. Thomas are matters of intention, centrally, not situations or consequences. See S.T. I-II, q. 72.
12. On God's requirements for us being for our own good, see C.G. III, 24, [8]; and 122, [2 and 4].
13. On the resurrection of the body, see C.G. IV, 79-81.
14. See S.T. I, Q. 1, a. 8, ad. 2; and Q. 62, a. 7.
15. On the unknowability of the existing singular, see S.T. I, Q. 86, a. 1; and De Veritate, Q. 10, a. 5.
16. See S.T. I, Q. 84 and 85. My understanding of St. Thomas' theory of knowledge owes much to Bernard Lonergan, S.J. for his excellent treatment of St. Thomas's theory of knowledge, see Verbum: Word and Idea in Aquinas (Notre Dame: University of Notre Dame Press, 1967); for the distinction between static and dynamic viewpoints, see his Philosophy of God and Theology (Philadelphia: Westminster Press, 1973), Chap. 3.

EDUCATION IN THE LATE TWELFTH AND EARLY THIRTEENTH CENTURIES: THE WITNESS OF HÉLINAND OF FROIDMONT

Beverly Mayne Kienzle

INTRODUCTION

Hélinand (1160-1237), monk at the Cistercian monastery of Froidmont, authored several Latin works: the *Chronicon* (a history of the world), some short treatises, various letters, and a collection of primarily liturgical sermons.[1] His works, by their method of composition and their content, reveal much about medieval learning and teaching. Hélinand provided some information about his own schooling, identifying his childhood teacher. In his sermons he expressed opinions about education in the twelfth and early thirteenth centuries. We see reflected there a distrust of the university and the city, and the use of preaching as instruction to combat heresy. This study reviews Hélinand's life and schooling, and then focuses on writings, especially sermons that include ideas on education, teachers and students. Highlighted in the analysis of Hélinand's schooling and of his writing is the place he accorded classical or pagan literature. His own monastic humanism is viewed against the background of patristic and monastic attitudes towards the classics.

BIOGRAPHY

To summarize Hélinand's life, I draw on his works: he himself recounted most of what we know.[2] He tells in his *Chronicon* that his young father and uncle (*pueri nobiles et pulcherrimi*) lost their inheritance in 1127 and were forced to flee Flanders because of reprisals following the assassination of Charles, Count of Flanders (PL 212: 1028D). The uncle, Hellebaut, was later to become chamberlain of Henry (PL 212: 733B), who was the brother of Louis VII and the archbishop of Reims (1162-1175). Few dates in Hélinand's biography are certain. He gives us no information on the date of his birth, but he was probably born around 1160. He had definitely entered Froidmont by 1190,[3] and thus probably did so sometime during the 1180s.[4] But in his *Chronicon* he does identify his boyhood teacher Ralph of Beauvais, a pupil of Abelard (PL 212: 1035D). Following his studies, Hélinand acquired fame as a poet. In a letter written five years after his conversion, but not dated, he states that no spectacle was held anywhere without him (PL 212: 749A, 748D). Once a monk, Hélinand turned his flattering and chiding to praising God and rebuking the wealthy and mighty. Between 1193 and 1197, he composed the *Vers de la Mort*, where he allied himself with a personified Death, urging the powerful to reform their lives in preparation for the Judgment. After the 1199 Cistercian General Chapter ruling against monks who were writing satirical poetry in the vernacular[5] Hélinand must have refrained from composing such verse, but his sermons are filled with decrials of the outrages inflicted by unnamed kings and nobles. Alluding to Qo 12:11, he defends the preacher's duty to strike and puncture, using his words as goad and nail.[6] In 1229 we find Hélinand in southern France, in Toulouse, involved in efforts to preach against heresy. We have little information about his life between the *Vers de la Mort* and the sojourn in Toulouse. In a reference to a work on the life of the saints from Beauvais, I rediscovered a date for his death: February 3, 1237.[7] Hélinand's feast was celebrated for a time in the diocese of Beauvais, from 1854 until Pius X's reform of the breviary in 1911.[8]

RALPH OF BEAUVAIS AND HIS METHOD

From simply knowing the name of Hélinand's teacher, it is possible to glean some information on how Hélinand was taught and how that method influenced his own manner of composition. The 1142 *Chronicon* entry on Peter Abelard identifies Ralph, an Englishman, known as the Grammarian. He taught at Beauvais and, according to Hélinand, was as learned in divine literature as in secular (*tam in divinis quam in secularis litteris eruditus*) (PL 212: 1035D). Hélinand's wording indicates that Ralph achieved a balanced knowledge of sacred and secular texts, a balance that is reflected in Hélinand's works.

Ralph expressed his ideas in glosses, the preferred form of discourse for twelfth-century grammarians. Richard Hunt, in his studies on twelfth-century glosses, reconstructs some of the life and work of Hélinand's master. He finds that Ralph's name occurs in two anonymous glosses on Priscian (*Promisimus* and *Tria sunt*) with sufficient frequency to conclude that these glosses represent the methods of his school. Hunt also finds contemporary references to Ralph that indicate his importance.[9] Gerald of Wales, in his *Speculum ecclesiae*, speaks of Ralph as one who stood out above others as a grammarian and an authority on literature. Peter of Blois corresponded with Ralph who must have reproached Peter for leaving the schools and joining the *curia* of the Archbishop of Canterbury. Peter's reply defends the *curia* and chastises Ralph for not having moved on in his old age to knowledge higher than grammar. Together these references with their approximate dates indicate that Ralph was at the height of his fame in the late eleven sixties and seventies and that he was an old man when Peter wrote his letter, between 1182 and 1185.

Examining glosses and medieval library catalogues, Hunt finds three works by Ralph: the *Summa super Donatum*, a grammatical *summa*, the *Verba preceptiva*, a series of grammatical rules often illustrated with lines from classical poets, and the *Liber Titan*. The *Liber Titan*, unusual in form, contains long grammatical notes on lines from Ovid's *Metamorphoses* and Lucan's *Pharsalia*. Classical and biblical quotations illustrate the notes.

Comparing Ralph's school to earlier glossators (especially Petrus Helias), Hunt points out various characteristics of Ralph's method, among them the reapplication of the study of authors to grammar, seen in the free use of illustrative quotations.[10] The frequent use of classical quotations is a characteristic of Hélinand's style that distinguishes his sermons from those of his contemporaries. Ralph's school used illustrative quotations more frequently than earlier glossators and the classical quotations chosen demonstrate that the glossator made selections from his own reading instead of merely taking them from Priscian. It is not surprising then to observe the frequent use of illustrative classical quotations in Hélinand's work, nor to learn that researchers studying his classical borrowings and trying to imagine the contents of his library conclude that he probably used many works directly instead of simply plucking sayings from *florilegia*. In fact, correlations between his sermons and *Chronicon* point to his writing the last five books of the *Chronicon* as a preacher's aid.[11] Perhaps he was a compiler of other sources as well.

EDUCATION IN HELINAND'S SERMONS

While Hélinand tells in the *Chronicon* what few facts we have on his education, in the sermons he expresses views on instruction. His concerns are traditional, stated in Gregory's *Regula Pastoralis* and expressed in many thirteenth-century treatises,[12] but they reflect the climate and tensions of his own day: a society where university and city together were seen as threats to Cistercian life, and where instruction had as one of its purposes the refutation of heresy. Three sermons include denunciations of current practices, and two of those also offer prescriptions for education. One, delivered to a clerical and university audience on the occasion of the founding of the University of Toulouse, is expressly concerned with the purposes of education and has as its background the Albigensian war.

Hélinand did not like what he saw in the universities. He denounced hypocritical teachers and greedy students. One could imagine him today joining those who lament that students are no longer interested in public service but instead pursue courses of study aimed only at obtaining high salaries and material wealth. University masters are criticized in Sermons Eighteen for Pentecost and Twenty for the Assumption. In Sermon Eighteen, Hélinand chides teachers of Scripture who dress and act in a way that demonstrates that the world is topsy-turvy—a frequent medieval literary topos. To support his assertion, he states that owls fly by day and no longer flee the sun, and he describes the vanity and gluttony of these teachers with lively and even crude details. He calls them rosy doctors (*rosei . . . doctores*, PL 212: 634B), and accuses them of reducing their tonsures to a minimal size, curling their hair, and looking in mirrors all day. Gluttonous, they feed on the patrimony of the church while serving their stomachs more than Christ. In a world upside down, they wear shoes on their hands, gloves on their feet, and have various body parts reversed. These preachers and teachers are condemned as pleasure-seekers who without the practice of good works have but worthless learning to offer (PL 212: 634D). In Sermon Twenty, Hélinand turns to those he calls delicate masters (*delicati magistri*, PL 212: 651). They too are denounced for gluttony and vanity. With full stomachs, they debate about fasting, and while wrapped in silver and stuffed with gold, they recommend poverty (PL 212: 651BC). They also practice unchastity while preaching about chastity. Various images illustrate the emptiness of their preaching: bark without sap, a lamp without oil, a wedding without a bridegroom, and food without seasoning.

The fullest statement of Hélinand's views on education, teachers, and students is found in his Sermon Fifteen for the Ascension.[13] This is also the most studied sermon of Hélinand because it has interested historians who investigate the founding of the University of Toulouse. The Treaty of Paris, signed on April 12, 1229, contained a clause providing for the foundation of a new university in Toulouse. Presumably the teaching of orthodoxy would help to combat heresy. The abbot of Grandselve, Helie, was responsible for organizational details, including recruiting the university masters. Recruitment was facilitated by a quarrel in Paris, where in late March the university issued an ultimatum demanding redress of its grievances within a month after Easter, thus by May 15. Unsatisfied students and masters began to leave Paris, and some, including John of Garland, journeyed to Toulouse. It is usually agreed that the university's opening ceremony took place on Ascension Day, May 24, 1229, and that Hélinand preached for that occasion in the Church of Saint James to an audience of students and university masters.

In this Ascension Day sermon, Hélinand cautions against learning undertaken without a spiritual dimension, attacks proud philosophers, and criticizes students whose studies are motivated by the desire to earn money. The first half of the sermon contains a general treatment of the theme: Ps. 24:3-4, "Who shall climb the mountain of the Lord, or who shall stand in his holy place? One with innocent hands, and a pure heart." Our earthly lives must be led in innocence and purity of heart, and our efforts here, including our pursuit of knowledge, must be directed towards the true knowledge that dwells with God in heaven (PL 212: 603C). In the second half of the sermon, Hélinand is more specific and attacks those who study in order to swell their heads with pride or their pocketbooks with lucre. His first target is philosophers. Be they followers of Pythagoras, Plato, Epicurus, the Stoics, or any others, they join Lucifer, Alexander, and Simon the Magician in a precipitous pursuit of falsehood. They are driven and will be destroyed by ambition (PL 212: 602). Hélinand next addresses the students in the audience in a style deliberately more simple. He warns that they travel great distances and endure many hardships to study and earn money, the reward for which will be insanity, the inevitable outcome of pursuing worthless letters (*nihil salvantes litterae*, PL 212: 603B). The preacher laments that virtue and life are not sought anywhere. In a frequently quoted passage, he cries, "the clerics in Paris pursue liberal arts, in Orleans, authors; in Bologna, codices; in Salerno, medicine boxes; in Toledo, magic; and nowhere, virtue" (PL 212: 603B). Thus, the cities where major universities were located are associated with vice and vain pursuits. Literature, law, medicine, magic — all are worthless if not focused on God.

A nineteenth-century historian suggested that Hélinand was attacking a letter issued by the university masters. The letter was addressed to schools of other regions and affirmed the possibility for studying freely and living well in Toulouse — a promise which seems difficult to fulfill in a region ravaged by war and about to see the beginnings of an inquisition. A short study published for the 1979 anniversary of the university credits Hélinand's inaugural sermon with establishing an "astonishingly retrograde" program for the university, one that denounces the lies of philosophy and exalts holy ignorance.[14] Jacques Le Goff says less severely that Hélinand can in no way be considered an avant-garde thinker, and finds his assessment of education in 1229 about fifty years out of date.[15]

The assertion that the sermon establishes a program of study, retrograde or not, seems to be exaggerated, but certainly the sermon's theme stands in opposition to the message of the university masters in their praise of free study in Toulouse. And in such an environment, a message that education should combat heresy is obvious by implication even though heresy is not explicitly denounced.[16] To deliver his message, Hélinand generously employs classical citations, figures of rhetoric and wordplay. With its deliberate display of erudition, the sermon argues not that holy ignorance is bliss, but that erudition ought to be placed at the service of God.

SACRED AND SECULAR LITERATURE

The implicit background for Hélinand's statement on the purpose of study is the medieval attitude toward its twofold heritage of patristic and classical literature. Patristic writers expressed conflict over their preference for the style of classical literature over Scripture. Whether that conflict was genuine, born of conventional rhetoric, or both, is another question. But Jerome imagined rhetorical tortures because of his fondness for Ciceronian eloquence.[17] Augustine's advice on pagan literature was to be echoed over the centuries. In *De doctrina christiana*, he counseled the Christian exegete to profit from whatever of value was found in pagan learning, just as Moses learned from the wisdom of the Egyptians (Acts 7:22).[18] Gregory the Great, himself well schooled in the *trivium*,[19] asserts the practical value of the liberal arts when he repeats the example of Moses and the wisdom of the Egyptians, associating the study of secular books with the Israelites' going down to the Philistines when they needed a smith (1 Sam. 13:20).[20]

Monastic writers expressed both admiration and distrust for pagan literature, and their remarks are often contradictory. As Jean Leclercq points out, Alcuin uses a verse from the *Aeneid* to reproach a friend for his great love of Vergil, and Bernard uses the authority of Persius to speak against vain learning.[21] Adding to the complexity of this problem is the conflict among the orders themselves.

We might expect twelfth-century Cistercians to intensify the monastic emphasis on the interior life and to reject the liberal studies of Benedictines. The dispute would still be alive in the seventeenth century.[22] In the *Dialogue Between a Cluniac and a Cistercian*, the Cistercian upbraids his Benedictine brother for poring over poetry and teaching it at times which should be set aside for spiritual reading and manual labor. The Cluniac justifies the reading of secular books as a way to acquire a better understanding of scripture.[23]

Yet scholars and poets joined the Cistercian order (Alain of Lille is perhaps the best known), and many produced significant works after entering the cloister. In the thirteenth century, Cistercian houses were founded near universities. Derek Baker interprets this as a response to an eventual lack of well-educated recruits for the order, when its very organization made it dependent on them.[24]

In Bernard of Clairvaux, whose influence Hélinand felt deeply, we also observe expressions of both admiration and distrust for

pagan classics. According to John R. Sommerfeldt, Bernard distinguished levels of knowledge suitable for different states of life and
considered learned those who had been trained in the epistemological method suitable for their state of life: mystical contemplation
for the monk, dialectics for the secular cleric. Sources are few for
his opinions on the education of the laity.[25]

Bernard's works contain numerous references to knowledge and
the methods of attaining it; here I shall cite some examples from his
sermons *On the Song of Songs* and from his Ascension Sermon Four.
Precedence was to be given to all that aided spiritual progress.[26] For
Bernard, inheritor of Anselm's introspective method, the self-
knowledge essential for acquiring humility leads to the knowledge
of God essential for salvation. He says that "knowledge of God and
of self are basic and must come first . . . ."[27] But nowhere does
Bernard condemn the classics. He states: "I am far from saying . . .
that knowledge of literature is to be despised, for it provides culture
and skill, and enables a man to instruct others,"[28] and again: "Perhaps you think I have sullied too much the good name of knowledge, that I have cast aspersions on the learned and proscribed the
study of letters. God forbid!"[29] Yet he warns strenuously against the
dangers of knowledge that swells pride and contributes to self-
importance. In his Ascension Sermon Four he describes persons
striving after knowledge of culture, or of management of secular
matters, and says that they build a tower of Babel.[30] In the sermons
On the Song of Songs and elsewhere he notes the benefits scholars
confer on the church when they refute her opponents and instruct
the simple. He also commends those who long for knowledge in
order to serve others,[31] and he supported the education of many
among the secular clergy.[32] Some of his remarks that seem directed
against education are probably influenced by his distrust of the city
university and his preference for monastic culture. For example, in
a letter he chides a monk who was living in Paris, advising him that
the woods and rocks of the forest would teach him more than
university masters.[33] But this is not equivalent to a rejection of
education. Bernard himself obviously received a strong classical
education, for his language reflects an impressive command of rhetorical technique and he does cite ancient writers.[34]

How are these currents of distrust and admiration reflected in
Hélinand's works? Clearly he distrusted all learning that was not
put to God's service, but most certainly he did not shun secular

literature. He entered the monastery after receiving an education in the liberal arts that, from what we know of the school of Ralph of Beauvais, was probably more steeped in the classics than the norm for that time. He attacks *litteras nihil sonantes*, but his criterion for worthlessness rests on the purpose the literature serves, not the nature of the literature itself. In the Toulouse Ascension sermon, he quotes frequently from pagan authors to introduce his message of seeking divine wisdom. In other sermons, the number of classical citations varies considerably, but even in sermons obviously directed to a monastic audience we do find classical authors, for example, lines from Ovid and a reference to Pliny in a Purification sermon.[35] He both agrees with and goes beyond the recommendation of his Cistercian predecessor, Alain of Lille, who was open to occasional references to pagan writers in sermons when their sayings made an apt point and provoked a fresh illumination.[36]

In Book Eight of the *Chronicon*,[37] Hélinand takes a position. A date for this work has not been established, but a *terminus ante quem* and a *terminus ad quem* can be set from the text. Hélinand refers to Henry, bishop of Orléans and brother of our bishop of Beauvais (*nostri Belvacensis episcopi frater*) who used to tell (*referre solebat*) a certain story that he had heard from John, canon of Orléans (PL 212: 731D). Philip, bishop of Beauvais, was Henry's brother and from that reference was obviously living. Hélinand also recounts with humor a visit of the same Philip who, he says, has sometimes stayed at the monastery (*apud nos aliquando hospitatus est*) (PL 212: 730C). Hélinand's use of the imperfect for Henry doubtless indicates that Henry is deceased. The use of the perfect tense with its value of completed present and more importantly the phrase "brother of our bishop" clearly indicate that Philip was still living at the time Hélinand was writing. Henry died in 1198 and Philip in 1217; this part of Book Eight must belong to the years between 1198 and 1217. Furthermore, the writing of Hélinand's *Chronicon* has been dated between 1211 and 1223. We can therefore date this part of Book Eight between 1211 and 1217.[38]

In it Hélinand deals with the soul and theories about hell and the afterlife. He surveys pagan theories, including those of Macrobius, Hesiod, Vergil, and others. He quotes from various classical authors — including Ovid, Persius, Seneca and Juvenal, affectionately called *satyricus noster*. But he advises his reader that true knowledge of self can be obtained only from scripture. He also points out the falsity of Vergil's opinion on the state of the souls of the departed. He refers the reader to two more perfect works than his: Gregory's *Moralia* and Bernard's *De consideratione*. Hélinand's exaggerated praise of Bernard sums up a sort of hierarchy of literature. Hélinand obviously knows and enjoys classical authors, but he affirms that Christian writers surpass them for attaining the knowledge of self that leads to knowledge of God. Bernard, praised for his style and thinking, is elevated above the greatest of the ancients — Apollo himself, Demosthenes, Aristotle, Seneca and Plato (PL 212: 731BC).

Thus we find that Hélinand is following Augustine's advice and profiting from Egyptian treasures, so to speak. Wisdom and enjoyment can be obtained from pagan works, but caution should be exercised because of errors like Vergil's and because, for Hélinand, the true purpose of learning was being lost in the new world of the universities. The sacred page remains the greatest source of knowledge, and Christian writers should be esteemed above others. Yet Hélinand clearly enjoys the classics, much in the spirit of the school of Chartres.[39] His extensive use of the classics in a variety of writings justifies his inclusion in studies of monastic humanism. Moreover, while his preference for sacred over secular page has a limited following in our day, his overarching caution to subordinate education to higher goals is still timely for a wider audience.

NOTES

1. Hélinand's works, first published by Bertrand Tissier in the *Bibliotheca patrum cisterciensium* (Bonnefontaine, 1669) were later printed in the *Patrologia Latina* 212. New editions are being prepared for the *Corpus Christianorum*: the *Chronicon* by Edme R. Smits at the University of Groningen, the *Vers de la Mort* by William D. Paden, Jr., and the *Sermones* by Beverly Mayne Kienzle.

2. See my summary of Hélinand's life in "The Sermon as Goad and Nail: Preaching in Hélinand of Froidmont," in *Goad and Nail*, Studies in Medieval Cistercian History, X, CS 84 (Kalamazoo: Cistercian Publications, 1985), 230-31.

3. He is listed as a witness in a document from 1190 edited by William Paden in "Documents concernant Hélinant de Froidmont," *Romania* 105 (1984):332-341.

4. Hélinand entered Froidmont under the abbacy of Guillaume I (1181-1193), according to L.-E. Deladreue, "Notice sur l'abbaye de Froidmont," *Mémoires de la Société*

Académique d'Archéologie, Sciences et Arts du département de l'Oise 7, part 3 (Beauvais, 1870), 514, 522.

5. William D. Paden, Jr., establishes dates for the poem and discusses the 1199 ruling in "De monachos ritmos facientibus," *Speculum* 55/4 (1981), 669-85.

6. PL 212: 571C: ". . . quia praedicator verbi Dei non palpare peccata debet, sed ferire et pungere, sicut scriptum est: Verba sapientium quasi stimuli, et quasi clavi in altum defixi." See my "The Sermon as Goad and Nail," Preaching in Hélinand of Froidmont," 228-40.

7. Abbé Sabatier, *Vie des saints du diocèse de Beauvais*, cited in Deladreue, "Notice," 523.

8. See Anselme Dimier, "Elinando di Froidmont," *Bibliotheca sanctorum* (Rome: Istituto Giovanni XIII-Pontificia Universita Lateranense: 1964) IV: cols. 1073-1074; and Seraphin Lenssen, "Aperçu historique sur la vénération des saints cisterciens dans 'Ordre de Citeaux,' " *Collectanea o.c.r.* 6 (1939):272.

9. Richard W. Hunt, "Studies in Priscian in the Twelfth Century II: The School of Ralph of Beauvais," *Medieval and Renaissance Studies* 2 (London, 1950; reprint Liechtenstein: Kraus, 1969):11-16.

10. Hunt, "Studies," 23-39. Other methods include greater length, more precision in the division of the text, a more critical attitude towards the text, some changes in the technique of argument, and applying logical analysis to the meanings of words.

11. See Edme R. Smits, "Hélinand of Froidmont and the A-Text of Seneca's Tragedies," *Mnemosyne* 36 (1983):339. Dr. Smits is continuing research on Hélinand's sources. M.M. Woesthuis, University of Groningen, is also investigating this topic; he presented "The Chronicler as Preacher: Hélinand of Froidmont and the Last Five Books of the Chronicon," at the Conference on Cistercian Studies, May 1989.

12. See Jean Leclercq, "Le magistère du prédicateur aux iiie siècle," *Archives d'histoire doctrinale et littéraire du moyen age* 21 (1946):59-67.

13. For an analysis of this sermon and its historical circumstances, see my "Erudition at God's Service," in *Erudition at God's Service*, Studies in Medieval Cistercian History, XI, ed. John R. Sommerfeldt (Kalamazoo: Cistercian Publications, 1987), 277-90.

14. P. Bonassie and G. Pradalie *La capitulation de Raymond VII et la fondation de l'Université de Toulouse 1229-1979: Un anniversaire en question* (Toulouse, 1979), 16, 55.

15. "Les universités du Languedoc dans le mouvement universitaire européen au xiiie siècle," *Les universités du Languedoc au xiiie siècle*, Cahiers de Fanjeaux 5 (Toulouse, 1970);317-18.

16. Heresy is not explicitly mentioned in this sermon, while it is in others Hélinand delivered in Toulouse. See my "Cistercian Preaching Against the Cathars: Hélinand's Unedited Sermon for Rogation, B.N.M.S. Lat. 14591," *Citeaux: commentarii cistercienses*, 39,3-4 (1988):297-314.

17. *Epistola ad Eustochium, Epis.* XXII,#30.

18. *De Doctrina Christiana*, II, 60-61.

19. See Paul the Deacon's *Vita*, PL 75:42.

20. See his *Commentaries on the First Book of Kings*, PL 79:355-57.

21. Jean Leclercq, *The Love of Learning and the Desire for God: A Study of Monastic Culture*, trans. Catharine Misrahi (New York: Fordham University Press, 1982), 113. See also pp. 112-150 on this topic.

22. See, for example, Pt. III of Jean Mabillon's reply to Rancé, translated and printed as "The Aims and Attitudes of Monks at Study," *Monastic Studies* 12 (1967):175-90.

23. Idung of Prufening, *Cistercians and Cluniacs: The Case for Citeaux. A Dialogue between Two Monks, An Argument on Four Questions*, trans. Jeremiah F. O'Sullivan, Joseph Leahey and Grace Perrigo, CF 33 (Kalamazoo: Cistercian Publications, 1977), 27-28.

24. Derek Baker, "Heresy and Learning in Early Cistercianism," in *Schism, Heresy and Religious Protest*, Studies in Church History, 9 (Cambridge: University Press, 1972), 93-107. For current research on Cistercian houses near universities, see Caroline Obert-Piketty, "La promotion des études chez les cisterciens à travers le recrutement des étudiants du collège Saint-Bernard de Paris au moyen âge," *Citeaux* 39 (1988):65-77; and "Benoît XII et les collèges cisterciens du Languedoc," *Les Cisterciens du Languedoc (XIIe-XIVe siecle)*, Cahiers de Fanjeaux 21 (Toulouse: Privat, 1986): 139-50.

25. See John R. Sommerfeldt's excellent article, "Epistemology, Education and Social Theory in the Thought of Bernard of Clairvaux," in *Saint Bernard of Clairvaux*, Studies Commemorating the Eighth Centenary of his Canonization, ed. M. Basil Pennington, CS 28 (Kalamazoo: Cistercian Publications, 1977).

26. *On the Song of Songs II*, trans. Kilian Walsh, CS 7 (Kalamazoo: Cistercian Publications, 1983), 36:2, 176.

27. *Ibid.*, 37:2, 182.

28. *Ibid.*

29. *Ibid.*, 2, 174.

30. *Sancti Bernardi Opera*, ed. Jean Leclercq, Henri Rochais and C.H. Talbot, 8 vols. (Rome: Editiones Cistercienses, 1957-1977), 5: 141-142; my translation appears in *Liturgical Sermons III* (Kalamazoo: Cistercian Publications, 1990).

31. *Song*, 36:2-3, 175-76.

32. See Sommerfeldt, "Epistemology," 173-75.

33. *Epistola* 106, PL 182:242. See also Lester K. Little, *Religious Poverty and the Profit Economy in Medieval Europe* (Ithaca, N.Y.: Cornell University Press, 1978), 92-93.

34. See Bernard Jacqueline, "Répertoire des citations d'auteurs profanes dans les oeuvres de saint Bernard," CHOC, *Bernard de Clairvaux* (Paris, 1953), App. IV, 549-54; and the review by E. Franceschini in *Aevum* 28 (1954):571-73.

35. Bib. Nat. MS. Lat. 14591, 132vb-35va. I am now preparing this sermon for publication.

36. *The Art of Preaching*, trans. Gillian R. Evans, CS 23, (Kalamazoo: Cistercian Publications, 1981), 23.

37. Parts of bk. 8 were excerpted by Vincent of Beauvais for the collection of *Flores* and are printed in PL 212:721-736 as *De cognitione sui.*

38. I am currently preparing a short article, "Dating Book Eight of Hélinand's *Chronicon*," with Edme R. Smits, University of Groningen. I am grateful to him for pointing out that the PL 212 passages are part of the *Chronicon*, and for the reference to the only dates set so far for the *Chronicon*. Those dates are proposed by J.N. Carman, *The Relationship of the 'Perlesvaus' and the 'Queste del Saint Graal'* (Chicago, 1936), 11-13.

39. Edme R. Smits is exploring the influence of the school of Chartres on Hélinand, and presented "Hélinand of Froidmont, Science, and the School of Chartres," at Helsinki in 1988. On the school of Chartres in the context of monastic education, see Luke Anderson's excellent article "Enthymeme and Dialectic: Cloister and Classroom," in *From Cloister to Classroom, Monastic and Scholastic Approaches to Truth*, The Spirituality of Western Christendom III, CS 90, ed. E. Rozanne Elder (Kalamazoo: Cistercian Publications, 1986), 242-43. For Richard Southern, however, the typical twelfth-century humanists had no genuine feeling for their sources. See "Peter of Blois: A Twelfth Century Humanist?" in R.W. Southern, *Medieval Humanism* (Oxford: Basil Blackwell, 1970), 125-26.

LEARNING AS EXPERIENCING HADEWIJCH'S MODEL OF SPIRITUAL GROWTH

Ulrike Wiethaus, Ph.D.

This essay consists of two parts that focus neither on Hadewijch the theologian nor on Hadewijch the mystic, but on her role as a spiritual teacher. First, I discuss ways in which she constructed her teaching authority. Second, this essay suggests a new interpretation of her model of spiritual growth based on the pattern of initiation developed by the anthropologist of religion Victor Turner. I will propose how Hadewijch's model reflected at least in part the specific situation of thirteenth-century Beguines in the Low Countries in terms of social change and a feminine sense of self.

*

We have very little biographical data about the Flemish mystic. Living in the duchy of Brabant around the year 1250 and well-educated she was, we may assume with some certainty, the mistress and leader of a group of Beguines until she was exiled from her position for unknown reasons. Her religious life among the Beguines unfolded within a larger circle of religious and lay people that included not only Beguines, however, and that transcended national borders. If we trust her list of those that she saw as spiritual models, the "perfected," her peer group was mainly composed of socially marginal women and men. Wealthy people were specifically noted as such.[1] Although Hadewijch's texts reveal a subtle and well educated theological thinker who very likely belonged to the patrician or noble class,[2] the author herself faced an immediate audience that was not all too conversant with the theology of the religious elite nor even perhaps interested in subtle theological discourse. One advantage of the relative lack of knowledge on the part of her audience is that it freed Hadewijch to articulate bold new formulations and to develop unusual genres as pedagogical vehicles. She is among the first religious writers in the vernacular who used rhymed letters, secular love poetry, and highly personalized visionary texts as modes of religious communication and instruction. The fact that Hadewijch was *not* a member of the ecclesiastical teaching hierarchy, due to the simple fact of her gender, forced her also to create a basis of her teaching authority outside (but not necessarily in opposition to) the male-identified orthodox lineage.

Hadewijch's Construction of Female Lay Authority

Hadewijch used three "building blocks" to consolidate the foundation of her authority. To begin with, her extraordinary visionary texts, in terms of their narrative plot a documentation of her spiritual growth, served at least partially to establish her credentials. In these texts, a number of supernatural or divine authorities affirm the extraordinary character of her insight, purity, and leadership qualities.

Secondly, she assured her students of the trustworthiness of her teachings by stressing their divinely inspired *moral integrity*. Both visionary, epistolary, and poetic texts stress repeatedly the goodness of God and the power of Love that she was meant to transmit to her students. In Letter 17, e.g., she writes:

> The things I order you in these verses were ordered me by God. Therefore I desire in my turn to order you the same things, because they belong perfectly to the perfection of Love, and because they belong perfectly and wholly in the Divinity.

> Dese dinghen waren mi van gode verboden, die ic v in desen worden verbiede. Daer omme beghericse v voert te verbiedene, om dat si volmaecteleec ter volcomenheit van Minnen behoren, Ende omme datse inder godheit volcomeleke ende gheheeleke behoren.

Thirdly, divine authorization through esoteric visions and her writings' moral integrity is complemented by her own creation of a perhaps shockingly motley lineage of already "perfected" people and those who are on their way to "perfection." All the members of this list, famous or not so famous, are seen as supportive examples of Hadewijch's own teachings. "Perfection," *volkomenheit*, is the *terminus technicus* (not only used by Hadewijch) of a state of being that has fully in-corporated the power of Love, *Minne*. This interesting list of fifty-six people, found at the end of Vision Thirteen, is inclusive of both men and women. As such, it diverges remarkably from the traditional makeup of ecclesiastical teaching authorities, the "Fathers" and the "Doctors" of the church. The list is modeled after the more popularized family of saints which is more inclusive of both sexes. Hadewijch's own creative lineage begins with the Virgin Mary, Mary Magdalen, and some apostles, and ends with a survey of contemporary holy people in Northern Europe, most of whom are women and some of whom are personal acquaintances. It is noteworthy that these acquaintances communicate with Hadewijch not only by natural, but also by supernatural means. None of her famous mystical women compatriots of the Low Countries, however, are mentioned by name. Among well-known religious women, only Hildegard of Bingen across the Rhine is noted surprisingly briefly as "Hildegard, who saw all the visions, is the twenty-eighth" ("Hildegard, die al de visioenen zag, is de achtentwintigste").[3] Although Richard and Hugh of St. Victor, William of St. Thierry, Guerric of Igny, Bernard of Clairvaux, and a number of fathers of the Church were found to have been the source of much of Hadewijch's writings, only Augustine (one of her favorite inspirations and challengers), Gregory, Isidore and Hilary among the church fathers, and Bernard of Clairvaux among the twelfth-century writers are mentioned. Despite her use of Bernard's teachings on love,[4] he is only listed laconically as "St. Bernard was the eighteenth, of whom I also know very little" ("De heilige Bernardus is de achttiende: over hem weet ik ook weinig"). The church fathers, on the other hand, receive more attention and are praised very highly, assuming somewhat superhuman dimensions: St. Gregory "was supremely perfect" ("Hij was . . . zeer volmaakt"). St. Hilary "was very just in all things" ("en in alles was hij zeer waarachtig"), St. Isidore "was so perfect in all virtues . . . so supremely great" ("zo volmaakt was hij in alle deugden . . . zo uitnemend groot . . . ").

Hadewijch's lineage, then, is projected backwards to the almost mythical foundations of the early formation period of Christianity and, with a large temporal leap, fastened in the nooks and crannies of a contemporary "culture from below" of locally renowned saintly people that existed at the margins of the high ecclesiastical culture to which Hildegard and Bernard belonged. Hadewijch's contemporary frame of reference of saintly teaching authority is made up of a network of recluses, hermits, a defrocked priest, a "forgotten master" in Paris, and a Beguine put to death by the inquisition. What Michel de Certeau has written in another context holds true here as well as a characterization of these saints, at least from the perspective of church authorities and university pundits: "An analogous situation today would be if the down-and-outs of our society, the fixed-income elderly or alien workers, were the eponymous heroes [and, I like to add, heroines] of knowledge."[5]

In sum, the great temporal gap in her list of the perfected illustrates clearly her sense of belonging and a counter-tradition of religio-social authority, even if she herself did not begin her life in this class in terms of her own upbringing and education.

Hadewijch's Texts

The large body of writings that Hadewijch left behind are judged today as among the very best of medieval Flemish literature. Her oeuvre comprises thirty-one prose letters, sixteen rhymed letters, fourteen visionary texts, and forty-five strophic poems. We can assume with some probability that Hadewijch compiled her works in the form in which we find them today.[6]

As has been suggested elsewhere (Willaert, op. cit.), and I agree with this view, all of Hadewijch's writings served the function of instruction. This is most obvious in her letters that (with one exception) are directed formally to a young Beguine and her circle of women friends.[7] All teachings are intended to lead her circle towards a bold goal that radicalized the imago dei anthropology of the twelfth century and found its way almost verbatim into Ruusbroec's teachings: to become God both in his humanity and his divinity. In Hadewijch's mysticism, this transformation deeply affirms femininity and defines it in surprising and uncompromising terms, a fact that gains in significance if we remember that her immediate audience was predominantly female.

Jan van Leeuwen, a mystic from Ruusbroec's circle, attested to Hadewijch as an authentic teacher whose writings are divinely inspired ("een heylich glorieus wijf heet hadewijch een ghewareghe lereesse; want hadewijch's boeke die sijn seker goet ende gherecht wt gode gheboren ende gheoppenbaert"). He adds, however, that her radical teachings are too esoteric, too "noble" and too "subtle" for most people ("want hadewijchs leerinhe es in vele steden alle menschen te edele ende te subtijlijc verborghen").[8] Hadewijch herself seems to have been convinced that her teachings were reserved only for a small circle of chosen people (see, e.g., Vision 13). What she and her group lacked in social or ecclesiastical status was thus compensated by a spiritual elitism.

Liminality, Language, and the Sacra

"Learning as experiencing," the title of my paper, is the core of the ascetical and mystical tradition of both Eastern and Western Christianity. What I wish to highlight here are a few features that I perceive as Hadewijch's unique contribution: her femininization of the transformatory process (exemplified in her interpretation of the Virgin Mary and the abyss) that affirmed the feminine identity of her audience, the use of four different genres that allowed her students to access her mystical knowledge on a number of levels, and the archetypal "rootedness" of her mysticism that connects her vision with that of other cultures and times — i.e., her teachings interpreted as initiation device.

Initiation can take many forms. The theoretical model that is most helpful to understand Hadewijch is Victor Turner's theory of liminality. I will briefly summarize the major features of Turner's model and show how it is helpful in understanding the psychological depth-dynamics of Hadewijch's mystical teachings.

In studying rites of passages in pre-literal societies, Turner and others noted a certain pattern that informed many ritual processes. The pattern consists of three basic phases: separation, liminality, and aggregation.[9] A rite of passage does not only delineate biological and social changes (e.g., puberty, marriage, death), but any transformation from one state to another. In Hadewijch's case, the desired change is described as becoming God in his humanity and his divinity. According to Turner, during the stage of separation, the initiates shed their previous social status and role and enter a state in which they are beyond any category of identification; they are neither "male" nor "female," neither "old" nor "young," neither "wealthy" nor "poor," etc. It is a state that is anxiety-provoking, yet fertile with rich new possibilities, and that allows the neophytes to experience themselves as free of any social persona. Turner explicitly states the potential for creativity that the state of liminality holds as a promise: "[Liminality is] a realm of pure possibility whence novel configurations of ideas and relations may arise" (p. 7). Within the context of stable societies, however, this creative potential is channeled into a deeper exploration of already given tribal teachings that results in a firm anchoring of the individual into tribal customs and traditions. I argue that for the women who joined the religious lay movements in the thirteenth century, however, rapidly changing social structures, in particular in the cities, had repercussions on the level of their religious imagination and modified this ancient pattern. Hadewijch's gynocentric model of spiritual transformation promised a new identity that could only be expressed and explored through a new language. This language necessarily had to be a hybrid that merged already existing religious and secular terminologies in an innovative manner.[10] This fusion reflected another kind of incorporation and absorption that took place on the social level: religious knowledge, traditionally guarded by a specialized social elite, began to pass into the hands of lower-class lay people of both sexes who — as in the case of Hadewijch — constructed their own legitimacy in part through highly creative and often women-inclusive lineages that drew on marginal religious authorities. These authorities — recluses, hermits, failed priests — were certainly not remarkable because of their command of the theological canon, but for deeds that were accessible to public scrutiny and verification. Acts of fasting, good works, and seclusion from others were much easier to appropriate, imitate, understand, and use as a sign of legitimacy than an already monopolized, specialized theological knowledge that depended on the relatively inaccessible skills of writing and reading.

I propose that this new type of religious lay identity could more easily be developed and articulated through the exploration of a liminal ecstatic state. The unusual patterns of intensive religious experiences displayed by their leaders or saintly models functioned both as legitimization of lay authority and as the creative ground from which new formulations were wrought. Unlike liminality in tribal societies, however, the state did not lead the individual *back* into traditional patterns, but aided in the formation of a new pattern of (self-)knowledge.[11] For Hadewijch, this included an experientially based shift — may we ask theologically, through an act of grace? — of feminine symbols from margin to center, thus aiding in the consolidation of a new role for lay religious women on a theological and existential level.

Our own knowledge about similarities in theological outlook among the Beguines, which would help us in determining the paradigmatic value of Hadewijch's specific model, is still poor, but we can say that their experiment succeeded at least socially and economically: they were able to construct a powerful new social identity, that of a lay group of religious women living independently and in self-government. Beguines were able to carve out a significant economical niche for themselves that survived in some parts of northern Europe until the early decades of this century. The Beguines' economical prosperity marks, in my opinion, the successful completion of the liminal period on a larger scale, that is, the "re-introducing" of the initiated into society. The initiates now have not only new identities, but also new (economic and social) duties and roles to play.

At the core of the liminal period is what Turner, indebted to Jane Harrison for the coinage of this term, calls the "communication of the *sacra*" (p.12), the elders' display and explanation of the most sacred objects and beliefs of the tribe. This communication takes place through three modes: exhibitions, actions, and instructions. Since Hadewijch had no control over the sacred objects of her cult community, e.g., the Eucharist, we may assume that her teachings did not include any traditional exhibitions. On the other hand, we can interpret the display of physical symptoms during ecstasies as the creative productions of new *sacra* that rivaled the status of church-approved symbols of the Holy such as relics and the Eucharist.[12]

The mode of ritual actions can be deduced from her visionary texts which are the most explicit in terms of religious practices. We find here (as in the case of other medieval women mystics) an understanding of the church service as a truly transformative, deeply moving ritual rather than a ceremony with little or no intense psycho-spiritual involvement. Unfortunately, we do not know whether Hadewijch's church experiences had paradigmatic value for her students or not. Visionary experiences among women mystics during mass were not uncommon. That they were correctly understood as challenges to set patterns of authority becomes clear if we read that ecstatic women were often seen as a nuisance and their convulsions, levitations, tears, and screams as unwelcome interruption. However, there is another, less conspicuous type of ritual action that we can interpret as particularly suited to a "lay-monastic" lifestyle. To do good works can be considered a deliberately performed ritual act since good works are explicitly intended to bring the individual closer to a realization of the *imago dei* ideal. Letter 17, e.g., deals extensively with the topic. Hadewijch first offers her students a poem, and then proceeds to interpret it line by line.

> Be generous and zealous for every virtue,/
> But do not apply yourself to any one virtue/ . . .
> Have good will and compassion for every need/ . . .

[Explanation:] The attributes I mentioned here are perfectly the divine Nature. For to be generous and zealous is the Nature of the Holy Spirit; this is what is his proper Person . . .

> Te alre doghet wes onstich snel;/
> En onderwinter di niet el./ . . .
> Te alre noet hebbet onste ende ontfermen/ . . .

Die wesene die ic daer noeme, die sijn volcomeleke hare nature/: Want gheonstech ende snel, dat es de nature vanden heileghen gheest; Daer met es hi proper persoen . . . .

The third mode of communicating the *sacra* is the most accessible to contemporary readers, the category of instruction. Hadewijch's instructions artfully weave together traditional Christian motifs and subtly new, original imagery. The *Strofische Gedichten* ("Poems in Stanzas"), for example, are built upon the structures of courtly love poetry, whose well-known techniques of meter, rhyme, assonance, stanza structure, courtly metaphors, and figures of speech are brilliantly employed (Hart, *op.cit.*, p.19). Mother Columba Hart suggests that the poems served the function to "recall her young Beguines to their early fervor" (*op. cit.*, p.20). Although this interpretation might very well be true, there is such richness in meaning and imagery that another view can also be supported: the exploration of the *early stages* of the mystical process, that is, being seduced and stripped by the major transformative force, Love, or *Minne*. It has been suggested that the poems are artistically organized around a numerical structure by Hadewijch, with Poem 29 as the key text and hub of the collection.[13] All other poems, with the exception of the first and last poem, which contain a few liturgical formulae in Latin, can be read as purely secular love poetry. It is the twenty-ninth poem that explains what Hadewijch means by spiritual rather than secular courtship, desire, and loving. As such, it is the key that unlocks the hidden meaning of all other seemingly secular poems.

Poem 29 explores the salvivic significance of the Virgin Mary. Given the centrality of the poem in the cycle, the Virgin Mary is thus crucial to a correct spiritual understanding of Hadewijch's use of courtly love metaphors. True *Minne* for the first time was disclosed to Mary rather than the prophets, their disciples, and David. In the following quotation, note the subtle gender symbolism that is woman-identified and allows Hadewijch's reader to identify with Mary rather than with a group of male authorities. Also, what is stressed is not Mary's virginity and purity, but formidable mental qualities such as steadfastness and single-mindedness. In contrasting the prophets with Mary, Hadewijch writes:

> They saw visions:
> They spoke beautiful parables,
> Concerning all that God would give us later on.
> > But, in my opinion,
> > Genuine, lavish Love
> Remained wholly unpracticed by them.
> For their manner of life was commonplace,
> Now here, now there, now off, now on;
> Mary, however, said no words but these:
> Be it done to me as God wills.
> It was by deep longing
> That this mystery happened to her,
> That this noble Love was released
> > To this noble woman
> > Of high praise
> In overflowing measure;
> Because she wished nothing else and owned nothing else,
> She wholly possessed him of Whom everybody had read.
> > Thus she became the conduit
> Open to every humble heart.
>
> Si saghen visioene;
> Si spraken parabilen scoene:
> Wat ons god noch soude doen.
> > Maer, na minen sin(n)e,
> > Die clare, vrie minne

Bleef van hen al ongheploen.
Want sij hadden haere seden als andere man
Nu hier, nu daer, nu af, nu an;
Mer Maria en sprac el niet
Dan: 'miej werde dat god versiet'.

Dat was bij diepen nyede
Dat haer dat groote gheschiede,
Dat die edel minne uut wert ghelaten
    Dien edelen wijve
    Van hoeghen prijse
Met overvloedegher maten;
Want sij el Niet en woude noch el niet en was,
Soe hadse al daer elc af las.
Dus heeft se dat conduyt gheleyt,
Dat elcker oetmoedegher herten is ghereyt.

The underlying spiritual process of the poems is a search for "high Love," a *terminus technicus* used in the courtly love tradition. For Hadewijch, it is an inner opening without complaints or remorse modeled after the exemplary attitude of single-mindedness and determination of the Virgin Mary.

If courtship as religious surrender to High Love is the central motif of the *Strofische Gedichten*, the *Mengeldichten* (or "Poems in Couplets") move beyond the courtly code into a more direct discussion of religious psychology. They are much less esoteric, and openly employ religious jargon. Their mixture of poetic and epistolary styles represents a "transitional genre" between the purely poetic *Strofische Gedichten* and the purely epistolary prose letters. The *Mengeldichten*, it has been noted, "impress the reader by their terse aphoristic style, which offers a wealth of memorable lines" (Hart, *op. cit.*, p.32). Hadewijch's words of advice are mixed with a strong dose of humility:

I pray God that he may direct your understanding
In his veritable Love,
And that he may enlighten you with himself,
And lead you by his deeper truth.
For from me you shall much lack this,
Although I also wished to speak for your profit.
                                        (Poem 6)

As in the *Strofische Gedichten* with its emphasis on the Virgin Mary, we note here as well a decidedly woman-identified spirituality. One text might serve as example. In her poetic version of the pre-Christian legend of the three bodyguards of King Darius, who argue about who or what has the greatest power (wine, a king, a woman, truth), she grants the highest position to woman. Mother Hart comments that "her handling of the third subject—that the most powerful of all things is woman—would seem to be one of the most astonishing passages she ever wrote" (p.33). And yet this version of the legend is only another variation of a theme that is displayed consistently in her writings. In this context as in Poem 29, the virtue of humility is a crucial element of her construction of femininity. However, humility is not weak and self-abasing. It has its own active force that reminds one of the Taoist principle of yin or the ancient Greek goddess Ge: humility's force is the force of depth, an unfathomable chasm that attracts, a boundless capacity to receive and absorb divine energy. Hadewijch writes:

Woman indeed is rightly the strongest:
She made the Lord a slave (Phil.2:7);
Although he was the noblest in heaven,
Her deep humility made him so submissive
That he fell from his sublimity
Into this unfathomable chasm.
For her humility was so great
That she summoned the King to come to her.
She was the strongest, that is undeniable.
                                        (Poem 2)

And in the next poem, she depicts the Virgin Mary as the first teacher, thus strengthening and affirming what has been said before:

This the Mother of Love truly showed:
In her could a person first learn to know it (Love).
Although others before her strove for Love,
Men could best understand it through her.

. . .
Justly then did Love exalt her,
When love made her the Mother of Love.
Why did not some wise man think of this?
                                        (Poem 3)

Certainly one wise man, Bernard of Clairvaux, thought of this, namely in his Sermons on the Song of Songs. But when we read Sermon 29 on the Song of Songs, in which he describes Mary actually as the Mother of Love, we find religious associations that do *not* speak of unfathomable depths and great strength associated with femininity. Furthermore, Mary is not seen as an active learner and teacher, but solely as a passive virgin, a status that defines a woman solely through her relationship to men. Bernard's imagination here is haunted by violence. Mary is pierced "through and through" by a "polished arrow." Cutting keener than "any two-edged sword," this weapon is the "special" love of Christ. The masochism of Bernard's sense of feminine "humility" comes through clearly in the closing passage on this victimized virgin/mother:[14]

> How I long not only to be wounded in this manner but to be assailed again and again till the color and heat of that flesh that wars against the spirit is overcome.

Let me cite one more remarkable elaboration of Hadewijch's spiritual path of humility, which is a powerful letting go of the ego's concerns, if we like to use contemporary psychological terminology, and simultaneously a boundless opening up to the energy conduit of depth. Giving up one's ego concerns and accepting suffering with as much equanimity as joy is difficult and painful. It can only be achieved if the all-embracing reality of cosmic Love is understood. Hadewijch writes in Poem 14:

> For Love can very well repay
> Those who painfully follow her paths.
> Provided anyone sinks low enough in humility—
> Lower by far than the thought of all men
> Who are born into the world—
> Greatness of love will come by this means.
> If you were willing to fall thus and to bow in all things,
> You would obtain perfect Love.
> For that brought God down into Mary,
> And he would yet acknowledge the same in one
> Who could hold himself so humble in love:
> . . .
> But such a one would receive him and carry him for as long
> As a child grows within its mother.

Hadewijch then continues to use each of the nine months of pregnancy as a metaphor for her stages of growth. At the completion of the spiritual pregnancy "is brought to term that Child/Which has lain in that great place: in the depths of lowliness, in the heights of love,/Where with all, in every way,/The soul lives for God with all power,/In new love, day and night./So its whole life becomes divinized" (Poem 14).

Humility, because it is explored in a way that is saturated with feminine metaphors of strength, paradoxically affirms the female identity and self-worth of both teacher and audience, and yet functions as a way of separating the neophytes from their previous identity (humility as a necessary letting go of social identities and norms). According to Turner, the process of transformation during the liminal process is often described in symbols of gestation and parturition. As Hadewijch's changing inner self, the neophytes of preliterate cultures "are likened to or treated as embryos, newborn infants, or sucklings by symbolic means which vary from culture to culture" (op. cit., p.7). Given the positive nature of Hadewijch's feminine imagery, we can reformulate what Turner observed in regard to sex-stereotypes. He noted that during the liminal period, traditional gender patterns were suspended, and the initiates were treated as either genderless, bisexual, or transsexual. His reasoning is that "since sex distinctions are important components of structural status, in a structureless realm they do not apply" (p. 8). Turner's view on this issue might only hold true to kinship-dominated societies, and perhaps mostly so for males.[15] In Hadewijch's case, the experience of liminality leads to the abandonment not of sex distinctions, but of sex discriminations in the form of misogynist views of women (see as example Bernard's violent treatment of Mary's arrow-pierced "wound" of motherhood). Rather than forming an entrance to a sexless realm, liminality frees Hadewijch to articulate femininity in a positive way. And, I would like to add, without devaluing masculinity either, since masculine images are allowed to re-emerge in the vision of the bridegroom. Violent masculinity (expressed by Bernard in a language of rape and warfare) is abnegated. Hadewijch experiences Christ as a paradoxical totality that includes child, lover, "His" feminine form (Minne), and formless energy (abyss).

Liminality as fruitful feminine depth is imagined as both an inner and an outer space—outer because she can see it, inner because of the metaphor of being swallowed into it. It is fecund with possibilities of rebirth. Turner points out the fact that the unstructuredness of the abyss allows neophytes to experience what is described as a "close connection with deity or with superhuman power, with what is, in fact, often regarded as the unbounded, the infinite, the limitless" (p. 8). The most extensive discussion of this kind of depth can be found in the visions. In comparison to her other texts, we may characterize her tightly structured and numerically arranged visions as esoteric texts clad in *religious* language in contradistinction to the esoteric text of her *Strofische Gedichten* which are disguised by *secular* courtly language. In other words, the visions move beyond a play with courtly terminology into a sharply delineated religious dimension, but without the sparse sententiousness of the *Mengeldichten*. The visionary texts are filled with rich images and mysterious speeches that often recall the visionary accounts of the Hebrew Scriptures. I would like to comment only on one imaginational cluster, that of the abyss. Psychologically, the abyss is the belly of the whale, the symbol of being swallowed with Jonah, the re-connecting with pre-natal realms. Joseph Campbell, the controversial scholar-magus of myths, comments on this act of metamorphosis in regard to the hero's journey: "[the hero's] secular character remains without; he sheds it, as a snake its slough. Once inside he may be said to have died to time and returned to the World Womb, the World Navel, the Earthly Paradise."[16] Hadewijch's abyss resembles the cosmic cavern, the *uterus mundi*, which grants rebirth and as such is a much more feminine symbol than the erected *axis mundi* of the cross[17] with its masculine undertones.

Hadewijch describes the process of being in-corporated a number of times. What makes her descriptions so interesting is that the act of being swallowed in the abyss is also a sexual experience, a version of the archetypal *hieros gamos* with an interesting role reversal. Now it is not the goddess who mates with a priestly king, but the divine bridegroom who unites himself with a human woman. As the goddess bestows sacred power on the priestly king through sexual union, so marks the *unio mystica* a power-charged transformation of the human nature into its archetypal image, the divine. In Hadewijch's visions, the swallowing and merging as identity transformation takes place in the first visionary cycle[18] on the human level which is sensual and physical, and at the end of the second cycle on the archaic, non-human level, which is represented by the divine abyss. Here is her description of the human dimension of the *hieros gamos* experienced during a celebration of the Eucharist:

> ...looking like a Human Being and a Man, wonderful and beautiful, and with a glorious face, he came to me as humbly as anyone who wholly belongs to another. Then he gave himself to me in the shape of the Sacrament ... After that he came himself to me, took me entirely in his arms, and pressed me to him; and all my members felt his in full felicity, in accordance with the desire of my heart and my humanity ... after that I remained in a passing away in my beloved, so that I wholly melted away in him and nothing any longer remained to me of myself. (7:64, 94)

> ...also ghedane mensche/ende man/Soete ende scoene/ende uerweent ghelaet tonende/ende also onderdanechleke te mi comende/Alse een die eens anders als es/ Doe gaf hi mi hem seluen in specien des sacraments...Daer na quam hi selue te mi ende nam mi alte male in sine arme/ ende dwanc mi ane heme/ ende alle die lede die ic hadde gheuoelden der siere in alle hare ghenoeghen/ na miere herten begherten/ na miere menscheit...Hier na bleef ic in ene veruarne in mijn lief dat ic al versmalt in heme/ende mi mijns selues niet en blief.

Compare this fully humanized sensual description with the second, divine experience of merging that is devoid of anthropomorphic imagery, stark and frightening in its alienness, yet encompassing all of life:

> There I saw a deep whirlpool, wide and exceedingly dark; in this abyss all beings were included, crowded together, and compressed. The darkness illuminated and penetrated everything. (11:1)
> (Daer saghic enen ouer diepen wiel/ ende enen widen/ende ouerdonker/ ende in dien wiel/ die soe wiit was/Sowas alle dinc besloten/so vaste/ende so na bedwonghen/Dat donkere uerlichte/ ende dore sach alle dinc.)

> And the abyss in which the disk ran as it circled about was of such unheard of depth and so dark that no horror can be compared to it. (12:1)
> (Ende die wiel daer die sciue in liep daer hi in draiede die was so onghehoerdelike diep ende so doncker dat en ghene eiselecheit waer ieghen gheliken en mach.)

> In that abyss I saw myself swallowed up. Then I received the certainty of being received, in this form, in my beloved, and my beloved also in me. (12:172)

(Jn die diepheit saghic mi verswolghen/Daer ontfinghic sekerheit met diere vormen ontfaen te sine in mijn lief/ende mijn lief also in mi.)

In both transformatory unification episodes, femininity is positively affirmed and accepted—once in the symbol of Hadewijch as anthropomorphic, sensual bride, the second time symbolized in the primeval abyss that functions as a divine epiphany of God/ess as the whirlpool/womb of all life. The positive interwovenness of masculine and feminine metaphors in these initiation experiences, especially the fluidity of gendered forms the divine takes on according to the stages of Hadewijch's spiritual development, are both reflective of Hadewijch's self-confidence and the gyno-centric character of her mysticism. Whether this aspect of her teachings added to making them "too noble" and "too subtle" for readers outside of her circle, we will probably never know.

NOTES

1. For a discussion of the social aspects of women mystics in Western Europe in the thirteenth century, see Bernd Ruediger, "Zur Reflexion der Frauenfrage in der deutschen Frauenmystik des 13./14.Jahrhunderts", in *Untersuchungen zur gesellschaftlichen Stellung der Frau im Feudalismus*, Historiker-Gesellschaft der Deutschen Demokratischen Republik, vol. 3 (Magdeburg 1981), 13-47. The following primary sources were used: *Het Visioenenboek van Hadewijch. Uitgegeven naar handschrift 941*, edited, with a commentary and translation by Herman W.J. Vekeman, Nijmegen, (Brugge, 1980); *De Visionen van Hadewijch. Middelnederlandse tekst*, edited, with a commentary and translation by Paul Mommaers, Nijmegen, Brugge, 1979; *Hadewijch: Van Liefde en Minne: de Strofische Gedichten*, edited, with a translation by Marc Ortmanns-Cornet, 1982; *Hadewijch: the Complete Works*, translated, with an introduction, by Mother Columba Hart, New York, 1980.

   In the essay, I have juxtaposed Mother Hart's translation with the original text when possible; thus the reader can judge the degree of accuracy of Mother Hart's translation which is, unfortunately, not always close to the original. For her masterly use of courtly language, see Tanis M. Guest, *Some Aspects of Hadewijch's Poetic Form in the "Strofische Gedichten."* The Hague, 1975. Many thanks to Connie Gundersen at St. Olaf's Rolvaag library for her assistance.

2. Frank Willaert, "Hadewijch," in: *Mein Herz schmilzt wie Feuer*, (Stuttgart, 1988), 110-124.

3. The list has been recently translated into English by Sr. Helen Rolfson: "These are the Perfect, Clad as Love . . ." in *Vox Benedictina*, 5:2,3, April/July 1988: 201-211. Mother Hart excluded the fascinating text from her edition, since in her opinion, it "lack[s] the mature discretion that characterizes all her other writings" (*op.cit.*, 2).

4. For example, in Letter 10 and in the Stanzaic Poems 1 and 12:19-20 (Mother Hart, *op. cit.* ,374). For an alternative reading of the brevity of this statement, see Theodor Weavers, *Poetry of the Netherlands in its European Context 1170-1930* (London, 1960). Weavers argues that Hadewijch must have written her list not too long after 1174, the date of his canonization, because St. Bernard should have been better known to her after the canonization became part and parcel of the liturgy and lore of each parish (see n.3:28).

5. Michel de Certeau, "Mystic Speech" in *Heterologies: discourse on the other* (Minneapolis 1986), 80-101.

6. On the arrangement of her texts, see, e.g., Hart, *op.cit.*, 18.

7. See Frank Willaert, "Hadewijch and ihr Kreis in den 'Visionen'", in: *Abendlaendische Mystik im Mittelalter. Symposium Kloster Engelberg 1984*, Kurt Ruh, ed. (Stuttgart, 1986), 368-388, and Hans Schottmann, "Autor und Hoerer in den 'Strophischen Gedichten' Hadewijchs", in ZfdA, (1973, 102:20-37). Most recently, Ursula Peters discussed Hadewijch's audience and her literary personna in *Religioese Erfahrung als literarisches Faktum: Zur Vorgeschichte und Genese frauenmystischer Texte des 13. und 14. Jahrhunderts* (Tuebingen, 1988), 48-53.

8. Quoted in Esther Heszler, "Stufen der Minne bei Hadewijch" in *Frauenmystik im Mittelalter*, Peter Dinzelbacher and Dieter R. Bauer, (Ostfildern bei Stuttgart, 1985), 99-123. For a summary of the medieval *imago Dei* conceptualization, see Bernard McGinn and Lars Thunberg, "The Human Person as Image of God" in *Christian Spirituality*, ed. Bernard McGinn, John Meyendorff, and Jean Leclercq. *Origins to the Twelfth Century*, (New York, 1987), 291-331.

9. Victor Turner, "Betwixt and Between: The Liminal Period in Rites of Passage", in *The Forest, of Symbols* (Ithaca, N.Y.: Cornell University Press, 1967), reprint in: Louise Carus Mahdi *et al.*, eds., *Betwixt and Between: Patterns of Masculine and Feminine Initiation*, (La Salle, 1987), 3-23; all references are made to this edition. See also Turner, *The Ritual Process. Structure and Anti-Structure*, (Ithaca, 1977).
   For a critique of Turner's model in regard to medieval women, see Caroline Walker Bynum, "Women's Stories, Women's Symbols: A Critique of Victor Turner's Theory of Liminality" in *Anthropology and the Study of Religion*, ed. Frank Reynolds and Robert Moore, (Chicago: Center for the Scientific Study of Religion, 1984), 105-125. Bynum, however, is concerned about women's discovery of their religious calling and their attempt to comply with it. Hadewijch is concerned about the next step, how to understand spiritual growth once the choice for a religious life-style has been made. My thanks to Kari E. Borresen for directing my attention to Bynum's article.

10. The exploration of new languages is an acute issue in today's feminist spirituality, since it is felt that the language of patriarchy cannot convey women's experiences. For a brilliant juxtaposition of "old" and "new" languages and their impact on women's sense of self, see Susan Griffin, *Woman and Nature: the Roaring Inside Her* (New York, 1978).

11. In mystical language, the "dark night of the soul" parallels in some ways the function of a liminal state.

12. I should add here that Beguines ordered many art works for their beguinages which took the place of sacred objects in their devotional practices. We can read medieval women's devotion to the Eucharist as an attempt to appropriate more publicly acknowledged sacrosanct objects as part of women's fight to remain within the male cult community. Ultimately, women lost this fight, however, and the question of what gender group within the church defines what sacred objects are, and who has access to them has not been solved even today.

13. J. Bosch, "Vale milies: De structuur van Hadewijch's bundel 'Strofische Gedichten', *Tijdschrift voor Nederlandse taal - en letterkunde*, 90 (Leiden, 1974):173-175, quoted in

Hart, *op. cit.* For an interpretation of the poem as a paradigm of mystical experience, see Wilhelm Breuer, "Das mystische Praesenzerleben des Frommen: Zu Hadewijch, Strophisches Gedicht Nr. 29" in *Studien zur deutschen Literatur und Sprache des Mittelalters*, ed. Werner Besch *et.al.* eds., *Festschrift fuer Hans Moser zum 65. Geburtstag* (Berlin 1974), 169-184.

14. Bernard of Clairvaux, *On the Song of Songs II: Sermons 21-46*, trans. Kilian Walsh, OCSO, Cistercian Fathers Series: no. Seven, (Kalamazoo: Cistercian Publications, 1983), 109. Breuer acknowledges that Hadewijch's interpretation of Mary's humility "seems to reverse the theological teachings on Mary of the high middle ages" (p. 177, my translation), and quotes as an example of this tradition Thomas Aquinas, who, for once unisono with Bernard, wrote, "in ipsa conceptione Christi B. Virgo nihil active operata est, sed solam materiam ministravit." Breuer does not ask, unfortunately, *why* Hadewijch chose to depart from this tradition.

15. Joseph Campbell, *The Hero with a Thousand Faces* Bollingen Series XVII, (Princeton, 1949), 92. See Bynum, "Women's Stories." For an example of the violent construction of male gender in a primal patriarchal society, see Gilbert Herdt, *The Sambia. Ritual and Gender in New Guinea* (New York 1986).

16. See Micea Eliade, *Cosmos and History. The Myth of the Eternal Return* (New York, 1959); and Eliade, *Rites and Symbols of Initiation. The Mysteries of Birth and Rebirth* (New York, 1958). Eliade stresses that for women, initiation rites point out the sameness of their sex with the procreative sacred matrix of all life, thus empowering women in a way inaccessible to men: "The woman receives the revelation of a reality that transcends her although she is part of it . . . it is the revelation of the feminine sacredness; that is, of the mystic unity between life, woman, nature and the divinity . . . The girl or inititated woman becomes conscious of a sanctity that emerges from the innermost depths of her being;" quoted in Eliade, *Myths, Dreams, and Mysteries* (New York, 1960), 217. For Hadewijch, this sameness allowed her to feel self-confident in her role as female lay teacher.

17. I have argued elsewhere ("Hadewijch's Visions as a Medieval Account of Female Individuation", unpublished paper presented at the Conference on Jungian Psychotherapy and Christian Spirituality, Buffalo, New York, 1985) that the fourteen visionary texts were deliberately organized in two cycles of seven text units each. The first cycle focuses on becoming one with God in His humanity, the second cycle on becoming one with God in His divinity.

GREGORIAN CHANT
AND THE POWER OF EMPTINESS
Calvin Stapert

I must confess to a certain presumptousness on my part in thinking a lifelong Calvinist might have something to offer at a conference celebrating the St. Anselm College Centennial. And yet I
make bold to do so because I think we are deeply united in the
common goal of Christian liberal arts education. I like to think that
fides quaerens intellectum is no less descriptive of Calvin College than of
St. Anselm College, just as I am sure that *Cor meum tibi offero Domine
prompte et sincere* is no less true of your commitment than it is of ours.

A second aspect of my presumptousness is my topic, Gregorian
Chant. Gregorian Chant has never been an ingredient in my liturgical life and although my area of specialization in graduate school
was medieval music, I am a long way from being a chant specialist.
But I do love the Chant and I hope you will at least be interested to
hear some of the ideas that have grown out of my peculiar perspective and that you might even find something valid and useful in
them.

I am here to praise Gregorian Chant, the repertory of music that
is at the heart of Catholic musical tradition. I praise it because I
hope it is an ingredient in music education that will never be bur-
ied. More specifically, I praise it because I see it as an ingredient in
music education that is particularly well-qualified to teach an
important spiritual truth, a spiritual truth that the contemporary
world has largely forgotten.

I have been teaching music history for twenty years. Like many
who teach music history, I spend a fair amount of time teaching
Gregorian Chant. There was a time when no respectable music

curriculum ignored this treasure of Catholic tradition. Until recently I was naive enough to think that such would always be the case. I thought music students, and even general students in music appreciation courses, would always get at least a bit of exposure to Gregorian Chant.

I am no longer so optimistic. A colleague from a respected state university recently informed me that their music students are no longer required to take any courses that deal with medieval music. I do not know how widespread that curricular practice is, but I am uneasy about the pressures that the inclinations of this generation are exerting toward the elimination of the study of the ideas, artifacts, and deeds of the past. Whether my fears are well-founded or not, however, is not at issue here. What I wish to suggest is a reason why I think the study of Gregorian Chant is particularly beneficial in this day and age.

In speaking about benefits of *studying* the Chant, I am not forgetting that the benefits of *practicing* it in worship are greater. But I live and work and worship in a situation where its practice does not exist and I would like to see the benefits spread beyond the few places where the practice still exists. Where the practice does not exist, study is the best alternative.

In thinking about rationale for studying Gregorian Chant, especially in a non-Catholic setting, one could, of course, fall back on its historical importance. Donald Grout, in his stellar and heavily used *History of Western Music*, does just that. Gregorian Chant, he says, was "one of the seeds from which, in the fullness of time, our Western music developed."[1]

There can be no question about Gregorian Chant's historical importance. To understand much of the music of the Middle Ages and Renaissance (and even beyond), one needs to understand the place Gregorian Chant has in the life and thought of those periods. But one could say that this is question-begging; it simply pushes the question ahead to the music of a later time.

Even though I am convinced that medieval and Renaissance music also have relevance for today, I am not comfortable merely to rest a claim for the importance of Gregorian Chant on its historical importance, especially not on the sort of historical importance that maintains that something is of value merely because it led to and helps us to understand something else. Herbert Butterfield eloquently pointed out the weakness of history that is only interested in what gave birth to or paved the way for some later thing.

It has been said that if a lamb should die in May, before it had reproduced itself, or contributed to the development of the species, or provided a fleece for the market, still the fact that it frisked and frolicked in the spring was in one sense an end in itself, and in another sense a thing that tended to the glory of God.[2]

Gregorian Chant, to continue Butterfield's metaphor, certainly "contributed to the development of the species" and "provided a fleece for the market," but if that is the only importance one sees in it, he is missing its essence. Even if Gregorian Chant has no impact on the history of music it would still be worthy of study. It would be worthy of study because it is something that "tended to the glory of God."

Music history textbooks usually make a gesture in that direction. They point to the Chant's integral relationship to worship. Let me quote Grout again: "Gregorian Chant . . . is not meant to be listened to for its own sake; as an adjunct to worship, it is strictly functional music."[3] To study Gregorian Chant in order to learn something about proper musical function in worship is indeed a worthy undertaking. It can teach us much on that score and for that reason alone would be worthy of study.

But its value does not stop there; it has value as a teacher of spiritual truth. Here I am treading slippery ground but I am far from being alone in having sensed something along these lines from my first exposure to the Chant. Recently I have been struck by two contrasting ways Gregorian Chant has been received. This contrast has opened the way for me to a better understanding of Gregorian Chant as a musical embodiment of a spiritual principle that Peter Kreeft calls "the power of emptiness."[4] But before discussing that principle and the way the Chant embodies it I must describe two contrasting "receptions" of the Chant.

The first reception is the one described by Grout.

When we hear Gregorian Chant for the first time, we may perhaps have a negative impression of it. We may be struck not so much by what is there as by what is not there. We feel the lack of supporting harmony or accompaniment; or we miss clearly defined time values and regular accents; or we notice that the melodic line sometimes turns strangely and often does not cadence on the expected note; or we are perhaps resentfully conscious that the music makes no attempt to thrill our senses or entangle our emotions.[5]

Grout is right. There is seemingly very little to Gregorian Chant. All the ingredients that modern listeners expect and even demand in their music are missing. There can be no denying that an antiphon like *Hodie Christus natus est* is musically impoverished compared to the musical resources used by, say, Vaughn Williams in his setting of the same words.

Now compare the reception described by Grout with the following statements from Thomas Merton's autobiography, *The Seven Storey Mountain*.

> Those psalms, the singing of the monks, and especially the ferial tone for the Little Hours' Hymns: what springs of life and strength and grace were in their singing![6]

> [*Salve Regina* is] the most stately and most beautiful and most stirring thing that was ever written, that was ever sung.[7]

> What measure and balance and strength there is in the simplicity of that hymn [*Conditor alme siderum*]! Its structure is mighty with a perfection that despises the effects of the most grandiloquent secular music—and says more than Bach without exhausting the whole range of one octave.[8]

> How mighty they are, those hymns and those antiphons of the Easter office! Gregorian chant that should, by rights, be monotonous, because it has absolutely none of the tricks and resources of modern music, is full of a variety infinitely rich .... Those Easter "alleluias," without leaving the narrow range prescribed by the eight Gregorian modes, have discovered color and warmth and meaning and gladness that no other music possesses.[9]

Those are extravagent claims, especially because Grout told the truth (which Merton admits) when he listed all the things the Chant does not possess. It does not have harmony or counterpoint, dramatic melodic shapes, rhythmic diversity, a sense of drive to clearly defined goals, wide-ranging dynamics, or a rich pallet of tone-color. Even if we allow for a generous dose of hyperbole in Merton's statements, their claims remain extravagant. Can the difference between these two receptions then be explained by debunking Merton's experience? Hardly. He was an exceptionally intelligent and sensitive man with a wide range of artistic experience and knowledge and an uncommon gift for writing. Besides, he is not the only witness to such riches in the Chant. Those who have lived with the Chant seem to be unanimous in praising it as liberally, if not as eloquently, as Merton did. Often even a brief encounter with the Chant in its proper setting of worship will elicit extraordinary praise. I have occasionally had students who, after having been exposed to Gregorian Chant in one of my classes, spent a week or two at a monastery with another professor. After returning they have sought me out to tell me, "You should have heard that music!"

So how can this apparent contradiction be explained? How can music so devoid of resources be so overwhelmingly rich? Two common answers take us a little way toward bridging the contradiction. One is that the Chant, even at its simplest, is artistically "right." I like the way Richard Crocker put it:

> Psalmody is not intended as an artistic experience . . . . Nonetheless, even these tones have . . . artistry . . . . The inflections are simple, but they are right; they have to be, to stand up under the use they have been getting day and night for over a thousand years.[10]

A second answer is to point out that the Chant needs to be heard in the right environment for its beauties to be perceived. Of course there is truth in such a claim. Chant is heard to its best advantage when it is heard in a place of worship as part of the act of worship. But I am not convinced that artistic rightness and proper surroundings alone build a bridge long enough to span the chasm between the Chant's paucity of musical resources and Merton's extravagant claims. Remember what he said — "[*Salve regina*] is the most stately and most beautiful and most stirring thing that was ever written," and "Those Easter 'alleluias' . . . have discovered color and warmth and meaning and gladness that no other music possesses," and *Conditor alme siderum* "says more than Bach without exhausting the whole range of one octave."

If there is a bridge across the gap between the apparent emptiness and the witnessed riches of the Chant, it has to be sought in the spiritual realm. It is understandable that the music history textbooks do not venture into this realm, but occasionally they do allude to it as, for example, in Joseph Kerman's *Listen*: "Hearing Gregorian chant . . . , we feel less like listeners in the modern sense than like privileged eavesdroppers, who have been allowed to sit in at a select occasion that is partly musical but mainly spiritual."[11] Or in Richard Hoppin's *Medieval Music*: "The chants . . . must be taken as a musical embodiment of the spiritual values inherent in the various acts of collective worship.... "[12]

I make no pretense that what follows in this paper is the key that unlocks the door into the spiritual realm of the Chant. The entering of that realm requires faith and obedience, without which all knowledge and understanding is for naught. At best I can point the understanding in the right direction as it tries to comprehend the spiritual dimension of Gregorian Chant. To that end I attempt to link the Chant's musical features to the spiritual principle of the power of emptiness.

The power of emptiness is a spiritual principle that finds its most direct expression in various paradoxical sayings of our Lord recorded in the Gospel of St. Matthew. Here are two of them:

> Blessed are the poor in spirit, for theirs is the kingdom of heaven (5:3).

> And everyone who has left houses or brothers or sisters of father or mother or children or lands, for my name's sake, will receive a hundredfold, and inherit eternal life (19:29).

The power of emptiness is one of the mysteries of the Kingdom of God. It cannot be understood by the thinking of this world. On that basis it is nonsense. But the Beatitudes turn all worldly thinking and all worldly values upside-down; or, rather, they turn them right-side-up. At the head of the Beatitudes we hear, "Blessed are the poor in spirit, for theirs is the kingdom of heaven." This, according to many commentators, "is the root from which the others grow," the one that "strikes the key of the kingdom-music."[13] In some way poverty or emptiness is the key to the abundant riches of the Kingdom of God, riches that belong to those "fully conscious of the poverty of all human resource...."[14]

Matthew returns to this theme when he reports Jesus' encounter with the rich young man who wanted to know how to inherit eternal life. When Jesus tells him to sell all his possessions and give to the poor, the young man goes away sadly. This prompts another of Jesus' enigmatic sayings:

> "I solemnly tell you, it will be hard for a rich man to enter the Kingdom of heaven. Further, I tell you that it is easier for a camel to go through the eye of a needle than for a rich man to enter God's Kingdom." (19:23-24).

The disciples are bewildered but Peter responds by saying, "We have left everything and followed you. What therefore will become of us?" To this Jesus answers, "Everyone who has left homes, brothers, sisters, father or mother, children or lands, for my name's sake, will receive a hundredfold, and will inherit eternal life" (19:27 and 29).

Here is the incredible promise again, but how is it possible? How can such riches come from all this poverty, emptiness, and self-denial? It is in an attempt to answer such questions that Peter Kreeft introduces the power of emptiness, a spiritual principle that is the foundation for both Christ's beatitude about the poor in spirit and his enigmatic saying about the camel going through the eye of a needle.

> The objector to poverty of spirit fails to understand the power of emptiness. The power Jesus refers to on the spiritual level is the same power that makes bowls, windows, and rooms useful on the physical level. Fill them up and they become useless; you take away their potentiality, their possibility. That power makes motherhood great on the biological level; it is the empty womb that can generate life. So spiritually, our strength is our receptivity, our passivity to God, our emptiness, our motherhood . . . . We must let God be God in us. If we come to God with empty hands, He will fill them. If we come with full hands, He finds no place to put Himself. It is our beggary, our receptivity, that is our hope.

> Thus comes the stinging paradox of Christ's negative statements. A rich man can enter the Kingdom only as a camel can go through a needle's eye. The Needle's Eye gate in the Jerusalem wall was barely wide enough for a camel, but not for its baggage. Merchants had to unload all their saddle bags for inspection before entrance to Jerusalem. We must do the same . . . .[15]

I maintain that Gregorian Chant is the music that more than any other embodies that spiritual principle. It is music emptied of all glitter and gimmicks. Its musical materials are at a minimum — a small range of diatonic pitches, a severely limited number of melodic intervals that overwhelmingly favors simple steps over dramatic leaps, only two or three rhythmic lengths for its notes, a narrow dynamic range, and monochrome tone color. It presents itself without fanfare and eschews a blatantly rhetorical posture. It refuses to grab our attention by "sound and fury" or by ravishing beauty or by sheer technique. It never seeks to impress or over-whelm. It is humble music; it avoids calling attention to itself. As Merton says, it is music that "should, by rights, be monotonous, because it has absolutely none of the tricks and resources of modern music."[16] But it is not monotonous; on the contrary, those who have sung or heard it in worship bear witness to its riches. Those riches, it seems to me, can only be the result of the working of the power of emptiness.

Our society is particularly ignorant of the power of emptiness. To be sure we are not entirely without our prophets who preach a simple way of life and peddle "more with less" cookbooks. But we do not heed their voices. We are a society that refuses to acknowledge limits and that believes more is better. We define value in quantitative rather than qualitative terms; we measure worth by possessions. We are a society that idolizes self, that claims greed is good, and that assumes that everyone has the right to acquire as many things as he possibly can. We are a society that continues to build bigger and bigger barns.

But for all our wealth, we are poor. We acquire more and more and find we have less and less of what we truly need. In our want we turn to, among other things, music. As a society we are madly enamoured of music; we truly "believe in music." But the music we turn to, for all its glitz, has nothing to offer, and for all its brute strength, is powerless to satisfy our needs. We are like the person in Ernest Dowson's poem.

> I cried for madder music and for stronger wine,
> But when the feast is finished and the lamps expire . . . .
> I am desolate and sick of an old passion,
> Yea, hungry for the lips of my desire.[17]

We need a music instead that is rich in its poverty and powerful in its emptiness. We need Gregorian Chant. We need a music whose poverty and emptiness reflects our own poverty and emptiness, a music that will turn us from our pride in our selves and our trust in our own human resources. Gregorian Chant, I think, can do that better than any other music. I hope this treasure of Catholic tradition will always be an ingredient in musical learning.

NOTES

1. Third edition with Claude V. Palisca (New York: W.W. Norton and Co., 1980), 27.
2. *Christianity and History* (New York: Charles Scribner's Sons, 1950), 6.
3. *A History of Western Music*, 36.
4. *For Heaven's Sake: The Rewards of the Virtuous Life* (Nashville: Thomas Nelson Publishers, 1986), 103.
5. *A History of Western Music*, 36.
6. New York: Harcourt Brace Jovanovich, 1948, 324.
7. P. 335.
8. Pp. 379-380.
9. P. 401.
10. *A History of Musical Style* (New York: McGraw-Hill Book Company, 1966), 14.
11. Third edition (New York: Worth Publishers, Inc., 1980), 74.
12. New York: W.W. Norton and Company, 1978, 91.
13. *The Interpreter's Bible*, vol. VII (New York: Abingdon-Cokesbury Press, 1951), 280.
14. *The Anchor Bible: Matthew*, introduction, translation, and notes by W. F. Albright and C. S. Mann (Garden City, New York: Doubleday and Company, Inc. 1971), 46.
15. *For Heaven's Sake*, 103-104.
16. *The Seven Storey Mountain*, 401.
17. *"Non sum qualis eram bonae sub regno Cynarae,"* 11. 19-20, 22-23, in *The Poems and Prose of Ernest Dowson* (New York: Boni and Liveright, 1919), 39.

ANSELM AND THE FALL OF LUCIFER IN THE WAKEFIELD CREATION PLAY

Thomas J. Jambeck

For the Englishman of the later Middle Ages, the Corpus Christi play was a play about the history of mankind. Specifically, it played out those significant scriptural events which trace God's providential plan for man's salvation. It is hardly surprising, then, that the four extant play cycles (Wakefield, York, Chester, and N. Towne) share a narrative structure which is striking in its homogeneity: each cycle begins with the Creation and the subsequent fall of Lucifer and Adam; each emphasizes the Passion and Crucifixion as the central redemptive act of human history; each ends with the Last Judgment. It is hardly surprising, too, given the long tradition of patristic biblical commentary, that each of the Corpus Christi playwrights dramatizes a given scriptural episode according to a well-established, apparently authoritative, exegetical convention. All of the extant Creation pageants reflect such a tradition, one which circumscribed the several events of the creation story into a relatively stable design. The Wakefield play of the Creation is no exception. It conforms substantially to what is clearly a received dramatic formula. What is striking in the case of the Wakefield play, however, is that despite the very small number of formal and, in several cases, verbal similarities that it shares with the other creation pageants, it diverges from the dramatic tradition in one significant respect — the dramatist's analysis of the nature of Lucifer's fall.

Since most readers of the Wakefield Creation regard Augustine's exegesis of Satan's revolt as the doctrinal touchstone of the pageant, a brief summary of his interpretation provides an appropriate starting place for this paper. In the *City of God*, the first fully developed account of Lucifer's fall, Augustine defines the angel's abandonment of God as originating in his "deficient will."[1] That is, Satan's decision to contravene the will of God had no efficient cause, in that his evil willing could not arise from a nature created as good. Rather, Lucifer erred in turning away from a being which is absolute to one that is relative. By deflecting his will from the immutable to seek out the inferior, by preferring himself to Him, the angel vitiated his nature, and this, according to Augustine, was "the first failing, the first weakness, the first defect of that nature" which, created for happiness, turned from him who has "supreme being" and so was doomed to unhappiness.[2] R. W. Hanning notes in this regard that since Augustine's treatment of Satan's rebellion was the dominant theory in the Middle Ages, it was therefore the primary influence in the shaping of the Fall of Lucifer plays. Hanning continues: "It is the originality of the opening plays of the Corpus Christi cycles . . . . to present Augustine's exegesis as a discrete dramatic action, in which an improper act of mimesis — Lucifer's seating himself in God's throne — expresses the corruption of the angel's will, its fateful turning toward a lower rather than a higher object of adoration."[3]

As an index of the current critical opinion on the Creation and Fall plays, Hanning's remarks provide a convenient focus for this paper. What I would like to argue is this: while Augustine's interpretation of Satan's sin informs the Fall of Lucifer plays of the other cycles, it does not describe what happens in Wakefield on at least two counts. First, Augustine's notion of the "deficient will" does not explain the nature of Satan's defection in the Wakefield episode. Second, while Lucifer's ascent to the throne of God witnesses his sin and thereby occasions his fall in the analogous plays, that is not the case in Wakefield.

My first objection is based on the fact that in Wakefield Lucifer's sin is not defined, in Augustinian terms, as a simple turning away from the contemplation of absolute beauty and power to the angel's own created and therefore relative attributes. Rather, it lies in the angel's misapprehension that he is the very source of his own beauty and power. For example, in his very first speech, Lucifer announces:

> If that ye will behold me right,
> this mastre longys to me.

I am so fare and bright,
  of me commys all this light,
  this gam and all this gle;
Agans my grete myght
  may no thyng stand ne be.[4]

(80-86)

Here, the Wakefield playwright departs from the other cycles in a significant way. In the analogous plays, Lucifer praises himself as the epitome of creation. The other playwrights regard Satan's desire to be like God, according to the Augustinian interpretation, as emanating from his prideful sense that he is the best of kind. For instance, the York Lucifer boasts: "All the myrth that is made is marked in me."[5] Later, he exclaims:

O! what I am fetys and fayre and fygured full fytt!
  þorme of all fayrehede apon me es feste,
All welth in my weelde es, I wete be my wytte,
  þemes of my brighthede are bygged with þe beste.

(65-68)

So, too, the Chester Lucifer proclaims his created perfection: "The mighte of God is marked in me . . . that ame repleth with heavenly grace."[6] What becomes apparent in these plays is that the audience never loses sight of the fact that Lucifer's desire to be like God issues from his pride in his creatureliness. But in Wakefield, Satan's sin is not simply a matter of deserting the absolute goodness of the Creator to contemplate his own created and therefore relative attributes. His apostasy arises from an entirely different principle. He sets his will over against that of God. He claims for himself an independence not only from the Creator's will, but also from his power:

My strengthe may not be told,
  my myght may no thyng kon;
In heuen, therfor, wit I wold
  Above me who shuld won.
ffor I am lord of blis,
  ouer all this warld, I-wis,
  My myrth is most of all;
therfor my will is this,
  master ye shall me call.

(90-98)

For the Wakefield playwright, therefore, the devil's desire to be like God inheres not in his deficient will—his turning toward a lower rather than a higher object of adoration—but in his delusion that, subject to no higher will, he might achieve "mastery" through the power of his own nature.

Since the Wakefield concept of Lucifer's sin diverges so radically from that which characterizes the other versions, it is necessary to ask whether a medieval antecedent exists that might account for the playwright's analysis. One need not go too far afield; for, the scholastic theologians, adapting Anselm's interpretation in his *De Casu Diaboli*, develop a theory of the Fall which, alongside the Augustinian version, was widely accepted in the later Middle Ages. In the *De Casu Diaboli* Anselm starts from the scriptural dictum that Lucifer's sin originated in his willing to be like God. However, the student, to whom Anselm is directing his explanation, objects: "If God cannot be conceived except as a unique being, so that nothing else can be conceived to be like Him, how was Satan able to will what he could not conceive?" Anselm's answer becomes the classical formulation of the problem for the scholastics: "Even if he did not will to be completely like God, but willed to be something less than God which was against God's will, then he still willed inordinately to be like God — for he willed something by his own will, which was subject to no one else." And, Anselm continues, "It is a characteristic of God alone to will something by his own will and to obey no higher will. Therefore, Lucifer presumed to have his own will — to will something that God did not will for him to will; in other words, he placed his will above that of God (156-157)." Unlike Augustine who regards Lucifer's desire to be like God as arising from the object of his will, Anselm discovers Satan's depravity in his mode of willing. While the angel could not wish to be like God as the object of his will—since God cannot be conceived—he could venture to act as if his will were independent of a higher order. Thus, Lucifer attempted to "absolutize" his will, to arrogate to himself a prerogative which is God's alone. In that way, he "sought to elevate himself to the position of God."[8] Eager to avoid any suggestion that the creation of the angel was somehow defective, Anselm argues that Satan's willing what God had not intended for him to will preceded any deficiency and therefore was its own efficient cause (Hopkins, 171). Anselm explains: in the first moment of their creation, God offered all the angels a perfect will, one which empowered the rational nature with the freedom to accept or refuse the divine gift of persevering in righteousness. Endowed with a faultless will, Satan must have sinned by willing to deny that gift. In other words, Lucifer's defection originated not in a "deficiency which came from God," but in the very power of his will to accept or refuse the gift of perseverance (155).

Faced with the dramatic problem of how to depict the nature of Lucifer's fall, the Wakefield dramatist has two options open to him: the Augustinian interpretation in which, inflated by the pride of his own creatural excellence, Lucifer wishes to be like God; and the later Anselmian account wherein Satan presumes independence from the divine will, chooses to act as if he were his own authority, aspires to divine likeness as something he could win by his own power. The playwright opts for the second. That he does so goes a long way to explain Lucifer's unconventional fall in the Wakefield play.

In all the analogous plays, Lucifer's occupation of the throne of God occasions his fall. That is, according to the Augustinian exegesis, the devil's attempt to ascend to God's throne symbolizes the angel's prideful attempt to become like God and, therefore, immediately elicits the Lord's reassertion of his divine authority. In Wakefield, however, Satan's actual fall occurs not when he seats himself on the Lord's "solio" but some sixty lines later when he proposes an action unique to this pageant, his fateful resolve to "take a flyght" (1. 131). Once again, Anselm — particularly as his theology of the angel's sin is later clarified by Thomas Aquinas —provides the exegesis by which we may understand the logic of the episode. Adopting Anselm's conclusions, Thomas observes that the angels, having witnessed the act of creation, perceive two bits of information. First, they realize that their existence owes its splendor to the Creator's might; their joy but reflects his bliss. Second, having glimpsed the glory of God through his creative act, the cherubim intuit, albeit obliquely, that a further bliss is possibly theirs, a beatitude which promises a direct and immediate participation in the divine life. Every creature, Thomas continues, naturally inclines to its source as the "final end at which nature is aimed."[9] And the angels are no exception. They fervently seek to embrace the eternal joy as the ultimate perfection of their existence. But while it befits an angel to turn to God as the source of his natural happiness, it is beyond the angel's capacity to turn to him as the origin of supernatural bliss. To see God in his essence, to experience the joy of contemplating him "as he is," transcends the creature's native powers. Because the cherubim aspire to a good that they cannot immediately apprehend, an object which may be attained only if it is accepted as a gift, the angels could will to possess it wrongly. Thus, Thomas concludes, in the first moment of creation, the angels experience what is theirs; in the second, what could be theirs. In the first instant, turning to God as the author of nature, the cherubim are all good; in the second, seeking him as the author of grace, they separate into the good and the evil.[10]

The dramatic boundary between these successive intervals of the angels' existence is clearly marked in the Wakefield episode. With the stage direction, "Hic Deus recedit a suo solio, et Lucifer sedebit in eodem solio," the playwright removes God from the scene (1. 77). He creates the metaphorical occasion wherein the angel's usurpation is made dramatically possible. He also creates the metaphysical moment in which the angel encounters the opportunity to achieve the beatitude that his nature promises but only God can bestow. Since the bliss which the throne represents is beyond the angels' purview, since they cannot see God himself but only the reflected image of his glory, they must judge for themselves how they are to merit the beatific union which is the ultimate purpose of their creation. And where there is room for judgment, there is room for error.

Therefore, as the Wakefield Lucifer seats himself on the throne, he contemplates the two realities, the two bits of information, which comprise the data of his choice: his own natural eminence and the supernatural joy which, glimpsed but unknown, heralds the fulfillment of his nature.[11] What is interesting here, particularly since it underscores the distinctively Anselmian nature of the Wakefield theology of the fall, is that, unlike the other plays, Lucifer's choice is not between these realities. In the analogous plays it is. There Satan chooses one over the other. He chooses his own natural perfection over the absolute good, his sin inhering in his inordinate attraction to his created and therefore relative excellence. For the Wakefield dramatist, however, the problem of Lucifer's choice is rather more subtle. That Satan should reject the goodness of the Creator is precluded by the very brilliance of his intellect. Like his fellow angels, Lucifer recognizes that the eternal joy is a divine gift which proclaims the ultimate destiny of the rational creature. Too, that Lucifer should desire the eternal bliss which the throne promises is in accord with the Creator's plan. Thomas points out, for example, that the good Satan seeks is that "for which his nature was ordained."[12] One proviso obtains: He must choose to achieve the promised end as God intends. Where the Lucifers of the other plays choose between God and themselves, the Wakefield angel has as his option not whether he should will what God in effect offers, but how he should will the object of his desire. Either he may elect to embrace the ultimate good in God's way, according to his will; or he may pursue that good in his own way, through the force of his native powers alone, without regard for God's will. The Wakefield angel puts it this way:

> Syn that we ar all angels bright
> and euer in blis to be;
> If that ye will behold me right,
> This mastre longys to me.
> I am so fare and bright,
> of me commys all this light,
> this gam and all this gle;
> agans my grete myght
> may nothyng stand ne be.

> (78-86)

While the Anselmian analysis of Lucifer's sin clarifies the playwright's portrayal of the angel's desire to be like God, his misguided intent to achieve "mastery" through the "might" of his own natural powers, it also provides the doctrinal logic for the way in which the Wakefield angel makes his fateful choice. For the playwright, the angel's defection involves a two-fold process. First, even though he has witnessed the act of creation, Lucifer fails to consider what he knows full well to be true: his existence is contingent upon the will of God. Ignoring this rule of creation, Lucifer takes the first step toward sin:

> ffor I am lord of blis,
> ouer all this warld, I-wis,
> My myrth is most of all;
> therfor my will is this,
> master ye shall me call.

> (94-98)

At this juncture, already seated on the throne, Lucifer wilfully asserts his sovereignty, but he has yet to sin. By desiring lordship "ouer all this warld," Satan does not venture to usurp what is beyond his native might. Clearly, if his willing to be master entails a certain aspiration to pre-eminence, that pre-eminence is sought by virtue of the powers which are naturally his. Lucifer is, after all, the crowning achievement of creation; the noblest of God's creatures, he is quite literally the lord of "all this warld." Therefore, while Satan's pride vaults perilously near heaven itself, the angel has not willed to cross the frontier which separates the natural from the supernatural orders; he has yet to reach out for that "mastery" which belongs to the Lord alone. What he has done, however, is to err seriously but not sinfully. Thomas explains: "Not paying attention to the rule of creation . . . in itself is not an evil . . . . What formally constitutes the evil comes into being in the fact that without the actual consideration of the rule, the will proceeds to the act of choice."[13] For the Wakefield dramatist, then, Lucifer's occupation of the throne does not occasion his fall. And for good reason. Lucifer has yet to sin; he has yet to make that choice by which he asserts the independence of his will. Therefore, the playwright depicts the angel's second and fatal step, his actual fall, only when Lucifer proposes to "take a flyght."

Having announced the rule which governs creation—"all maner thyng" is accomplished "after my will,/ that I haue thoght I shall fulfill/ And manteyn with my myght"—Deus withdraws (11. 13-18). The doctrinal implication is clear. While the angels recognize God as the "alpha et omega" of the universe, they lack that vision of "god himself" which alone could preclude defection from his will. Destined for a glory that exceeds their grasp but endowed with the powers which are the means to that glory, the angels are free to win or lose the prize of beatitude. With the Creator's departure, then, the dramatic focus is wholly upon the angels themselves and their capacity to perceive and, therefore, obey the rule which orders creation to its proper end. In such a universe wherein all that exists is contingent upon the will of God, the rational creature has only to contemplate the fact of his existence to verify his role in the order of things. Created to serve the will of God, the angel must keep to his appointed place, to will as God intends him to will. As long as the angel perseveres in his rightful "degree," he fulfills the purpose of his existence and, therefore, achieves the end of beatitude for which he was created. But, as the playwright also makes clear, the process can be short-circuited by pride. Caught by his own splendid but inadequate experience, the angel could fail to consider all that he should. In such an instance, if the angel proceeds to choose without heeding the higher rule, he in effect seeks to establish his will as the sole norm of behavior and thereby presumes to a prerogative that belongs to the Lord alone. Thus, refusing to submit to the will "that has maide all," the Wakefield Lucifer attempts to rise above his proper station, to possess what God does not intend for him to possess, and flies headlong into the will "that all shall deme" (1. 113):

> Now, therof a leke what rekys us?
> Syn I myself am so bright
> Therfor will I take a flyght.
> *Tunc exibunt demones clamando* . . . .
>
> (129-32)

Lucifer's "flyght," then, is a dramatic metaphor which captures neatly the Anselmian notion of the angelic attempt to vault the will of God. Reassured of his pre-eminence, confident that the glory which his nature promises is within his grasp, the angel reaches out to what lies beyond his native powers. Earlier, in the first moment of his creation, Lucifer sought "mastery" over "all this warld," a primacy for which his nature was ordained. Now, in the instant of choice, he ventures to leap the metaphysical boundary which separates the creature from his Creator. Because he would rise above his station, seeking his final joy not by the Creator's will but his own, Lucifer wilfully excludes himself from the glory he was destined to possess.

The Wakefield playwright's adaptation of Anselm's analysis of Lucifer's fall is unique among the extant Corpus Christi cycles. Why he should have rejected the established dramatic and doctrinal tradition is not at all clear. That he does so, of course, raises some interesting questions about the place of Anselm in the popular theology of fourteenth and fifteenth century England. What is clear, however, is that the dramatist discovers in Anselm, particularly in his analysis of sin as an integral feature of his theory of the atonement, the doctrinal context which not only describes Lucifer's fall but also prepares for the eventual restoration which the Corpus Christi drama celebrates. By following Anselm's account of the angel's sin, the dramatist also defines what for the later Middle Ages is the paradigm of the rule of behavior prescribed for all rational creatures by the very act of creation. To submit to the will "that has maide all," to serve one's appointed role in the providential order of things is to pay the debt of worship that every rational creature owes his Creator. Thus, at the outset of a cycle the purpose of which is to chronicle the redemptive history of mankind, the Wakefield dramatist advances the first principles of the divine economy which, ordained by the Creator at the very beginning of time, establishes the measure and rule of all subsequent events in salvific history.

NOTES

1. R. W. Hanning, "'You Have Begun a Parlous Pleye': The Nature and Limits of Dramatic Mimesis as a Theme in Four Middle English 'Fall of Lucifer' Cycle Plays," *Comparative Drama* 7 (1973-74):25. His term "deficient will" follows from Augustine's discussion in *The City of God*, XII, 6.

2. Saint Augustine, *The City of God Against the Pagans*, trans. Philip Levine, 7 vols. (Cambridge: Harvard University Press, 1966), 4:25.

3. Hanning, 26.

4. George England and Alfred W. Pollard, eds., *The Towneley Plays*, Early English Text Society, e.s. 71 (London: Oxford University Press, 1966), 3-4.

5. Lucy Toulmin Smith, ed., *The York Plays* (Oxford: Clarendon Press, 1885; New York: Russell and Russell, 1963), 3-4.

6. R. M. Lumiansky and David Mills, eds., *The Chester Mystery Cycle*, Early English Text Society, s.s. 3 (London: Oxford University Press, 1974), 1:8-9.

7. Anselm of Canterbury, "The Fall of Satan," *Truth, Freedom, and Evil: Three Philosophical Dialogues by Anselm of Canterbury*, tr. and ed. Jasper Hopkins and Herbert Richardson (New York: Harper, 1967), 156.

8. Jasper Hopkins, *A Companion to the Study of St. Anselm* (Minneapolis: University of Minnesota Press, 1972), 170.

9. St. Thomas Aquinas, *Summa Theologiae*, trans. Kenelm Foster O.P., (New York: McGraw-Hill, 1968), 9:136.

10. *Summa*, 269.

11. Jacques Maritain, *The Sin of the Angel*, tr. William L. Rossner, S.J. (Westminster, Md.: The Newman Press, 1959), 59. See also Edward J. Montano, *The Sin of the Angels*, The Catholic University of America Studies in Sacred Theology, Second Series, No. 89 (Washington: Catholic University of America Press, 1955), 230.

12. Montano, 136.

13. Montano, 63.

DID ANSELM ENCOUNTER
A DETOUR
ON THE WAY TO GOD?

Thomas A. Losoncy

> Thank you, dear Lord, thank you for this: what I believed before
> you by giving, now I understand by your enlightening: in such a
> way that if I were unwilling to believe I would be unable not to
> understand.[1]

This familiar but nonetheless remarkable comment conludes
chapter four of St. Anselm's *Proslogion*. It is remarkable for a
number of reasons. For one, many concerned about the philosophical purity of Anselm's argument for God's existence can cite this
passage against Barth[2] and company as proof that Anselm is not
simply engaged in exercises of religion in the *Proslogion*. It is also
remarkable for its location. Chapter Four is quite distant from the
end of the *Proslogion*. This fact, however, would hardly provoke a
stir among the devotees of chapters two through four as Anselm's
Proslogion argument.[3] Finally, there is a problem of meaning and/or
interpretation. Just what has Anselm now understood and *how* did
he come to understand it? Placing chapter four's concluding proc-
lamation in perspective contextually and establishing its meaning
will tell one something about how Anselm came to encounter a
detour on his way to God in the *Proslogion*.

Anselm's statement in chapter four seems puzzling when one
first encounters chapter fifteen and reads: "You are not only that
whose greater is unthinkable; but you are something greater than
the thinkable." One strongly suspects that the puzzling has turned
into "troubled waters" when Anselm next writes in chapter
sixteen:

O highest and inaccessible light: O whole and blessed truth: how far off you are from me, and how close I am to you! Beyond reach of this sight of mine you are, and thus I am present to that sight of yours! Everywhere and totally present you are, and I do not see you.[4]

What is particularly significant about these words is how closely they echo Anselm's very observations in chapter one of the *Proslogion*. Consider the following lines from chapter one:

Therefore now you, my Lord and God, come now teach my heart where and how to seek you, where and how to find you; Lord, if you are not here, where do I seek you in absence? And if you are everywhere, why do I not see you present?[5]

This tone of frustration or desperation, whichever, that appears in chapter sixteen continues in later chapters of the *Proslogion*. For whatever it is Anselm is missing in chapter sixteen, he rings out his plight in chapter eighteen by writing:

Behold, once more confusion; one more sorrow and grief stand in the way of one seeking joy and gladness! For my soul hoped for fulfillment, and behold once again it is overwhelmed by its need.... In the name of your goodness, help me, Lord! 'I have sought your face, O Lord, your face I will still seek! Do not turn your face away from me' (Ps. 31,7). Lift me up from myself to You! Cleanse, heal, sharpen and illumine the eye of my mind that it may behold you! Let my soul collect its powers once more, and with its whole understanding once more strive towards you, O Lord![6]

If chapter eighteen seems to place Anselm back at his beginning, chapter one, where he describes his understanding in much these same words, chapter twenty-six makes one wonder if Anselm has pursued all in vain. Consider his petitions in this final chapter of the *Proslogion*:

I pray, O God, that I shall know you and love you and rejoice in you. And if I cannot do this fully in the present life, may I from day to day until that day of fulness shall come ever progress. Let the knowledge of you progress in me here, and there be made complete. Let the love of You grow and there be made complete, so that here my joy may be great in hope, and there be complete in reality.[7]

When one reflects on these further passages they suggest a steady retreat from Anselm's confident assertion at the end of chapter four. Moreover they echo chapter one's desperate beginnings rather than the confidence of chapter four's conclusion. In short, the conclusion is indeed remarkable.

What has happened to the *intellectus* of this Christian thinker who would undertake to give understanding to belief by means of necessary reasons? Has this daring and precocious thinker turned upon himself, delivered a kind of *coup de grâce* to his own argument? Was whatever transpired in chapters two through four all for naught? Was it ultimately no more than an aberration, an endeavor fated to reach no higher than the setting from which it took flight? And what was that setting?

In chapter one of the *Proslogion* Anselm makes it abundantly clear that the existence of God is not self-evident to the intellect. For Anselm observes:

> Therefore now you, my Lord and God, come now teach my heart where and how to seek you, where and how to find you; Lord, if you are not here, where do I seek you in absence? And if you are everywhere, why do I not see you present?[8]

Where then is one to look for help in resolving this impasse? What is a human intellect to do in the face of such discouraging odds?

Instead of helping matters Anselm proceeds to compound the difficulties confronting one when, in chapter one, he notes that the intellect itself must recognize not one but two further problems; its own weakness and the immensity of the being it would seek to know:

> I do not try, Lord, to reach your heights, for there is no way at all to measure this intellect of mine against them . . . [9]

Given these added obstacles what is one to do? Surprisingly, Anselm makes an adjustment in chapter one when he says:

> . . . I do desire to understand in some measure (*aliquatenus*) your truth; the truth this heart of mine believes and loves.[10]

It is here that Anselm furnishes a clue to the product of chapters two through four of the *Proslogion* and to the subsequent difficulties which were described previously. For chapter one sets a very specific task for the *Proslogion*, to gain "some measure of knowledge" about God.

If one can take Anselm at his word he began this search as one whose intellect would ponder the things of this world. From them he would endeavor to ascertain whether, in addition to them and himself, there also existed a God. This much he explains at length in his *Rejoinder to Gaunilo*, section eight. After giving the details of his procedure Anselm replies to Gaunilo:

> Or is this then not among the things than which the greater is validly thinkable: to conjure up[11] that than which no greater is thinkable? There is therefore a way in which "that than which no greater is thinkable" can be conjured up. And just that easily can the Fool be refuted who does not accept the sacred saying when he denied "that than which no greater is thinkable" can be conjured up from other things.[12]

One learns, from Anselm's explanation in the *Rejoinder*, that the knowledge reached in chapter three of the *Proslogion* is the realization that somewhere in the universe of beings there is a highest being. This being is not merely the highest of beings that can exist in a hierarchy of beings but so high or supreme as to be wholly separate and distinct from all the rest. This information is developed at length in chapters eighteen through twenty-two of the *Proslogion* where it is noted that this being has no parts and so cannot come apart. It has no past or future existence but enjoys all its existence in one eternal now. It does not exist partly here or partly there but all and entirely at once. Anselm summarizes what separates such a being from all others and indicates such a being's distinctive features in the following manner:

> ...whatever is one thing as a whole and another thing as to its parts, and contains something mutable in it, is not wholly what it is. So too in the case of that which rose from nonbeing and which can be thought not to be and which returns to nonbeing unless it subsists through something else; and the same holds for that which has a past that no longer exists and a future that does not yet exist: such a thing does not exist in a *strict* and *absolute sense*. But you are what you are, for whatever you are at any time or in any way, that you are wholly and always.
> Furthermore you are he who properly and *absolutely* you are, because you have neither a past nor a future, but only a present, nor can you be thought not to be at any time.[13]

Such a being, or such a way of being, is unthinkable as nonbeing and in this singular way God more truly is than all other beings of the universe. Such an insight is the obtaining of "some measure of truth" about God. Moreover, such knowledge fully satisfied Anselm's quest as he stated it in chapter one of the *Proslogion*. But Anselm's intellect (*intellectus*) did not rest here. It quite naturally and humanly sought more. When one examines chapter five of the *Proslogion* and the subsequent eight chapters one discovers an entirely new program of inquiry. Anselm inaugurates this new search with the question, "What (*Quid*) then are you, Lord God, than whom a greater is unthinkable?"[14] This will introduce a host of queries about *what* it means to call God sensible, omnipotent, compassionate, impassible and so forth. The curious thing about these queries is that Anselm both makes them and yet, in a way, never answers the queries he makes precisely. He always informs one in which way or how God is all these things but not what God is. Thus he will say God is sensible, not as beings who possess bodily senses, but as the highest of intellectual and knowing beings who, in a way, must include the knowledge of sensible beings and much more in an all-encompassing knowing.[15] Similarly, God is omnipotent in the highest fashion, not being one who has the power to do something disadvantageous to oneself but always able to do what is in keeping with the highest intelligible being's nature.[16] It is this sequence of reflections that finally overtakes Anselm in chapter fourteen of the *Proslogion* when he says:

> Have you, then, my soul, discovered what you are seeking? You were seeking for God and you discovered him to be a thing, the highest of all things, a thing whose better cannot be thought . . . . Lord, God, why does my soul have no sense of you if my soul has discovered you? Has my soul not discovered you? Has my soul not discovered that you are light and truth? . . . Or is it the truth and the light that it saw; and for all that has not yet seen you because it saw you only to some extent (*aliquatenus*), but did not see you as you are? (Cf. I John iii, 2)[17]

It is in these lines that Anselm recognizes that he has embarked upon a path that has gone astray from his original quest. In fact, he then summarizes this realization in chapter fifteen of the *Proslogion* when he writes, "You are not only that whose greater is unthinkable; but you are something greater than the thinkable."

Such a realization is not a rejection of his original conclusion in chapter four but rather the frank admission that he has encountered a detour from his original purpose. For the human intellect naturally seeks to know what that being is which exists, to probe the richness of that being's nature and identity with all its power. It is this very natural intellectual longing that Anselm acknowledges he will have to forego when he observes:

> How great is that light in which everything true sparkles and which shines for the thinking mind! How vast is that truth in which there is only truth and outside of which there is only nothingness and the false. And how immeasureable the truth which in one glance sees everything that has been made; and sees by whom and through whom, and how all these things were made from nothing. What purity is there, what simplicity, what certitude and lightsomeness is there? Surely it is more than can be understood by a creature.[18]

NOTES

1. St. Anselm, *Proslogion*, chap. 4. All translations in this paper are my own, but they are made after consulting those of many others whose efforts are sincerely appreciated. The Latin text used is that of F.S. Schmitt. *S. Anselmi Opera Omnia*, vol. I (Edinburgh, 1946).

2. I refer here to K. Barth's influential *Fides quaerens intellectum* (Munich, 1931; 2d ed., Zurich, 1958; 3d ed., Darmstadt, 1966). English trans. I.W. Robertson, *Anselm: Fides Quaerens Intellectum:* (London, 1960; reprint, Cleveland, 1962).

3. One cannot entirely suppress some musings about this situation. How many smiles or smirks of disdain have been occasioned by the thought of those monks of long ago beseeching Anselm to replace the *Monologion* with something shorter and, perhaps, simpler? But what is to be said for those endless "Readings in Philosophy" which have no time for more than chapters two, three and four of the *Proslogion*?

4. *Proslogion*, chap. 16.

5. *Ibid.*, chap. 1.

6. *Ibid.*, chap. 18.

7. *Ibid.*, chap. 26.

8. *Ibid.*, chap. 1.

9. *Ibid.*

10. *Ibid.* Anselm's use of *aliquatenus* is of paramount importance here and for the entire argument of the *Proslogion*. Whether one renders the Latin as "in some measure,", "in some degree" or "to some extent," it is necessary to appreciate that the approach is adverbial and that Anselm is not attempting to gain a quidditative knowledge of God. For a lengthier study of this notion and Anselm's use of language in the *Proslogion*, see my "Language and Saint Anselm's *Proslogion* Argument," *Acta Conventus Neo-Latini Bononensis*, ed. R.J. Schoeck, (*Proceedings of the Fourth International Congress of Neo-Latin Studies*, Bologna 26 August to 1 September 1979) (Binghamton, NY: Center for Medieval and Early Renaissance Studies, 1985) 284-291.

11. *Rejoinder to Gaunilo*, sec. 8. Again, the word *coniicere* in this section is of key

importance. One may render it in English as "to conjure up," "to conjecture about," or even as "to puzzle out." The term occurs five times in this section, and its translation is of significance to the understanding of Anselm's *Proslogion* argument. For further discussion of this issue see my "Language and Saint Anselm's *Proslogion* Argument."

12. *Rejoinder*, sec. 8.
13. *Proslogion*, chap. 22. The underlining is mine.
14. *Ibid.*, chap. 5
15. *Ibid.*, chap. 6.
16. *Ibid.*, chap. 7.
17. *Ibid.*, chap. 14.
18. *Ibid.*

PART THREE

Modern and Contemporary

HISTORY AND TRADITION
IN AMERICAN CATHOLICISM:
A BICENTENNIAL REFLECTION

James M. O'Toole

Few years of western history were more significant than 1789. A new government was launched in the recently independent United States of America. Based on the largely untested principles of republicanism, this was an experiment that was just unusual enough to succeed even though none like it ever had before. In France a very different revolution was underway, launching a government that would prove considerably more tumultuous but that would nonetheless change the face of European civilization. Elsewhere that year, Belgium declared its independence, Alessandro Volta articulated the laws of electricity, and Mozart wrote *Così Fan Tutte*.

Inside the American republic, an event of lesser promise also occurred without much fanfare or notice. A priest named John Carroll, scion of an old Maryland family, was designated by Pope Pius VI as the first Roman Catholic bishop in the United States. This "gentleman of learning and abilities," as John Adams had called him, had been elected by his fellow priests to assume this role in May of the previous year, and in May 1789 the pope confirmed this election. Carroll presided over the uncertain missionary enterprise that was the Catholic church in America from then until his death in 1815, by which time other bishops and dioceses had been designated and the American church had established itself as a lasting presence. In this year of 1989, American Catholics celebrate the bicentennial of their church.

In recent times Americans have become accustomed to celebrating bicentennials. A decade ago we survived the bicentennial of the

Revolution, not without a certain degree of hoakum, and we are at present marking the 200th anniversary of the Constitution and the Bill of Rights with a thankfully greater degree of decorum. These celebrations require us to think, if only briefly, about our past, our history, and our traditions. But what do we really know of that history and, more important, what do we make of it? Many point to evidence that we are losing our collective memory. Alan Bloom tells us that serious understanding of our past is drowned out in the noise of cultural relativism and rock music. Lynne Cheney and Diane Ravitch offer depressing examples of young adults who may have heard of the Civil War but cannot place it in time or tell what it means. E. D. Hirsch concludes sadly that too many Americans, young and old, are simply culturally illiterate.[1] In the era of the bicentennials, how do we recover the historical sense? How do we come to grips with our past and extract its meaning for the present?

For American Catholics, this effort at historical understanding is both more critical and more difficult, if only because the consequences of forgetting are more serious. Catholics, after all, belong to a church that places a positive value on the power and meaning of tradition. Indeed, they look to tradition as a source of divine revelation, an expression of what God wants for his "pilgrim people on earth." Shouldn't Catholics be more ready to study and reflect on their history as the serious side of the otherwise celebratory occasions of their bicentennial? Shouldn't they be able to find in that history the themes and patterns that provide not only insights but also guideposts?

*   *   *

American Catholic history offers no shortage of material for study and reflection, though until recently both the outlines of that history and its larger meaning seemed entirely clear. The story of Catholicism in the United States was one of steady growth, of hardships overcome through a combination of vision, perseverance, and divine assistance. American Catholic history was above all a tale of progress. Beginning with Carroll himself, both the size and the institutional role of American Catholicism expanded steadily throughout the nineteenth and twentieth centuries. Churches and dioceses sprang up in places where they had previously seemed impossible or unlikely, even in aggressively Puritan (that is to say, aggressively anti-Catholic) New England. Periodic episodes of nativism notwithstanding, the church followed the frontier west, absorbing and offering a home for the successive wave of immigrants who fled agricultural crisis and political turmoil in Europe. In the more recent past, American Catholics began to exert their influence in the wider community, in politics and the professions, moving up into the middle class and out into the suburbs. By 1960 they were able to grasp the brass ring of acceptance, as "one of their own" was elected president. That event changed the role of Catholics in American society just as surely as the opening of the Second Vatican Council two years later changed the face of Catholicism around the world.[2]

This somewhat oversimplified historical picture is now being refined, as American Catholic historians have identified other themes. The assumption that Catholic history in this country was a deliberately edifying story in which everyone was good and getting better, everyone was holy and getting holier, is yielding to a more nuanced view. Three particular trends in recent Catholic history stand out. First, historians are showing that the American church was more culturally diverse than we had previously assumed and that tension and turmoil were at least as characteristic as unanimity of purpose. We now have descriptions of the trustee movement of the nineteenth century, a largely unsuccessful effort by the laity to assert their role in church affairs by sharing power with their priests and bishops. From the studies of contending clergy and laity, sometimes locking each other out of church buildings and even shooting at one another, comes a sense of the difficulties in accommodating a hierarchical church to a democratic civil state. In the same way, other historians have described the "theology of the streets" that Italians and other ethnic Catholics brought with them, often to the consternation of Irish hierarchs, who prized docile and decorous mass attendance more highly than lively, open-air, weeklong devotions to the "Madonna of 115th Street."[3]

Second, historians have at last begun to appreciate the role of women in the church's history. No longer confined to the pious ladies of the sodality or the "good sisters" who ran the parish school and obediently followed "Father's" orders, Catholic women even took on roles, like street preaching and other apologetical tasks, previously thought reserved for men.[4] Women always constituted at least half the church's membership, and nuns generally outnumbered priests by factors of three and four to one. Clearly, no accurate American Catholic history can be written if it ignores or minimizes them.

Finally, historical study is also devoting serious attention to the content and expression of religious belief. In the past, too much Catholic history was top-heavy, written from an institutional perspective as if the phenomenon under consideration were General Motors rather than a community of faithful believers. Catholic history was what priests and bishops did and what they said to one another. Now historians are looking deeper into what made the church different from other organizations in society. The mass and the sacraments provide the baseline, of course, but what was the nature and meaning of other practices that constituted for average Catholics the core of their belief and enduring identification with the church? Devotion to the Holy Spirit, the cult of the saints, connections between personal piety and Victorian ideals of domesticity are all receiving their proper consideration, and there is much more to be done. Perhaps because all Catholics recognize that the devotional world changed so markedly after Vatican II—when was the last time most Catholics attended rosary and benediction, a novena of grace, or the Forty Hours' Devotion? — historians are attempting to rediscover and describe the spiritual "world we have lost."[5]

The addition to Catholic history of these and other previously ignored subjects is surely beneficial, representing in its own way a kind of intellectual progress. But what is the significance of this expanded historical vision for the life of the church outside the academy? What connection do the particulars of this history have to the larger tradition that is and ought to be a guide for the church as a whole? The task of making connections is not an easy one, for the "lessons" of history are neither self-evident nor unchanging. "History is not a creed or a catechism," Cardinal Newman reminded us. It offers no ineluctable "rules."[6] As we know it today, history is, of course, a nineteenth century invention, a serious — even "scientific"—effort to assess critically the evidence of the past and then to codify it in narrative form. It focuses on particular people and events and then tries to generalize their meaning. Does history in this sense have any connection to the ongoing tradition of the church, which seeks in some measure to stand apart from the vagaries of change and intellectual fashion?

* * *

To begin to answer some of those questions, we might consider first what history is not. Too often in the past, Catholic history had a definite purpose, a sense of certainty, a set of clearly defined lessons. From the time of Eusebius, the first historian of the church, history was expected to serve an apologetic purpose. That author himself maintained that authentic teaching and doctrine had no history: they were true eternally. Only heresy—he called it "innovation"—had a history, and his investigation of it was necessary because it would show where heresy had gone wrong in deviating from the fixed standard. The Venerable Bede stated the matter equally succinctly: the study of history was useful because it "encouraged [the reader] to imitate what is good [and] to avoid what is sinful and perverse."[7] It fell to Voltaire, the great skeptic, to summarize the purposefulness of this approach with his famous aphorism that history was "philosophy teaching by example." By extension, too much earlier Catholic history tried to be "theology teaching by example." The final meanings and outcomes of history were already known in advance, derived from other sources, including an ancient tradition that the authority of the church kept alive and handed on. History offered merely a set of examples or case studies that demonstrated how true those truths were.

Catholic history can no longer be that, for history and tradition are not the same thing. Without history, tradition is the static deposit of Eusebius or Voltaire, a pool into which historians dip for proof-texts as needed. Such a tradition is ultimately lifeless. Consider again the insight of Cardinal Newman, who argued that any idea (including a religious idea) that was worth knowing, that "takes possession of the intellect and the heart," was "various [in] its aspects" and the result of a long, eventful "process" of development.[8] Without tradition, however, and the continuity it provides, history is merely a random collection of detail, devoid of any larger meaning. All is reduced to relativity, to cultural determinism. Every phenomenon is simply the generalized "product of its times," an all-purpose phrase that dismisses as much as it explains. Henry Adams is supposed to have answered an inquiry about what his discipline was by saying that "history is one damn thing after another." If it avoids the Scylla who cries that its meaning is already laid out for it in advance, history must likewise avoid the Charybdis who claims that it means nothing at all, that it is only a mental curio cabinet or a method that yields in the end only "one damn thing after another."

American Catholic history can and should be something more as it turns to its work beyond the present bicentennial. First, it must be a broadbased study of the people who have associated themselves with the church over time. We need more studies of what the church has meant to ordinary Catholic believers and why they continued to associate themselves with it. These questions take on special meaning when applied to America, where, from an early date, church membership had become a voluntary matter. How did American Catholics define themselves in relation to the church of which they claimed to be a part? What were the governing metaphors they used to express their religious identity at a time when other aspects of their identity (geographic, ethnic, economic) were changing? How did the church's particular patterns (its own calendar, for instance) weave into their lives? What was the larger whole of which individuals considered themselves a part? Simply put, what did it mean to say that one was a Catholic in 1815, in 1865, in 1920, or indeed in 1989? American Catholics in each of those years and the years in between would have thought the answer to that question perfectly obvious, but each would have found something strange in the answer of the others. Catholic history must begin to articulate both the differences and the similarities.

To do so, historians must expand their study of the nature of religious belief and practice in this country. It is belief and the things believers do, after all, that distinguish religious organizations from purely secular ones, even those with an avowedly charitable or educational purpose. Belief calls forth commitment and sacrifice to a degree that is unexplainable in purely practical terms. At the same time, belief yields a specific set of devotional practices that constitute an overarching religious culture that merges social structure with individual psychology. The believer remains an individual while at the same time participating in the larger whole. The forms of expression may change, but the underlying consistency remains. Different aspects of the larger body of tradition are emphasized in different historical circumstances because they speak to each age in a new way. The ups and downs of Marian devotion, for example, virtually unknown in John Carroll's day but everywhere a hundred years later, offer a model to be tested with other aspects of Catholic belief and practice. History can provide the evidence for how American Catholics have constructed their cultures and outlooks by focusing on particular and general cases at different periods.

Finally, Catholic history must adopt the canons of rigor and seriousness that have always been valued by other historians. It must be complete, unafraid of finding conflict, unsentimental, and mature. It cannot avoid certain subjects when they show human frailty if it hopes to be taken seriously when it describes others that reveal human achievement. Too often in the past, the desire to be narrowly edifying distorted the historical reality and rendered it harmless. The laity were assumed to be naive and easily scandalized, and they had in effect to be protected from their history. A pastor, planning an anniversary celebration for his parish, once told me that he wanted to write an "optimistic" history of it. Catholic history may sometimes be optimistic, but it is not necessarily so, for history, like life itself, is more complicated than that. Above all, Catholic history must be incarnational: if it is not the story of real people — people who get angry as well as inspired; people who are sometimes petty as well as noble; people who are, if we may borrow the Lutheran phrase, *simul justi et peccatores*, at once saved and sinners — then it has little to offer. History is not the lives of the saints; it is a study of the possibilities for God's action in human life and the possibilities for the range of human response.

In this way, Catholic history can and must be an open-ended process of seeking, a process for which Saint Anselm, under whose patronage we gather this weekend, provides the most useful guidance. When Anselm's faith sought understanding, he knew that what was important was the seeking, that in this life neither faith nor understanding would ever be as complete as they might one day be. Applied to the demands of Catholic history, this seeking of fuller descriptions provides the agenda for the future, and we do not know where it will lead us. If we resolve to make the journey, however, the current era of the bicentennial will have provided not merely an opportunity to reflect upon and rejoice in the past. It will have left us a clearer appreciation of how our own history contributes to the larger tradition that guides the church as a whole. That faithful understanding will be an achievement worth celebrating.

NOTES

1. Alan Bloom, *The Closing of the American Mind* (New York: Simon and Schuster, 1987); Lynne V. Cheney, *American Memory: A Report on the Humanities in the Nation's Public Schools* (Washington; National Endowment for the Humanities, 1987); Diane Ravitch and Chester E. Finn, Jr., *What Do Our 17-Year-Olds Know? A Report on the First National Assessment of History and Literature* (New York: Harper and Row, 1987); E. D. Hirsch, *Cultural Literacy: What Every American Needs to Know* (Boston: Houghton Mifflin, 1987).

2. From the late nineteenth century onward, American Catholic history has had many chroniclers. The classic interpretation was put in place by John Tracy Ellis, *American Catholicism* (Chicago: University of Chicago Press, 1956; 2d ed., 1969). For more recent surveys, which adopt different approaches, see James Hennesey, *American Catholics: A History of the Roman Catholic Community in the United States* (New York: Oxford University Press, 1981), and Jay P. Dolan, *The American Catholic Experience: A History from Colonial Times to the Present* (Garden City, N.Y.: Doubleday, 1985).

3. Patrick Carey, *People, Priests, and Prelates: Ecclesiastical Democracy and the Tensions of Trusteeism* (Notre Dame: University of Notre Dame Press, 1987); Robert A. Orsi, *The Madonna of 115th Street: Faith and Community in Italian Harlem, 1880-1950* (New Haven: Yale University Press, 1985).

4. No general history of Catholic women in America yet exists, but for a useful collection of essays outlining current scholarly activity, see Karen Kennelly, ed., *American Catholic Women: A Historical Exploration* (New York: Macmillan, 1989). For a summary of previous historical treatment of Catholic women, see James J. Kenneally, "Eve, Mary, and the Historians: American Catholicism and Women," in *Women in American Religion,* ed. Janet Wilson James (Philadelphia: University of Pennsylvania Press, 1976), 191-206.

5. For a summary of some of this recent historical work, see Joseph P. Chinnici, *Living Stones: The History and Structure of Catholic Spiritual Life in the United States* (New York: Macmillan, 1989). More specialized studies include Chinnici, *Devotion to the Holy Spirit in American Catholicism* (New York: Paulist Press, 1985), and Ann Taves, *The Household of Faith: Roman Catholic Devotions in Mid-Nineteenth Century America* (Notre Dame: Notre Dame University Press, 1986). Also helpful is the multi-volume *Foundations of American Spirituality* series currently being issued by the Paulist Press.

6. John Henry Newman, *An Essay on the Development of Christian Doctrine* (Westminster, Md.: Christian Classics, 1968; reprint of 1878 edition), 7.

7. Eusebius, *Ecclesiastical History,* trans. Roy J. Deferrari (New York: Fathers of the Church, 1953), 35; Bede, *A History of the English Church and People,* trans. Leo Shirley-Price (Baltimore: Penguin, 1955), 33.

8. John Henry Newman, *Development of Doctrine,* 29, 56. The distinction between history and tradition is treated succinctly in Jaroslav Pelikan, *The Emergence of the Catholic Tradition (100-600)* (Chicago: University of Chicago Press, 1971), 4-10.

J. H. NEWMAN AND THE RELATIONSHIP BETWEEN CATHOLIC BELIEF AND LEARNING

Peter J. Cataldo

This paper will address the reconciliation between, on the one hand, an open, universal conception of higher learning and, on the other, adherence to the magisterium of the Catholic Church in the thought of John Henry Cardinal Newman (1801-1890). My objective is not to concentrate on his *The Idea of a University*, but to combine concepts from both his *Idea* and other works, in particular his *Essay in Aid of a Grammar of Assent*, for a resolution to the problem. My procedure will be first to present Newman's view of the main components which enter into the problem. An epistemological and psychological resolution to the apparent dilemma is then suggested from Newman's account of that act of mind which he calls "complex assent."

I. *Newman's View on Catholic Higher Education.*

The nature of the university, or for that matter of higher learning in general according to Newman is founded on the structure of human knowledge, that is to say, on truth, which for Newman is a conformity of the mind with being. It is from this conformity with real being and not some received "canon" that Newman investigates the nature of higher learning, Catholic or secular. Newman writes in his *Idea*:

> Truth is the object of Knowledge of whatever kind; and when we inquire what is meant by Truth, I suppose it is right to answer that Truth means facts and their relations, which stand towards each

other.... All that exists, as contemplated by the human mind, forms one large system or complex fact, and this of course resolves itself into an indefinite number of particular facts, which, as being portions of a whole, have countless relations of every kind, one towards another. Knowledge is the apprehension of these facts, whether in themselves, or in their mutual positions and bearings.[1]

Try as it may, the human mind cannot with one glance or view possess the whole of reality but instead must view its facts under different aspects or abstractions. Only by such aspectual views of the whole, and in their interrelations, does the human mind begin to approach a mastery of the whole. These aspects in turn comprise the various branches of knowledge or sciences according to Newman. The operation by which this occurs is what Newman calls in the *Grammar of Assent* the instinct of notional apprehension. He uses this same operation of the mind to explain the generation of the sciences in his *Philosophical Notebook*, where he summarizes the sources of the unity of the sciences:

These separate abstractions are the matter of sciences because they are each of them an abstraction of what is one, the original individuum, and are therefore consistent with themselves. They are contemplations of that which is one under particular aspects respectively . . `.` . Each abstraction then retains with it the idea of unity and solidarity, and therefore of system and of science, and of harmony of attributes, each part being consistent (in communion) with each other and with the whole.[2]

Each science or branch of knowledge is complete with respect to its own aspect of the "original individuum," but because each is separate and partial, each is incomplete in relation to the whole as such. By reason of its incompleteness, each science requires what Newman calls the "external assistance" of the others, which is possible precisely because of both their independence and their common subject-matter. Hence, by viewing all of the various branches of knowledge together, the human mind is able to approach an apprehension of the objective whole of reality in proportion to the sciences it has mastered.

Conversely, the mind will possess a defective apprehension in proportion to the number and value of those sciences which are left absent from the circle of knowledge.[3] The exclusion of any one branch of knowledge will actually limit and impair the others, particularly if the science of God, viz., theology, is excluded, because as Newman shows, it is "of wide reception, of philosophical structure, of unutterable importance, and of supreme influence . . . "4 Moreover, it is further evidence of the university's intricate web of knowledge that the place of theology will not simply be neglected after its exclusion, but that other sciences will usurp it owing to a tendency of the human mind. "The human mind," Newman explains, "cannot keep from speculating and systematizing; and if Theology is not allowed to occupy its own territory, adjacent sciences, nay, sciences which are quite foreign to Theology, will take possession of it."5

For Newman, the university ought to be structured according to the ordered unity and universal character of knowledge itself, which is evident as he defines the task of the university with his typically lucid and alluring prose:

> in truth, it professes to assign to each study, which it receives, its own proper place and its just boundaries; to define the rights, to establish the mutual relations, and to effect the intercommunion of one and all... it is pledged to admit, without fear, without prejudice, without compromise, all comers, if they come in the name of Truth; to adjust views and experiences, and habits of mind the most independent and dissimilar; and to give full play to thought and erudition in their most original forms, and their most intense expressions, and in their most ample circuit. Thus to draw many things into one is its special function; and it learns to do it not by rules reducible to writing, but by sagacity, wisdom, and forbearance, acting upon a profound insight into the subject-matter of knowledge, and by a vigilant repression of aggression or bigotry in any quarter.6

There could not be a more clear affirmation from Newman of the freedom of thought in all of its import than what is found in this text. Unmistakably present also is the point that this freedom is not an end in itself but is for the sake of truth, i.e., the unified Truth of which he wrote at the beginning of the *Idea*. The importance of this condition on the freedom of thought is reconfirmed by Newman in his subsequent discussion of the problem of reconciling mysteries both divine and natural. Reconciling mystery is possible for Newman as long as we remember the cardinal maxims that truth cannot be contrary to truth, that truth often *seems* contrary to truth, and that one must be patient with such appearances.7 As for the Catholic scientific investigator, four things are presumed by Newman, which again follow from his general position that investigation be for the sake of truth. Newman stipulates that (1) the investigation have no collision with the dogmas of the faith; (2) that there is no interpretation of Scripture or conclusions of religion; (3) that no interpretation of religious paradoxes is attempted, and (4) that the weak are not recklessly scandalized.[8]

II. The origin of the Balance between Belief and Learning

The question may now be posed whether Newman has any means of distinguishing that sort of intellectual pursuit which abides by the conditions he cites from that which does not. Does Newman provide us with a measure of the balance between his unified view of knowledge and the proscription against collisions with the tenets of the Christian faith? It is clear from the text of the *Idea* that Newman finds these two components of higher learning quite compatible. He writes, for instance, that "we, none of us, should say that it is any shackle at all upon the intellect to maintain these [dogmas] inviolate. Indeed, a Catholic cannot put off his thought of them . . . . The habitual apprehension of them has become a second nature with him . . . . "[9]

This "habitual apprehension" of the Catholic believer is a good point from which to approach the compatibility of Newman's holistic conception of liberal learning with the integrity of Catholic doctrine. In the *Grammar*, Newman argues that the explicit assent of the Catholic to the propositions of the faith, such as can be found in the Creed, are at the same time assents of a sort to many other implicit propositions of the faith. One could for example make an assent to the explicit proposition, "One Holy Catholic and Apostolic Church," which would include an anticipatory or prospective assent to all the other propositions bound up with the explicit proposition but otherwise unapprehended. Moreover, an actual assent could still be given to the truth of each of the implicit propositions with the assent to the original. This is how the multitude of abstract notions and propositions which constitute the Catholic *credenda* and for which each Catholic is bound to believe, come within his reach, priest and layman, educated and uneducated alike.[10] This same kind of prospective belief can be found with secular and ordinary propositions. Newman cites the propositions, "Alexander conquered Asia," and "Veracity is a duty" as examples of commonly accepted assents in which there are many other implicit propositions included.[11] These kinds of secular analogues, as such, provide a rational warrant for Newman's explanation of prospective belief in the Catholic *credenda*. They also indicate that one and the same operation of the mind is at work in both religious and secular modes of belief.

More important for our purposes is to point out that which in the nature of the proposition allows for this kind of assent and ultimately for the balance between development of thought and integrity of doctrine. Newman's arguments in the *Grammar*, especially in the first three chapters, indicate that the proposition has an irreducible quality. I have found that Newman treats the proposition as being essentially different from, and not reducible to, the following four aspects: its internal and external modes of being held, the apprehensive sense of its terms, and its truth-value. I call this the "irreducibility of the proposition." Its independence from its internal and external modes is evident from the fact that one and the same proposition may be held as an interrogative, a conditional, or a categorical, and may also be held correspondingly as a doubt, inference, or assent — keeping in mind that for Newman assent is the unreserved and unconditional adherence to or acceptance of a proposition as true. One and the same proposition may also be apprehended notionally or concretely. Finally, Newman holds that one may assent to the truth or falsity of a proposition without necessarily apprehending the subject, *per se*, of the proposition.[12]

All this is necessary to understand the type of assent which allows for the desired balance in higher learning. For, if the proposition, which is the essential object of the act of assent, is irreducible in the ways just cited, then it is possible to assent to the truth of a proposition while at the same time being reflectively conscious of the causes of its truth. This type of assent Newman calls "reflexive" or "complex." To assent to the truth or falsity of a proposition unconsciously or without apprehending anything else about it is called "simple assent." However, we are able to engage in inferential reasoning and still preserve the unconditionality of the assent whose reasons we intend to clarify, because the proposition to which assent is given is not, by nature, inextricably bound up with the inference which has led to it. In other words, the conditionality of inference is compatible with the unconditionality of assent for Newman because the conclusiveness of a proposition is as he states only an "aspect" of it and not part of its intelligibility. Moreover, the irreducibility of the proposition means that the truth-value of the proposition cannot be equivalent with its conclusiveness, which is an equivalence assumed in John Locke's notion of the degrees of assent.

Newman sums up the matter stating, "[t]herefore to set about concluding a proposition is not *ipso facto* to doubt its truth; we may aim at inferring a proposition, while all the time we assent to it."[13] The reality of complex assent is borne out first by ordinary experience, as with beliefs such as "Great Britain is an island," or "India exists." One may hold such beliefs with an assent on what were sufficient reasons, but which have been forgotten or perhaps were never formally marshalled and by some occurrence are subsequently analyzed and reviewed. Such a review does not necessitate a suspension of the unconditionality of the assent according to Newman, and this is because of what I have argued is the irreducibility of the proposition.

III. *Investigation vs Inquiry.*

The occurrence of complex assent happens according to what Newman describes as "the claims and responsibilities of our education and social position."[14] Whatever the level of those claims and responsibilities, Newman argues that we must separate the complex assent of "investigation" from "inquiry." The specific act of complex assent can be seen as commonly occurring in the process of investigation, but this is often confused with inquiry, a process in which complex assent is not present. The "investigator" unconditionally accepts some truth while seeking to investigate its credibility by adducing proofs and arguments for it. The "inquirer" from the beginning questions whether a particular proposition is in fact true. Newman says of the "inquiry" into religion that we "cannot without absurdity call ourselves at once believers and inquirers also."[15] Newman grants that the general distinction can be blurred in cases of religious believers who claim to be inquiring when they are not, and with others for whom to investigate can only mean inquiry. Once these circumstances are taken into consideration, the general distinction may still be applied.

Investigation is also compatible with assent reversal and does not entail a resolution never to abandon assent. Investigation does not preclude the possibility of reversing an assent which the investigation was meant to confirm. This possibility does not detract from the unconditionality of the assent. It is not necessarily an admission of a condition, or the falsity of an assent to acknowledge the possibility that the state of affairs to which one gives assent might be otherwise. Moreover, to make an assent in the face of such a possibility is not a resolution "never to abandon that belief." Newman shows the self-referential inconsistency of such a resolution. The resolve never to change an assent would itself be a condition upon which the assent depended, but the essence of assent is the unconditional acceptance of propositions. "What belief, as such, does imply," Newman adds, "is not an intention never to change, but the utter absence of all thought, or expectation, or fear of changing . . . . We do not commonly determine not to do what we cannot fancy ourselves ever doing."[16]

It is very important to note that the process of investigation is not for Newman unique to theological questions but is a law of our nature with analogous applications. The assents which undergo investigation can be found in religion, social duty, politics, or in the conduct of life. In each case there is a gradual refinement and enlargement of our assents, or at times a formal revision.[17] The inferences for some assents may not survive a first wave of review, or may go on to a second round of scrutiny but eventually give way because of the cumulative force of arguments. In any case, the objections raised in an investigation are not as such inimical to the unconditionality of assent. The assent which is finally held at the completion of an investigation will differ from the original insofar as it is explicit and deliberate. That is to say, it is an assent with knowledge of its grounds. It is also worth noting that Newman's notion of investigation can be interpreted as analogous to several of his seven criteria for genuine development, given in his *An Essay on the Development of Christian Doctrine*. Moreover, both the development of an assent and the development of an Idea begin for Newman from the same starting point of the mind's aspectual view of an objective whole.[18]

The question of the compatibility and balance between the free development of thought in the university and adherence to doctrine has led us to an act of the mind and its analogous use. It seems entirely appropriate that the balance be preserved in the thinking and assenting individual who is teaching or learning. It is the indivi-

dual person who uses natural powers and acts in the acquisition
and expansion of knowledge. Ultimately, the balance in the development of doctrine cannot be forced externally, but should be the
result of the act of complex assent in investigation, which as I have
noted, is analogously present in many areas of human thought and
endeavor.

The controversy over the theology of liberation might serve
both as an example of the union between development of thought
and Church teaching in investigation, and as an example of inquiry
which becomes confused with this balance. In 1984 and 1986 the
Sacred Congregation for the Doctrine of the Faith issued two documents on liberation theology which represent the distinction quite
well. The first of the two documents outlines the common themes
of the several theologies of liberation and shows that those types
which incorporate Marxist analysis and hermeneutic fall into what
I would consider the category of inquiry since they, as it concludes,
"misunderstand" or "eliminate" seven teachings of the Church.
These are: the transcendence and gratuity of liberation in Jesus
Christ, true God and true man; the sovereignty of grace; the true
nature of the means of salvation, especially of the Church and the
sacraments; the absolute distinction between good and evil; the real
meaning of sin; the necessity for conversion; and the universality
of the law of fraternal love.[19] In each case it is argued that the
teaching is contradicted in some way by most liberation theologies.
What is actually doubt about the truth of these teachings is mis-
construed, through a reductionism, as their development.

The second document presents itself as a very good example of
what investigation should be.[20] All of the essential points of liberation theology are developed while an unconditional adherence to
the doctrine of the faith is maintained. The document speaks to the
concepts and issues of liberation in the modern world, or oppres-
sion, sin, the people of God, the kingdom of God, and preference
for the poor, among others. In doing so, the Congregation indicates
fruitful paths for legitimate investigation in this theology. In both
documents, the developmental character of liberation theology is
emphasized by noting its contemporary significance, its biblical
foundations, and its magisterial history. Moreover, the importance
of the experiential foundation of investigation into this question is
also recognized by the Congregation in its second document[21] and
by Joseph Cardinal Ratzinger. Ratzinger has written that a better

answer to the problem is "attested in lived experience," and that theological and Church authority alone are insufficient in the matter.[22] In Newman's terms, it is the complex assent of the individual person reflecting on his experience in which the richness of that assent is more fully grasped. The harmony of doctrine with enlargement of thought is true development, and cannot be adequately maintained by external sources alone, because it is a harmony grounded in what Newman has elsewhere called the "organum investigandi," the living, assenting mind.[23]

IV. Conclusion.

The open, holistic view of higher learning which Newman held and argued so eloquently in his *Idea* enjoys full compatibility with the magisterium of the Church for the fundamental reason that the unconditionality of assent to that magisterium is not bound up with modes in which the assent is held or expressed. As a result, the unconditionality of assent need not be diminished or weakened by the process of investigation. Church law certainly protects and preserves the balance between Catholic belief and progress in learning. In addition, this balance arises out of a law of our human nature, Newman's philosophical analysis of which may shed a helpful light on this important question of our day.

NOTES

1. *The Idea of a University*, with introduction and notes by I. T. Ker; ed. (Oxford: Clarendon Press, 1976), 52.
2. The Philosophical Notebook of John Henry Newman II, ed. Edward Sillem and Rev. A. J. Boekraad (New York: Humanities Press, 1970), 17-19.
3. *Idea*, 54.
4. *Ibid.*, 71.
5. *Ibid.*, 91.
6. *Ibid.*, 369.
7. *Ibid.*, 372.
8. *Ibid.*, 381.
9. *Ibid.*, 379-380.
10. See *An Essay in Aid of a Grammar Assent*, with an introduction by Nicholas Lash; ed. (Notre Dame: University of Notre Dame Press, 1979), 126-129.
11. *Ibid.*, 129.
12. See my doctoral dissertation, *John Henry Newman's Conception of Mind* (Ann Arbor: University Microfilms International, 1986).

13. *Grammar*, 158.
14. *Ibid.*, 159.
15. *Ibid.*, 158-159.
16. *Ibid.*, 160-161.
17. See James Collins, "Tasks for Realistic Theisms," in *The Emergence of Philosophy of Religion*, (New Haven: Yale University Press, 1967), for similarities to Newman's notion of investigation. Collins' outline of a realistic philosophy of religion is also quite helpful for studying Newman's philosophy of religion in the *Grammar*.
18. See *An Essay on the Development of Christian Doctrine* (London: Longmans and Green, 1878), 29, 33, 55, 71-72; for evidence of a similar starting point. One could argue that the *Essay*, the *Idea*, and the *Grammar* address Newman's aspectual view of reality in terms of development, knowledge, and the mind respectively.
19. *Instruction on Certain Aspects of the "Theology of Liberation,"* Vatican translation, *Origins: NC Documentary Service*, vol. 14 (September 1984), par. 17: 204.
20. *Instruction on Christian Freedom and Liberation*, Vatican translation, *Origins: NC Documentary Service*, vol. 15 (April 1986), see especially par. 70: 723.
21. *Ibid.*, 70.
22. *The Ratzinger Report*, trans. Salvator Attanasio and Graham Harrison (San Francisco: Ignatius Press, 1985), 186. James Collins' affirmative reflection on *Aeterni Patris* of Pope Leo XIII has an analogous application here. Collins states that the language of *Aeterni Patris* "underlines once more the cardinal role of the living human mind in achieving a genuine restoration of Christian philosophy. The latter cannot spring into being through decree, through curricular shifts, or through descriptive praise from the outside." He admits that these are important conditions, but adds that Christian philosophizing must "grow out of the mind's own acts and habits of studying philosophy and serving the truth of faith." *Three Paths in Philosophy* (Chicago: Henry Regnery Co., 1962), 307.
23. *Grammar*, 386-387.

LONERGAN ON CATHOLIC EDUCATION: A FEW SUGGESTIONS

Louis Roy, O.P.

"Lonergan's whole career was dedicated to the university ideal in Catholic studies."[1] This judgment made by Fr. Crowe, the leading expert on the thought of Bernard Lonergan, does not come as a surprise to those who know how close Lonergan was to North American higher education. Every year through the 1950s and 60s, he would give a summer workshop on a Catholic college campus; and during the 1970s he taught at Harvard University and at Boston College.

In this essay I should like to show how Lonergan's philosophical and theological ideas suggest a definite orientation for Catholic education. I shall begin each part of my paper by briefly referring to a particular educational problem, and then I shall select aspects of Lonergan's thought that can help us to address the problem. I will thus speak first of the learning activities in the humanities, science and philosophy; second of moral development and its religious underpinnings; and third of the renewal of Christian faith in a college setting.

1. Learning in secular fields of knowledge

In education circles an abundant literature currently laments such phenomena as the students' ignorance, hyperspecialization, inadequate use of textbooks, etc. The problem seems to be that teachers focus too much on concepts and formulas to the detriment of the students' intellectual activities. One concentrates on the objects to be learned rather than on the learning subjects. The implicit philosophy of the classroom is often conceptualism (emphasis on information instead of understanding) and pragmatism (stress on experience and practical rules instead of quest for meaning and truth).

In the marketplace of the innumerable data, hypotheses and theories that are offered to young learners, the problem of integration has become formidable. On the one hand, we can no longer have recourse to the narrow and static synthesis provided, until recently, by the Catholic schools' classicism, which had been shaped by Graeco-Roman humanism and modern scholasticism.[2] On the other hand, we cannot rest content with the prevalent relativism which, as Allan Bloom has recently argued, stultifies the minds of American students.[3]

What we need is a modest, partial, ongoing, revisable synthesis which, in order to be revisable not according to sudden, inexplicable shifts in incommensurable paradigms,[4] but according to a methodic control of meaning,[5] must be based on transcultural foundations. Realistic readers of this essay may wonder whether such foundations are attainable. But before stating how they can be reached, let me stress the necessity for intellectual foundations. The human mind spontaneously seeks unity. The complexities of contemporary natural and human sciences, however, preclude any well rounded system. But if the educational emphasis on objects to be studied is matched by an equally strong emphasis on the knowing subjects, students will get a sense of what it concretely means to be involved in a process of integration. Their efforts at elaborating a provisional synthesis will be situated in a context where the quest for truth is apprehended as a worthwhile journey.

Among the steps leading to a personal integration Lonergan commends active methods in education. At first, these must involve bodily and external activity. But as the child gives way to the teenager and the college student, active methods more properly consist in examining the relevant data and images, raising the right questions, counting on the human intellect's natural wonder, so that the learner will dynamically facilitate the occurrence of insights.[6]

Again, to train young minds for the task of integrating, Lonergan makes a second recommendation. After pondering Piaget's distinction between assimilation and adjustment, he highlights the chronological priority of the former over the latter. General education consists in developing one's assimilative power. This habit is acquired, first by learning the use of spoken and written language and by reading literature, and second by "the study of mathematics rather than natural science, and of philosophy and history rather than the human sciences."[7] This preference does not entail any disparagement of the sciences, especially by someone like Lonergan who spent so much time paying attention to their contents and understanding their methods. But when the young study the sciences only, they run the danger of resting content with simply memorizing what the most important thinkers of the last decades have said, and then with just keeping abreast. In contrast to this intellectual conformity, he praises the versatility of scholars such as Jean Piaget himself, the economist Colin Clark, the sociologist Talcott Parsons, the orientalist William Foxwell Albright, who could excel in more than one field of study because they had aquired a fundamental creative ability.

Lonergan also draws attention to the importance of philosophy in reinforcing the students' integration. He remarks that not all products of human intellectual creativity should be integrated.[9] Besides sense, truth and value, there are aberrations in the realm of action, in historiography, in the human sciences and in philosophy. The symbolic animal which is the human person naturally looks for meaning. It seeks understanding, asks about the truth-value of what it has grasped, and deliberates regarding its commitments. When adverted to, this basic quest constitutes the dynamic transcultural foundations. It is normative because it enables the knowing and acting person to discriminate between sense and nonsense. Students need to acquire this normative self-knowledge which is the core of philosophy. Thus they will get in touch with the part of themselves that is the source of genuine creativity and responsibility and that is open to the Mystery.

Although greatly aided by secular learning and by philosophy, full intellectual integration, because it is never purely cognitional, nevertheless lies beyond the ken of secular disciplines. Therefore, we must now discuss the moral and religious aspects of education.

2. *Moral development and religion*

The cultural world students live in raises problems of ethical formation. The Weberian separation between facts (examined by the sciences) and values (central to action) has generated what Alasdair MacIntyre calls "emotivism."[10] To the Western individualistic conscience, values are a matter of personal choice and cannot be really discussed. This stance entails a mixture of unfocused moral idealism, indifference with regard to relevant information, unexamined principles of conduct and hidden agendas in the minds of many students, especially with respect to their goal of quickly becoming successful and wealthy.

To face these issues, Lonergan's approach can be very useful. Again, it begins with the human subject, and indeed with the acting person. Most young people feel a need for personal authenticity. Full development as a human being can become one's "most prized achievement."[11] In all ages and cultures, good educators have spotted their best ally: the desire to excel which is so prominent in a healthy youth. Writing about the "good choices and actions" thanks to which a person does excel, Lonergan uses a suggestive metaphor when he characterizes such achievement as "the work of the free and responsible subject producing the first and only edition of himself."[12]

Moreover, as Walter E. Conn points out, Lonergan offers guidelines for authenticity. In his introduction to the theme of self-realization, Conn observes that "authenticity itself is not a criterion ... but rather an ideal which stands in need of a criterion."[13] And he explains: "The *criterion* of human authenticity, of the responsible person, is the self-transcendence that is effected through sensitive and creative understanding, critical judgment, responsible decision, loyal commitment, and genuine love."[14]

Some of my readers will have recognized here a typical Lonerganian listing of the cognitional and effective acts that make for authenticity. Lonergan characterizes the movement of human progress as going "from below upwards."[15] It starts with experiencing the data, then asks questions for understanding, which are followed by the need to check the truth of one's hypotheses, after which there emerge questions for deliberation regarding one's values and courses of action. However, being a self that continually develops in the right direction proves to be extremely difficult.

Important as this upward movement surely is in Lonergan's eyes, he nonetheless considers it to be hindered by four kinds of bias: the dramatic bias, which results from a malfunctioning of the psyche; the individual bias of egotism; the group bias of social and economic self-interest; and finally the general bias typical of the short-term pragmatism of common sense.[16] In the light of such threats to its ideal development, Lonergan concludes that the upward movement to human maturity encounters a radical "moral impotence."[17] It is impossible to find in oneself the motivation required in order to implement fully the transcendental precepts: be attentive, be intelligent, be rational, be reasonable, be in love. Not only are the psyche and the will inadequate to the task, but the intellect, having absorbed a lot of false ideas during the process of its socialization, easily falls prey to a wrong estimation (or sometimes even denial) of ethical issues, of sin, and of moral impotence.

Given the ambiguities that mark the upward movement of self-realization and self-transcedence, a second movement is needed, which can rescue the first. It is the movement "from above downwards."[18] It does not go, as the first does, from the data through acts of understanding, judgments of fact and judgments of value to decisions. Instead, this second movement proceeds from a basic state of religious love, which makes it possible to accept the judgments of value and of fact handed on by tradition, to try to understand the meaning of these judgments and eventually to arrive at expressing them in new words, symbols, artifacts, that is to say, data.

Such is the movement of grace; such is the general way Christian salvation is granted. Now it remains for us to see what this theological vision entails as corollaries for Catholic education.

3. *Education for Christian faith*

Faith seems to be very difficult to communicate. Even sons and daughters of Catholic parents show little understanding of the core doctrines professed by the church. They tend to be selective: they choose the beliefs they find interesting and discard the others. Emotional or practical relevance rather than truth has become the criterion for one's religious ideas. How, then, is it possible, in an age of individualism, to share the traditional doctrines with members of the young generation?

The movement "from above downwards," which has been described in the second part of this essay, can help us to understand how such sharing takes place. Although faith can be shared, strictly speaking it cannot be communicated by humans. Only God can communicate faith and he does so by pouring an unrestricted lovingness into people's hearts. Anthropologically Lonergan situates this God-given love at the top of human conscious intentionality. Faith is the awareness that accompanies such being-in-love. It is defined as "the knowledge born of religious love."[19]

Lonergan also distinguishes between faith and belief. He sees faith as an inner word, as the conscious and yet unthematized knowledge derived from unrestricted loving. He sees belief as an outer word, as the explicit knowledge handed on by a religious tradition. The link between faith and belief is the following: "Among the values that faith discerns is the value of believing the word of religion, of accepting the judgments of fact and the judgments of value that the religion proposes."[20]

So far as the downward movement is concerned, there is a dynamic that operates as follows. On the fifth and highest level of human intentionality, God grants love and faith. On the fourth level, the eye of faith discriminates between the values and disvalues that are apprehended in feelings, and greets the judgments of value that are offered by an authentic tradition. On the third level, it invites reason to accept the judgments of fact that the Bible presents as words of God and that are passed on by a truthworthy church. On the second and first level, it challenges the intellect to appropriate as much as it can the meanings transmitted by Christianity.

It seems to me that this vision entails three consequences for the education of faith. In the first place, students must be offered the possibility of experiencing living communities of faith. In the academic environment of the Catholic college, they should be able to single out individual believers or groups of believers whose personalities and ways of life are what Lonergan calls "incarnate meaning."[21] It is not necessary that, on a Catholic campus, everyone be a professed Christian. But one must find a sufficient number of significant believers in order to be challenged by a fundamental context of meaning. By such a context I mean credible persons, proposed activities, shared values, faith-symbols that are relevant to our culture, classes in which the contents of Christianity are presented in a coherent manner. Students will have access to their own experience of transcendent love provided this experience is activated by witnesses who are themselves loving, committed, dedicated, in solidarity and cooperation with others.

In the second place, a distinction between meaning and truth may help to differentiate two aspects of Christian pedagogy. Meaning is on the level of understanding. When students ask about the meaning of Christian texts, narratives, beliefs, practices, rituals, forms of art, etc., they raise questions for understanding these data and they are moving from the first and second level to the third and fourth, where they will eventually verify and appraise their ideas. So there must be ample room in Catholic cathechesis and theology for this upward movement in which sound information is offered and relevant questions are posed regarding Christian teachings, in relation to the students' life experience.

On the other hand, it is incumbent upon religious educators to make it clear that such apprehension of meaning cannot settle the question of whether Christian doctrines are true or not. Students should be guided towards raising this question for themselves and consider the option of responding affirmatively in the light of their awareness of the movement "from above downwards." That is to say, if they have an experience of a transcendent love brought home to them by Christian mediators and by the greatest of mediators—Jesus Christ—then faith as the knowledge born of religious love will allow them to discern the value of believing in the judgment of value and of fact proposed by the church. They will have to face squarely the dilemma of assenting to divine revelation. They will make a decision which is based, not only on the meaningfulness of what they understand, but, more significantly, on the credibility of God.

Assuredly nothing in this intricate and engaging process can be automatic or easy. What is at stake is the most important option in a person's life: the decision to believe or not to believe in the God of Jesus Christ. And this difficulty brings us to the third educational aspect to be underlined. Catholic educators must foster the development of questions and feelings. According to Lonergan, questions constitute the dynamism of the upward ascent from experiencing to understanding and to judging. In mathematics, in the various sciences, in literature, history, philosophy and theology, the right questions must be hit upon in connection with the appropriate information. Questions matter more than answers, norms and rules, because without the questions the latter do not make sense. Only by starting with questions can students develop their mind. And if they possess a well-trained mind, they will be more likely to greet the illuminating power of Christian teachings.

However, if their heart is to develop as well, an education of feelings is required. According to Lonergan, values are apprehended in "intentional feelings," that is, in feelings that are related to represented objects. Since both values and disvalues are apprehended, he is insistent that one should foster sound feelings and correct aberrant feelings.[22] Educators can have recourse to psychological techniques, either in class or in private conversation, in order to help students to take fuller cognizance of their feelings. As a consequence, students will be in a better position to deal with their transcendent experiences, in which a stable feeling of being in love is offered to them. Furthermore, cultivating the feelings that open them up to values will allow them to discover the necessity of a moral conversion and to engage in it.

I hope I have convinced my readers, in the course of this essay, that Lonergan's philosophy and theology suggest a definite way of tackling three sets of recurrent problems in Catholic education: the integration of learning, moral development, and the sharing of Christian faith.

NOTES

1. Frederick E. Crowe, S.J., "'The Role of a Catholic University in the Modern World' — An Update," *Communicating a Dangerous Memory*, ed. Fred Lawrence, supplementary issue of the *Lonergan Workshop* Journal (Atlanta: Scholars Press, 1987): 1.

2. On classicist education, see Bernard J.F. Lonergan, *Method in Theology* (New York: Herder, 1972), 301-302. See also p. 326: "What ended classicist assumptions was critical history."

3. Allan Bloom, *The Closing of the American Mind* (New York: Simon and Schuster, 1987).

4. See Thomas Kuhn, *The Structure of Scientific Revolutions*, 2d ed. (Chicago: University of Chicago Press, 1970).

5. As Lonergan has argued in *Method in Theology*, 28-29.

6. See his *Philosophy of Education* (Typescript, Cincinatti: Xavier College, 1959), 91-92. This emphasis on the learner's insights, in contrast to concepts, is characteristic of his book *Insight: A Study of Human Understanding* (First published 1957; paperback reprint; San Francisco: Harper and Row, 1978).

7. *Philosophy of Education*, 193-194.

8. See *Philosophy of Education*, 194-195.

9. *Collection*, vol. 4 of *Collected Works of Bernard Lonergan* ed. Frederick E. Crowe and Robert M. Doran (University of Toronto Press, 1988), 119.

10. *After Virtue*, 2d ed. (University of Notre Dame Press, 1984).

11. *Method in Theology*, 254.

12. *A Second Collection* (Philadelphia: Westminster, 1975), 83.

13. *Conscience: Development and Self-Transcendence*, (Birmingham: Religious Education Press, 1981), 5.
14. P. 6 (italics his).
15. *A Third Collection* (New York: Paulist Press, 1985), 180.
16. See *Insight*, 191-206, 218-242.
17. See *Insight*, 619-633.
18. See *A Third Collection*, 181. In *Old Things and New: A Strategy for Education*, (supplementary issue of the *Lonergan Workshop* Journal, ed. Fred Lawrence, (Atlanta: Scholars Press, 1985), Frederick E. Crowe has developed the implications for education of these two vector forces, which he calls "the way of achievement" and "the way of heritage."
19. *Method in Theology*, 115.
20. *Ibid.*, 118.
21. *Ibid.*, 73.
22. See *Method in Theology*, 30-34.

PÈRE SERTILLANGES
AND THE INTELLECTUAL LIFE:
A CLASSIC REVISITED

Francis J. Murphy

In 1889, at the time of the founding of St. Anselm College, a young Dominican theologian, Brother Dalmatius Sertillanges, was completing his doctoral studies at Corbara, on the island of Corsica. Père Antonin-Gilbert Sertillanges had been ordained a priest the previous year. Thirty years later, in 1920, Sertillanges wrote his most renowned work *The Intellectual Life: Its Spirit, Conditions, Methods.*[1] However, the theme which animated that work had long since become the characteristic force of his own development as a human, a Christian and an intellectual.

> The intellectual I have in view is a man of wide and varied knowledge complementary to a special study thoroughly pursued; he loves the arts and natural beauty; his mind shows itself to be one in everyday occupations and in meditation; he is the same man in the presence of God, of his fellows and of his maid, carrying within him a world of ideas and feelings that are not only written down in books and in discourses, but flow into his conversations with his friends, and guide his life.[2]

Underlying Sertillanges' life and thought was a fundamental, integrating unity. The human, the spiritual and the intellectual dimensions of his life were all deeply rooted in the thought of St. Thomas Aquinas. Although St. Thomas had died over six centuries earlier, his thought had assumed renewed importance during the formative years of Sertillanges.

In 1879 Pope Leo XIII issued his celebrated encyclical, *Aeterni*

Patris. With that letter, Leo XIII formally initiated the "Thomistic Revival," which shaped Catholic philosophy and theology until Vatican Council II. The Pope was convinced that the great problems of the age were the fruit of basically faulty philosophical principles. The sharp cleavages between reason and revelation, science and faith, nature and grace were seen by Leo XIII to be direly harmful to both society and the church. The remedy which he prescribed was Thomism, the system of thought in which St. Thomas synthesized the philosophy of the Ancients, the science of the Arabs and the faith of Christianity. Leo XIII extolled St. Thomas as "a lover of truth for its own sake, richly endowed with human and divine science, like the sun he heated the world with the warmth of his virtues and filled it with the splendor of his teaching."[3]

The young Sertillanges experienced an intellectual awakening, when he was twenty years old, that stimulated his desire to develop intellectually and to study St. Thomas passionately. That experience resulted from his reading of *Les Sources* by Père Alphonse Gratry, a priest of the Oratory. In the "Foreword" to the first edition of *The Intellectual Life*, Sertillanges acknowledge his great debt to Père Gratry as his mentor and model.

> This little work has no pretension to replace *Les Sources*; in part it is inspired by that book. The author, doubtless like many another, has not forgotten the stirring he experienced at twenty, when Père Gratry stimulated in him the ardent desire for knowledge.[4]

That "ardent desire for knowledge" found rich fulfillment in Sertillanges' life as a Dominican, from his last days as a novice at Belmonte (Spain) in 1883 until his death at Sallanches (France) in 1948. The French Dominicans, the order of St. Thomas himself, were the foremost figures in the "Thomistic Revival," which Pope Leo XIII had energized by *Aeterni Patris*. In turn, St. Thomas was to become the focal point of Sertillanges' study, research, writing and spirituality. In his long career of Thomistic scholarship Père Sertillanges became one of the leading figures in the philosophical and theological revitalization of modern Catholicism. His published works, comprising over seven hundred books and articles, embraced the fields of aesthetics and spirituality as well as philosophy and theology.[5] The spirit of St. Thomas permeated Sertillanges' life no less than his work.

One especially important contribution of Sertillanges to the

"Thomistic Revival" was his translation into French of many of the Latin works of St. Thomas. Among his many translations was that of a brief letter, entitled *De Modo Studendi*, written by St. Thomas to Brother John, an otherwise unknown Dominican confrere. In that letter, St. Thomas answered Brother John's question concerning "how one should set about to acquire the treasure of knowledge."[6]

In his book, *The Intellectual Life*, Sertillanges later sought to answer that age-old question. His continuity with St. Thomas and Père Gratry was evident in two all-encompassing respects. First, like Thomas and Gratry, Père Sertillanges had exemplarily lived the life of the Catholic intellectual before he set out to answer the question in writing. Second, he perceived the question in essentially spiritual terms, equating the pursuit of truth with the quest for union with God, who is total Truth. Thus for Sertillanges the intellectual life is seen as a special spiritual vocation, simultaneously professional and moral. That vocation involves every dimension of life and constitutes a total personal commitment to truth. It includes:

> Lectures, reading, choice of companions, the proper proportion of work and rest, of solitude and activity, of general culture and specialization, the spirit of study, the art of picking out and utilizing data gained, some provisional output which will give an idea of what the future work is to be, the virtues to be acquired and developed . . . [7]

But above all, for Sertillanges, the vocation of the intellectual requires the spirit of prayer.

> Intelligence only plays its part fully when it fulfills a religious function, that is, when it worships the Supreme Truth in its minor and scattered appearances. Each truth is a fragment which does not stand alone but reveals connections on every side. Truth in itself is one and the Truth is God.[8]

In his metaphysical concept of the convergence of truth and good, as in his emphasis on the unity of truth, Sertillanges reflected the mind of his master, St. Thomas. His position differed sharply from that of most of the secular intellectual elite of his day. The secular, scientific position had received recent (1918) expression in Max Weber's celebrated address, "Science as a Vocation." In that essay, the renowned German sociologist addressed the same question as did Sertillanges in *The Intellectual Life*. Weber formulated the question in the terms of the great Russian author, Leo Tolstoi: "What shall we do and how shall we live?"[9] That natural science could not answer this question was as "indisputable" for Weber as it was for Tolstoi. However, while Weber denied the possibility of a rational, scientific answer to the question, he also categorically dismissed even the possibility of a religious solution to the problem. In his blunt terms, "the tension between the value-spheres of 'science' and the sphere of 'the holy' is unbridgeable."[10] It was against precisely that spirit of intellectual fragmentation that Pope Leo XIII had directed his encyclical *Aeterni Patris*. It was against precisely that mentality that Sertillanges reacted when he described the intellectual environment of the early twentieth century in these words:

> More than ever before thought is waiting for men and men for thought. The world is in danger for lack of life-giving maxims. We are in a train rushing ahead at top speed, no signals visible. The planet is going it knows not where, its law has failed it: who will give it back its sun?[11]

The fullness of light, the sun, could be recovered not by reason alone, but only by reason illumined by revelation. Here was found the unique role of Thomism. Here was required the special vocation of the Christian intellectual. Here was the driving force for Sertillanges' essay on *The Intellectual Life*: "Let us often remind this age, which so sorely needs light, of the conditions which enable us to get light and to prepare its diffusion by our work."[12]

Looking back on *The Intellectual Life* seventy years after its first publication, certain of Sertillages' own qualities as a scholar and as an author are immediately striking. The breadth of his references reveals a mind of amazing culture. Contemporary philosophers like Bergson and Nietzsche are as familiar to him as Aristotle and St. Augustine; Leonardo da Vinci and Mozart are as present to him as Rodin and Péguy.

Equally striking is Sertillanges' imagery. He is a master of metaphor. In explaining the ultimate unity and convergence of truth, Sertillanges writes: "If I embark on the tributary, I reach the river, and then the sea."[13] In discussing the thirst of the young intellectual for knowledge, he avers: "The important thing for the man of truth is to understand that truth is everywhere, and that he is allowing a continuous stream to pass by him which might set his soul working."[14]

A third characteristic of Sertillanges' thought is his use of maxims: brief, pithy, memorable expressions of his ideas. For example, in his analysis of the asceticism required of the scholar, Sertillanges notes: "There is a luxury tax to be paid on intellectual greatness."[15] In his emphasis on wholesome personal associations, he states: "Friendship is an obstetric art; it draws out our richest and deepest resources."[16] In opposition to those who longed for the return to a romanticized earlier age — including many of his conservative French Catholic compatriots — he warns: "Let us not be like those people who always seem to be pallbearers at the funeral of the past."[17]

Certain aspects of *The Intellectual Life* seem very dated now. The constant, exclusive references to the masculine gender of the scholar, while standard practice in the 1920s, are jarring to a reader in the 1980s. Practical proposals concerning note-taking and research techniques seem almost primitive in the age of computers and word-processing. The psychological theory underlying Sertillanges' advice has been replaced, even in Catholic writing, by more dynamic, existential approaches, pioneered by Adrian van Kaam in *A Psychology of the Catholic Intellectual*.[18] Yet, despite these accidental limitations, the essential thesis of Sertillanges' study is as valid today as it was two generations ago.

Today, in the age of the "information explosion," the fundamental unity and coherence of truth needs desperately to be reaffirmed. That task requires both a philosophical system with the comprehensiveness of Thomism and a continuing corps of technically excellent, morally principled, socially concerned and spiritually integrated scholars, consecrated to the service of Truth. In all honesty, the vocation to *The Intellectual Life*, as presented by Père Sertillanges, was answered by a very few in his own generation. The dire results of what his contemporary Julien Benda termed *The Betrayal of the Intellectuals*,[19] are both a sobering reminder and a massive challenge to the Christian intellectual community. That challenge is especially relevant to St. Anselm College, students as well as faculty and administrators, as the second century of Catholic higher education in the Benedictine tradition begins on this campus, which has already so richly contributed to the life of both the Church and the country.

In conclusion, there are two brief quotations from *The Intellectual Life*, which seem singularly pertinent. The first is a compendium of Père Sertillanges' thought.

Man is multiple and each of us is a separate specimen of mankind; God is in all men; let us have the wisdom to honor man and to respect God in ourselves.[20]

The second quotation reveals that Père Sertillanges had a sense of humor to match his common sense. He wrote: "The listener brings you a soul to heal or to enlighten; do not put him off with words."[21] I defer here, too, to the sage counsel of Père Sertillanges.

NOTES

1. 1. A.-G. Sertillanges, *The Intellectual Life: Its Spirit, Conditions, Method*, trans. M. Ryan (Westminster: Christian Classics, 1980). Of the many editions of this work in both French and English, this edition is cited for both the quality of the translation and general accessibility.
2. Sertillanges, 241.
3. Leo XIII, *Aeterni Patris*, in J. J. Wynne, S.J., *The Great Encyclicals of Leo XIII* (New York: Benzinger, 1903).
4. Sertillanges, "Foreword," vi. See also A. Gratry, *The Well-Springs*, trans. S. Brown, S.J. (New York: Benzinger, 1931).
5. For a brief biographical sketch and a bibliography of the principal works of the author, see "Sertillanges," *Dictionnaire de Théologie Catholique*, III (Paris: Librairie Letouzey et Ane, 1972), 4034-35.
6. V. White, O.P., ed. and trans. *How to Study* (Thomas Aquinas, *De Modo Studendi*) (Oxford: Blackfriars, 1947), 5.
7. Sertillanges, 7-8.
8. *Ibid.*, 30.
9. M. Weber, "Science as a Vocation," in *From Max Weber: Essays in Sociology*, ed. and trans. H. H. Gerth and C. W. Mills, (New York: Oxford University Press, 1968), 143.
10. *Ibid.*, 154.
11. Sertillanges, 15.
12. *Ibid.*, vi.
13. *Ibid.*, 19.
14. *Ibid.*, 72.
15. *Ibid.*, 42.
16. *Ibid.*, 56.
17. *Ibid.*, 15.
18. A. van Kaam, *A Psychology of the Catholic Intellectual*, Synthesis Series (Chicago: Franciscan Herald Press, n. d.).
19. J. Benda, *The Betrayal of the Intellectuals*, trans. R. Aldington. (Boston: Beacon Press, 1955).
20. Sertillanges, 173.
21. *Ibid.*, 204.

FR. BEDE JARRETT, O.P.
AND THE ENGLISH
CATHOLIC INTELLECTUAL REVIVAL
Robert Nicholas Bérard

In September 1916, the thirty-five year old Fr. Bede Jarrett was unanimously elected Provincial Pior of the English Dominicans. For the next eighteen years, until his untimely death in 1934, Fr. Bede remained a major figure in the intellectual life of English Catholicism. As an historian, editor, homilist, social critic, and ecclesiastical administrator, he made significant public contributions to English Catholic thought in the years between the World Wars; as a friend, correspondent, and spiritual advisor he made an equally important, if less visible, impact on the intellectual leadership of his society.

Cyril Beaufort Jarrett was born on August 22, 1881 at Greenwich, the fifth of six sons of Col. Henry Sullivan Jarrett, a member of the Indian Civil Service and an Orientalist scholar of some repute, and Agnes Delacourt Beaufort. His parents returned to India in 1884, leaving five children under the care of Col. Jarrett's mother at the home of his brother-in-law, William Leigh, at Woodchester, Gloucestershire. Like his brothers, Cyril Jarrett attended Stonyhurst, although he began his formal education at the age of ten and did not complete the final year of his course. Despite his relatively late start, he was able to win the school's gold medal in 1898. In August of that year, in response to a vocation he later claimed he had had since his earliest memories, he asked to join the Dominican Order and was accepted into the Novitiate, taking the religious name Bede, the following month.

The new novice spent the next two years at Woodchester Priory, near his childhood home, where he studied under the brillant, eccentric social activist, Fr. Vincent McNabb, O.P., acquiring a firm grounding in Thomist philosophy and in the importance of giving public witness and expression to the faith. In late 1900 he moved to the Dominican House of Studies at Hawkesyard Priory, Staffordshire, where the next four years were spent in further study and preparation for his ordination, which took place in December 1904.

Just prior to his ordination, however, Bede Jarrett, was permitted to matriculate at Oxford, to pursue studies in history. It is clear that his Oxford years were particularly influential in his intellectual development, not only as an historian but as an advocate for a particularly English expression of English Catholicism. He attended the lectures of A. J. Carlyle, A. L. Smith, R. L. Poole, Paul Vinogradoff, and Charles Oman, among others, and developed a particular interest in the history of medieval Europe. He formed a close relationship with his tutor, Ernest (later Sir Ernest) Barker, who remarked, some thirty years later, on his "candid and lucid and open intelligence" and his "genuine passion" for scholarship.[1] In 1907 he took a rare First in the Modern History School at Oxford. He moved to the Catholic University of Louvain, where the most promising English Dominicans were sent to complete their theological studies. He completed the two-year course with distinction in just over a year, at the same time continuing research for his historical writing.

In 1908 Fr. Bede returned to England as an assistant at St. Dominic's Priory in London. There he occupied himself with preaching, parish duties, serving as chaplain and master to a group of Scouts, researching and writing such historical works as *Mediaeval Socialism* (1913) and *St. Antonino and Mediaeval Economics* (1914). There also he came into contact both with the face of inner city poverty and deprivation and the social reformers who sought to alleviate such conditions. These experiences were to sharpen his desire to seek in the Catholic faith practical and just solutions to the problems of industrial society. He was elected Prior of London in 1914, just before the outbreak of the war, which was to cost him three of his brothers.

In 1916 Fr. Bede assumed the duties of Prior Provincial; he was re-elected three times and served in this role until 1932. During these years he oversaw the expansion of the Dominican community, including the growth of the Second and Third Order religious, the establishment of houses in the university centers of Oxford and Edinburgh, and the development of missions in Grenada and South Africa. He was the motive force behind the founding of *Blackfriars* and its development into a stimulating and influential periodical. In 1929 his name came second — due, it is said to the defection of the Polish delegation — in the election held to choose a new Master-General of the Dominicans.[2] Alongside his almost crushing internal administrative duties, his heavy burden of retreats and other religious responsibilities, and continuing efforts at popular historical scholarship, Fr. Bede made time to involve himself in a variety of social causes, supporting the League of Nations Union and the St. Joan's Alliance, which sought to advance the rights of women, and speaking and writing widely on the social teachings of Popes Leo XIII and Pius XI.

In 1932 he lay down the burden of the Provincial's office, but within weeks he was elected Prior of the new foundation at Oxford for which he had so long laboured and asked to take on the editorship of *Blackfriars*. Reluctantly he accepted both of these heavy responsibilities, while continuing his periodical and scholarly writing, preaching across England and in the United States, and teaching in the Dominican house of studies. He was felled by a stroke in February 1934 and died a month later. Thousands of people filed by his casket to pay their respects, and both the Catholic and non-Catholic press were full of tributes to this charismatic friar, widely recognized as the greatest preacher in the English-speaking world.

Fr. Bede certainly believed not only that Catholicism held out the hope of personal salvation but that its social teachings offered humane and practical solutions to the problems of industrial society. He believed further that the Dominican order, the guardian of the treasury of St. Thomas Aquinas, could once again assume its pre-Reformation importance in the intellectual life of English society. These beliefs underlay much of his historical writing, as well as his efforts to re-establish a Dominican presence at Oxford, to reform observance in the order to mirror more closely that of the time of its foundation, and to interpret and popularize papal social encyclicals to his countrymen.

It is through his histories that Fr. Bede Jarrett is most widely known outside of Britain. Trained as an historian at Oxford, he wrote lives of St. Dominic, the Emperor Charles IV, and the scholar Contardo Ferrini, a history of the English Dominicans, and a history of Europe for use in Catholic schools. His most influential works, however, were likely those which explored medieval Catholic social and economic thought, particularly his *Social Theories of the Middle Ages* (1926), which explored medieval thought on topics as diverse as war, money-making, and the status of women. Although there is little evidence that he attempted to distort his historical accounts to support his political views, they are infused with the conception of history, entered in a list of quotations in his school history note-book, as "the science which teaches us to see the throbbing life of the present in the throbbing life of the past."[3]

His histories are engagingly written and true to the sources easily available to him, but they fell far short of the standards of thoroughness and criticism which the historical profession had come to demand by the end of the First World War. Fr. Bede never wrote history for its own sake, but always to instruct, always in response to a religious "call."[4] Furthermore, as his successor as Provincial, Fr. Bernard Delaney wrote, "All his histories bear the marks of having been written by a busy man."[5] Thus, although such works as *Mediaeval Socialism*, which he considered his best work, appealed to the intelligent general reader, they never were fully accepted by professional historians. Perhaps one of Fr. Bede's greatest disappointments was the negative reception which greeted *Social and Political Theories of the Middle Ages*, which he had written, in part, in order to further the reputation of Dominican scholarship in Britain.[6]

Yet if his historical writing did not make a lasting contribution to medieval scholarship, it did help to rescue a misunderstood age —and especially the medieval Church—from many popular notions of its backwardness and irrelevance to contemporary issues. Thus, while he never suggested—even had it been possible—as did Fr. Vincent McNabb, that society make a radical return to the medieval economic order embodied in the *Liber Moralis* of St. Antonino, he did insist that the great Dominican's application of ethical and moral standards to economic decision-making had never lost its relevance and was never more in need of emphasis.

Finally, whatever errors crept into Fr. Bede's histories, he never wavered in his deep respect for the people of whom he wrote, their insight, humanity, and wisdom. He could never understand, he once wrote, those historians who seemed so to hate the dead.[7] Many historians, of course, face the quandary of a conflict between their love of truth and of the people whose lives and work they chronicle. Despite his deep devotion to truth, he admitted that only one person had been able to write of men both completely sympathetically and truthfully, "and He wrote but once, and that in the dust."[8]

Fr. Bede Jarrett had a call not only to explain Europe's Catholic past to an increasingly secular and indifferent present, but also to bring its insights to bear on contemporary social, economic, and moral problems. His fearless and often fierce attacks on what he regarded as the economic abuses of his age helped to make him one of the best known Catholic leaders in England, especially to non-Catholics. In a society in which the Catholic hierarchy had only recently condemned socialism and forbade contact with unrepentant socialists, Fr. Bede seemed to go out of his way to defend those who clung to their socialist ideals.

Little in his upbringing — thoroughly upper middle-class and Tory—could have led him down this path. Perhaps it was his years at St. Dominic's Priory in London, which bordered on some of the poorer slums of the capital, where his duties included the care of souls in the great prison of Wormwood Scrubs; perhaps it was his deep personal sympathy with those who worked to improve the conditions for working people, or his intellectual revulsion at the irrationality and injustice of the economic system.

At any event, from his earliest days in London until his death, Fr. Bede returned repeatedly to the "social question," the huge gap between the rich and poor: "a little group, comparatively, possessed of national wealth, living in comfort and luxury, gathering all the good of the modern inventions that are so wonderful, to protect, to add comfort and luxury to their lives; at the other end, a great mass of population in straitened circumstances, struggling to escape from their circumstances, and again uncertain of tomorrow."[9] It was the comparative uncertainty of economic life in an age of triumphant individualism and materialism which he thought the greater crime. Such "pagan economics" he believed undermined the whole moral fabric of society, even one with a long Christian tradition. Thus he complained, "We rightly denounce those who practice birth-control; have we no denunciation for those who make birth-control almost an economic necessity?"[10] He had even greater fear for the export of modern capitalism to the less developed societies in the Empire, believing that the "seed of materialistic economics" sown in the non-Christian world would result, in time, in "violent antagonism to the inherited culture of the Western world."[11]

At St. Dominic's he began to read socialist papers and attend socialist lectures, and he always defended the value of socialist criticism, but there is no evidence that he ever embraced socialism —or any other ism—itself. Similarly, after the rise to power in Italy of Mussolini, Fr. Bede, was like most Englishmen of his time, completely bamboozled by Il Duce. While believing that Fascism could never be made to work in Britain, he did argue that its proclaimed attention to family life and the importance of the small trader, farmer, and shopkeeper gave it claim as *an* alternative to contemporary capitalism.[12] Similarly, he encouraged the rise of Guild Socialism, as a *via media* between Bolshevik state socialism and anarchic syndicalism,[13] but, again, he never suggested specific remedies. Rather, he urged both Capital and Labor to make terms with the church, to reform themselves along lines suggested in the great encyclical *Quadragesimo Anno* before it was too late. At the same time he opposed firmly the use of force or violence to attain such reform. For this reason, he supported Prime Minister Baldwin in his opposition to the General Strike of 1926, holding that "There is no right among the poor to extort alms by force,"[14] while condemning those capitalists who used the Church's teaching to condemn revolution, but ignored her calls for economic justice.

Still, he never became involved himself in politics nor endorsed any political programme. "Political remedies," he wrote, "are no business of a priest, for the Catholic Church has . . . cut, in our times, both the theatre and Parliament, to the loss, I . . . imagine, of both."[15] He accepted the Church's "grand refusal;" "I only urge people to think more unselfishly and tolerantly. As a priest, I advocate no measures, for so many are allowable and good, but only hope that supernatural motives will weigh with all."[16] He did, however, give special encouragement to Catholic socialists, in part because they received so little from either the hierarchy or their fellow partisans, in part because he wished to see Catholics active across the political spectrum. "We shall let in Labour again sooner or later. It's good to know that some of the Household of the Faith will be there."[17]

Although his social criticism was devoted largely to ethics and economics, Fr. Bede did take up other causes in his writing and preaching. He labored, through the League of Nations Union, to promote mutual arms reduction and a tempering of the spirit of aggressive nationalism in Europe. A patriotic Englishman himself, Fr. Bede was distressed by the agonies of his country's relations with Ireland. "It is like a Greek tragedy," he wrote, "with the quarrels of the Gods ruining the lives of men."[18] At first a Unionist, he became an advocate of Dominion Home Rule, complaining bitterly that British policy was driving Irishmen toward republicanism. He was horrified by the violence of the Black and Tans, "people of violence" who were "out of control." "No provocation," he wrote, "justifies in any way whatever the evil behaviour of the armed forces of the crown,"[19] which, he believed, was leading to the name of England "being dragged hatefully thro' the mud."[20]

He also supported, through the St. Joan Alliance, the cause of women's suffrage, although he viewed the results of contemporary feminism in the context of the prevailing social system with some concern. He supported a movement which would make it possible for a woman "to be wholly all that one was capable of becoming," but lamented that the emancipation of women seemed so far only to mean "that they are now more successful as typists than as wives."[21]

All of these social problems were associated in a general decline of absolute moral principles in favor of a flaccid relativism embraced by intellectual and political leaders in the West. Thus, despite their "generous impulses" they "show more modesty in their opinion as to the proper way to dispose of old razor-blades than of mental defectives."[22] Governed by "sentimentalism," fueled by "the overstimulation of feelings by a sensation-loving press,"[23] and a passion for "efficiency" — and here he lumps together Marxists, Fascists, and the leaders of the democracies — "they imprudently vote for imprisoning freedom."[24]

In Fr. Bede's view, the Catholic Church in general and the Order of Preachers in particular had a unique opportunity to play a leading role in the amelioration of the social and cultural malaise of the modern world. Although he seldom criticized them, he was impatient with the failure of the English hierarchy to seize that opportunity and sought to involve his own order in the work of reform. The English bishops, he believed, seemed capable only of "inaction or reaction", while Catholics were losing souls to the Communists.[25] "We put ointment on the sores, but we leave the social body's inner ailments timidly alone."[26] Similarly, the church saw increasing numbers "attracted by a shallow, comfortable mysticism, because we have not set in front of it true mysticism."[27]

Even more disturbed was he at the Catholic press in England. Most Catholics, he wrote, bought Catholic papers as a matter of duty, like eating fish on Friday, "as part of the general scheme of salvation,"[28] but Fr. Bede found them — particularly Ernest Oldmeadow's *Tablet* — stodgy, narrow, and timid in all but their hostility to England and Anglicanism. In his own journalistic work, he aimed to alter that image. When an assistant at St. Dominic's Priory he transformed *The Rosary Magazine*, originally given to devotional literature for Dominican tertiaries, into a forum for the discussion of current social issues. Similarly, when he created *Blackfriars*, against widespread opposition from many Dominicans[29], from the old *Catholic Review*, he intended to offer readers a popular, outward-looking, and topical journal. When publisher Basil Blackwell wrote that the magazine was "little more than respectable," Fr. Bede ordered its editor: "Would you please see that it is no longer respectable."[30] If England's Catholic minority were to make an impact on society, they required the necessary intellectual armor. The aim of *Blackfriars*, he claimed, should be "to provide the Catholic dining public with arguments they can employ after the soup to worsen their adversaries, Protestants, Pagans, and the Deadly Sins."[31]

Such formation and support of the laity, Fr. Bede believed, was essential to the life of the Catholic community and the society at large, especially given what he regarded as the failure of the clergy to match their priestly vocation with a prophetic one. "These P.P.s you meet are not likely to do much, nor Cardinals who weep and sigh, but we want an enthusiastic band of young men who accept tradition but are not content with it."[32] It was to the realization of this goal that he believed that Dominicans were specially called, but they could succeed only if they could reform themselves and re-establish their historic reputation for intellectual and religious rigor.

To this end, Fr. Bede made one of his chief goals the return of the Dominicans to Oxford and to other major universities. The greatest part of the nation's intellectual and political leadership passed through Oxford and at a time in their lives when they were most prepared to be influenced, inspired, even converted by men of zeal and learning. Not all in fun, he wrote, "The idea is to convert the young man there by pandering to his love for the picturesque

—a Priory to the Holy Ghost, the white forms, the chanted office, lectures, sermons, etc. . . . then, when he's least attentive, baptise him. We shall have to have very weak tea always served, so weak as to be valid matter for Baptism."[33]

This vision led him also to establish a house in Edinburgh, the centre of Scottish intellectual life, and influenced his direction of the Dominican mission to South Africa. There he argued for the establishment of a house at Stellenbosch, in an area of almost negligible Catholic settlement. It was, however, the seat of the country's most prestigious Afrikaaner university. The leadership of society was passing, he saw, to the Afrikaaners, and only by winning over their leadership could change be effected. He was well aware of the challenge. In the face of the injustices toward the black population, he wrote, "one simply boils with indignation,"[34] and he claimed that the "Boers are Dutch, farmers, and Calvinist, each most stubborn, all of them together the most stubborn combination in the world." Yet they were too important to be neglected, and their very hostility, he fancied, would have attracted St. Dominic himself.[35]

A connection with Oxford would also give Dominicans "a spirit of work" as it had done the Benedictines.[36] They were no longer, he admitted either good scholars or good preachers—"We have been a learned order," he wrote, "and nowadays we live on the reputation of our spiritual ancestors" — but "Oxford would cure all this,"[37] giving Dominicans the opportunity to study, teach, and preach — their particular vocations.

There is no doubt that Fr. Bede Jarrett made a significant contribution to the revitalization of Dominican life in England in this century. He was an audacious leader, whose personal courage and faith inspired his men. It is perhaps more difficult to gauge exactly his impact on the wider Catholic community. According to one reviewer, "He was probably the best known preacher in England, and in constant demand . . . "[38] as a retreat-giver. Although he was often criticized by some Dominicans for his "shallow theology and homely idiom,"[39] his preaching was done in "modern English only," larded more with references to Shakespeare than to the Fathers,[40] and it spoke to people on personal and practical terms. His own education and background left him well placed to reach England's intelligentsia, Catholic and non-Catholic, and his personal magnetism seemed to touch all races and classes.

Those who knew him personally were touched profoundly by Fr. Bede Jarrett. His personal asceticism never was manifested in dourness or harshness, but rather in an unfailingly positive and optimistic faith in God and trust in other people. He believed that man "was to be lovingly led, not bullied, towards God."[41] "His legacy", wrote Dom Hubert von Zeller, whom Fr. Bede had constantly supported and encouraged, "was not so much his books or his buildings but his friends."[42] Vera Brittain, whose marriage he solemnized, remarked on the beauty of his face, "like a spiritual flame" and his eloquence.[43] Gwendolyn Plunkett-Greene wrote in an obituary in *Pax* that he had a "supernatural element" about him; he was "specially a minister of the Holy Ghost" or rather, she wrote privately, he may have *been* the Holy Ghost.[44] His letters to elderly women struggling with loneliness, to children of suicides, to young monks in love shine out with wit and sympathy which cushions but never obscures his wisdom and orthodoxy. Perhaps the most illuminating memorial on his death appeared in the "Parish Notes" of the *St. Dominic's Parish Magazine*. "He helped you save your soul by seeming to ask you for it as friend might ask for a loan. You were too honoured by the request to refuse it. You at once gave all you had to give, and immediately he handed it back to you again . . . ."[45]

Fr. Bede Jarrett was by no means the sole or even chief author of the intellectual revival of English Catholicism in the first half of this century. It may be argued that such an honour is due to Newman alone, and some would give Belloc, Chesterton, or Ronald Knox primacy of place.[46] The variety of his activities, however, the regard in which he was held by those who did not share his faith, the power of his preaching, and the impact of his personality on so many souls have secured him a place in that company. In short, Fr. Bede Jarrett was, in the happy phrase of Pope John Paul II, who, in many ways he so much resembled, "a sign of contradiction"[47] in a world of strife, ambition, materialism, and relativism. He was always ready to leave the cloister to address the world in its own language, but only on the terms of his faith.

NOTES

1. Ernest Barker, "Introduction" in Bede Jarrett, O.P., *The Emperor Charles IV* (London: Eyre and Spottiswoode, 1935), x-xi.
2. Interview with Rev. Bede Bailey, O.P., August 1986.
3. From a MS containing quotations on history, Jarrett Papers (Carisbrooke, England, Carisbrooke Priory). The quotation is likely drawn from the mediaevalist Augustus Jessopp (1824-1914).
4. J. B. Reeves, "Bede Jarrett," Jarrett Papers, unpublished MS, 1935, 495.
5. Bernard Delaney, O.P., "Father Bede Jarrett, O.P.," *Blackfriars* (May 1934):310.
6. Reeves, 522.
7. Bede Jarrett, O.P., "Manichaeans, Ancient and Modern," *Blackfriars* (September 1, 1923):1062.
8. Bede Jarrett, O.P., *A History of Europe from the Earliest Times to the Present* (London: Sheed and Ward, 1929) 12.
9. Bede Jarrett, O.P., "Our Social Principles: from the Encyclical, *Quadragesimo Anno*" Jarrett Papers, draft MS, n.d.
10. Notebooks of drafts for leaders in *Blackfriars*, undated MS., Jarrett Papers.
11. Bede Jarrett, O.P., "Empire Restored," *Blackfriars* (1 March 1927):156-157.
12. Bede Jarrett, O.P., "Is Fascism the Answer to Communism," *Catholic Herald*, undated clipping in Jarrett Papers.
13. Jarrett to Joseph Clayton, June 18, 1919. Jarrett Papers.
14. Bede Jarrett, O.P., "What About the Rights of Property?" *Catholic Herald* (December 23, 1923):3, 13.
15. Reeves, 561.
16. Jarrett to Lady Margaret Domville, February 11, 1919, Jarrett Papers.
17. Jarrett to Joseph Clayton, October 17, 1931, Jarrett Papers.
18. Jarrett to Lady Domville, August 25, 1922, Jarrett Papers.
19. Bede Jarrett, O.P., "We English," *Blackfriars* (October 1, 1921):413.
20. Jarrett to Lady Margaret Domville, March 5, 1921, Jarrett Papers.
21. Bede Jarrett, O.P., "Since Then," *Blackfriars* (February 1, 1931):95.
22. Bede Jarrett, O.P., "The Fading Away of Christian Moral Principles Around Us," *Clergy Review*, vol. iv, no. 1 (July 1932): 4.
23. *Ibid.*, 3.
24. *Ibid.*, 4.
25. Reeves, 671.
26. Notebooks of drafts for leaders in *Blackfriars*], undated MS., Jarrett Papers.
27. Jarrett, "Fading Away," 8.   28. Bede Jarrett, O.P., "Catholic Newspapers," *Blackfriars* (October 1925):571.
29. See Delaney, "Father Bede Jarrett, O.P.," 311.
30. Jarrett to Rev. Bernard Delaney, O.P., July 23, 1925, Jarrett Papers.
31. *Ibid.*
32. Jarrett to Lady Margaret Domville, July 24, 1919, Jarrett Papers.
33. Jarrett to Lady Margaret Domville, January 1, 1919, Jarrett Papers.
34. Jarrett to Joseph Clayton, January 9, 1930, Jarrett Papers.
35. Kenneth Wykeham-George, O.P. and Gervase Mathew, O.P., *Bede Jarrett of the Order of Preachers* (London: Blackfriars Publications, 1952), 74-76.
36. Jarrett to Rev. Austin Barker, O.P., March 30, 1905, Jarrett Papers.
37. Jarrett to Rev. Austin Barker, O.P., September 1, 1906, Jarrett Papers.
38. Edwin Essex, O.P., "Review of *Meditations for Layfolk*," *Irish Rosary* (January-February 1948):35-36.
39. Reeves, 6:24-27.

40. See Jarrett to Sr. M. Frances, May 18, 1933, Jarrett Papers: Jarrett urges her to take Shakespeare and "go over him, idle, wherever the book opens, and go on. Some of his phrases are lovely, cull them, ruminate over them, learn them by heart, and work them into your prayers."

41. Essex, 38.

42. Dom Hubert von Zeller, *We Live with One Eye Open* (London: Sheed and Ward, 1949) 95.

43. Vera Brittain, *Testament of Experience* (London: Gollancz, 1957), 18.

44. Gwendolyn Plunket-Green, "Father Bede Jarrett, O.P.," *Pax*, v. XXIV, no. 154 (August 1934): 106; see also Gwendolyn Plunket-Green to J. B. Reeves, undated, Jarrett Papers.

45. "Parish Notes," *Saint Dominic's Parish Magazine*, v. IX, no. 46 (April 1934): 3.

46. See the discussion in Edward Hutton's essay, "Catholic English Literature, 1850-1950," in Rt. Revd. George Andrew Beck, *The English Catholics, 1850-1950* (London: Burns Oates, 1950), 515-558.

47. Karol Wojtyla, *Sign of Contradiction* (New York: Seabury Press 1979).

JOHN JULIAN RYAN AND
THE IDEA OF A CATHOLIC COLLEGE
Vincent J. Capowski

John Julian Ryan was born October 5, 1898 in Houston, Texas. This piece of factual information is the kind dear to the historian who usually would use it to locate a person in place and time. The use of this information in this paper is opposite. John Ryan was not a Texan in attitude, style or outlook. Neither was he the typical student of Brookline, Massachusetts High School from which he did graduate in 1917. He was *sui generis*, unique and not amenable to type casting. In appearance, especially in later years, he had the look of a genial Irish host. Smiling with a hearty laugh, he was a pleasant person to encounter on or off campus. But that *persona* was also deceiving. He was a man to whom ideas were of supreme importance. He wanted to know. He was hungry for God. It was this search for meaning that made him fascinating, a kaleidoscope of intellectual musings, and probing discussions of the latest political, economic, or cultural phenomena. He was a curious man who had tried to understand systematically how this life worked and what God wanted of us. The John Ryan I knew could not, therefore, be located in Houston, Brookline, Worcester, Conception, Missouri, South Bend, Indiana, or even Goffstown, New Hampshire. His location was marked not by place and time but by ideas, discoveries, and an integrated, holistic approach to reality.

The subject of this paper is his idea of the Catholic college. Unfortunately his ideas and hopes for what Catholic higher education should be or might be were so far removed from what was and what is, that those of us who were his friends were subject to his sense of frustration at opportunity missed or at the misunderstanding of what the mission of places like St. Anselm College should be.

Yet these outbursts never gave way to despair. To the last John exhibited an energy and a combative enthusiasm for the conversion of the heathen among the church's leadership and the creation of a just Christian social order. In 1975 he was invited to speak at the Notre Dame School of Engineering on the topic of humanistic work as a result of his 1972 book *The Humanization of Man*. In the peroration to this talk, he made the following statement that summarizes his attitude:

> Well, what I have been suggesting throughout here—this transition from one technology and way of life, to one in which *all* work, play and behavior will become, as far as possible humanistic because [it will become] artistic, professional and truly vocational—will such a transition be easy. Hardly. With human nature and the entrenched economic system what they are, it may well be extremely difficult, if not impossible. But, being as young as I am—I am only 77—I still have hopes.[1]

"I still have hopes." Hope, faith and charity are not easy virtues. They need constant cultivation and reinforcement and it is this need that John Ryan felt Catholic colleges should fulfill.

John Julian Ryan's intellectual estate is found in three books and countless articles. He once remarked that on most of the printed forms for academic *curriculum vitae* much space was left for degrees —all he held was a Bachelor of Arts and later an Honorary Doctorate — but very little space was left for publications; and John wrote, and wrote in all kinds of literary formats. He wrote poetry which may have been his first love. He wrote essays. He wrote an English composition text. He wrote letters to the editor. However, his three books and cognate articles are the basis of his reputation and significance. Each was written in response to a felt need and written with a passion and enthusiasm. His first book-length exposition was entitled *The Idea of a Catholic College*. Published in 1945 by Sheed and Ward, it was dedicated to "Mary the Mother of God." A foreword was written by Richard J. Cushing, then Archbishop of Boston. The book set out in a form most would regard as old fashioned today, a blueprint or design for a Catholic college. His second book was entitled *Beyond Humanism: Toward A Philosophy of Catholic Education*. It was published in 1950 by Sheed and Ward and continued his didactic and systematic explanation of what Catholic education should be. By this point in his career, his reputation as a

Catholic educator who dealt with first principles and was willing to talk of the Mystical Body of Christ as a reality was gaining attention among Catholic educators and Catholic college administrators. He was much like the little boy in the fable of the king with the clothes that only the good could see. All hid their knowledge of the king's nakedness until the little boy pointed it out to the consternation of all.

In this paper, I would like to begin with a consideration of John's last book-length work, *The Humanization of Man* published in 1972 by Newman Press. In the introductory note John discussed the problem he had finding a title for this work:

> The present title was settled on because the work offers partly a promise, but mainly a hope: a philosophically grounded hope. It is that we can forge a truly humane culture from our present ghastly one through learning to understand and follow the basic principles of a method which has been tragically overlooked and neglected.[2]

That hope for a truly humane culture informed all his work. John wanted a society imbued with Christian charity and the basic principles of the artistic method. It was this living dimension of the Mystical Body that was the true goal of society and he believed that society could be best taught these goals in the Catholic college. However, these are not the aims of most Catholic institutions of higher learning in the United States.

In a short essay response to a question posed by *Ave Maria* magazine in its October 19, 1968 issue "Why A *Catholic* College?" John voiced his reservations about Catholic higher education. He was one of six panelists who were asked this question "Why A *Catholic* College?" "To arrive at a satisfactory answer," he said, "we have first to consider what, ideally, such an institution might be like and might be expected to do."[3] He went on to say that such a college would be a community of apprentices in the liberal arts under the direction of masters who would try to equip them to deal with the problems confronting them in the world. They would learn to cope with this existential dilemma "in the light of the requirements of the Kingdom."[4]

> At such a college, the student would acquire not merely various kinds of knowledge, but also the forms of skill and the methods by which these kinds of knowledge could be made fruitful.[5]

At this point, two definitions are necessary. John made a basic distinction between arts and science. He felt that there was a radical misunderstanding of these terms embodied in the structure of all higher education that was basic. Science, he pointed out over and over again, in the phrase arts and science did not refer to that branch of philosophy devoted to studying the natural order of things, but rather came from the Latin root *scientia* or knowledge. While arts again did not refer to the fine arts, but rather, again reflecting its Latin derivation, meant skill. Therefore, in a College of Arts and Sciences one studied the knowledge available and then systematically practiced the skills necessary for a professional. He objected to the college which emphasized the mastery of knowledge without developing the skills necessary to apply that knowledge. One should not just study philosophy, but under the direction of a philosopher, attempt to philosophize. Theory without application tended to lead to the pedantry of the expert who knows but cannot practice. Both knowledge and skill are necessary for a truly educated person.[6] It is interesting to note that this ideal is more closely observed in the natural sciences than in the social sciences and humanities. Natural science students are expected to have some laboratory, hands-on experience in doing science. In the social sciences and humanities, we do try to develop skills and understanding of research methodologies by assigning an occasional research paper. Generally however, it can be said that theoretical knowledge and its acquisition is the main goal of higher education. In fact John Ryan wrote the *Humanization of Man* to try to reintroduce both to society and to higher education what he called the artistic method. Please note in his *Ave Maria* essay he said that ideally a Catholic college would be a community of apprentices and masters in the liberal arts. Apprenticeship is taken on to develop a skill under the guidance of a master. Knowledge alone is not enough. The student at the ideal Catholic college:

> No less importantly, . . . would acquire a philosophy and a theology of life that would enable him to integrate his other training in accordance with some high commitment to professional service, so that he could live as a fully human person in enabling others to do the same.[7]

In other words John Ryan wanted a Catholic education to contribute directly to the building of the Kingdom of God on earth. This

was not and is not happening. The typical Catholic college catalogue hardly mentions these qualities. The aims are to aid the
student for "success" by equipping him with the knowledge to be a
"worthy" citizen and "good" Catholic.

John Julian Ryan believed that the end of all Catholic education
was training in charity so that the student would learn to live a life
of service as a trained professional dedicating his work to God. The
terrible cleavage of the religious and secular spheres had to be
overcome. The necessity was for one to interpenetrate the other so
that the work one did was in itself a prayer and the fulfillment of
both the spiritual and mundane. We should all be laboring as if our
work was holy. No one should set out to become rich, eliminate the
competition, and be motivated by enlightened self-interest. In the
chapter on "Aims" in the *Idea of A Catholic College*, John stated:

> The way of life here described is not for the few only; it is the norm
> for every vocation, no matter how lowly. For every way of life not
> only should be, but can be, made professional: all men can follow,
> with professional skill, some richly charitable vocation.[8]

The question that remains is how does one become a professional,
dedicated to a code of ethical conduct and the advancement of one's
profession. The answer proposed by John Ryan lay in what he
described as the artistic method.

The remainder of this paper will be devoted to explaining what
John meant by the artistic method and how it was essential for a
Catholic college in creating a humane society. In his discussion of
higher education, John Ryan pointed out that what we have been
sold is an image. What we believe higher education to be hinders its
ability to fulfill the goal of educating students for professional service. As he said:

> ...students, parents, and teachers alike have come to adopt a narrow
> view of what a student is supposed to be doing. Being a student has
> come to mean: listening to lectures, doing homework, reciting, and
> taking written tests—all for the gaining of "credits." Once we adopt
> the right view of education, however, we see that it is a process
> quite different from this — a process in fact, aimed more at the
> development of wisdom than at the acquisition of knowledge.[9]

The student is in college to learn three things. First, how a thing is
done; second, how to do it himself; third, how to instruct others in
how to do it. This prescription means that teaching must be quite

different. It is more analagous to coaching than lecturing and classes should be viewed as practice periods where the students try out their knowledge among their peers and are willing to make mistakes and accept correction. The teacher should be a model and have the attributes of a good actor. Encouragement, positive reinforcement and praise for that which is done well must be part of his repertoire. It is at this point that an understanding of the artistic method is most necessary.

This artistic method is very simply the general principles of craftsmanship and pedagogy. First, technique follows intention. For example, the forms of research are dictated by the topic to be researched. Training of the body and learning of the required skills are necessary to the successful completion of the subject being mastered. It is a deceptively simple proposition that technique is determined by intention. Yet why is it that in the modern college one cannot distinguish one class from another unless told what subject is being taught? The techniques of teaching do not seem formed by the subject being taught except verbally, even then little or not at all. Second, students learn best what they learn on their own. A class in which the students contribute their knowledge of a topic from what they have learned on their own engages their interest and becomes part of their frame of reference in a way a lecture never can. How much better a practice session of learning in which the students demonstrate their mastery through trial and error. Learning can only be done by the student. At least 60% of class should be a matter of practice and no more than 40% to theory or explanation. To John Ryan a teacher's work was more supervisory than explanatory or disciplinary.

> The Catholic college of liberal arts, then, should be a community of workshops in which are learned the arts of conducting and sacramentalizing civilization; workshops in which artists-in-residence develop in their apprentices one or other scientifically grounded skill — this, by guiding them in their attempts to solve a unified and progressively more difficult array of normal problems. The training here is not simply in investigating what others have said or in learning how things are done; it is also a training in meditating on the truths of wisdom and in learning how to do things.[10]

Please note that the end of Catholic education is to conduct, in a professional manner, civilization and to sacramentalize it. The methodology is artistic and the locale is the workshop of the master-teacher. The student has as his goal "learning how to do things."

In illustration of this principle John once remarked how refreshing and shocking it would be if professors ran their classes as athletic coaches in those same colleges ran their teams. No student athlete would remain on the team very long if he did not demonstrate commitment, enthusiasm, dedication, and a desire to improve his skills. The coach is not interested in teaching his charges the general principles and systems by which the sport is played. The coach helps the athlete play the sport as well as he can and in the process demonstrates the rules, theory, and philosophy underlying that sport. The idea of having students with the enthusiasm of athletes in class would be both frightening and inspiring. John Julian Ryan felt that all teachers were coaches or artists. They should know the true purpose of their teaching activity. They should know the nature of the materials with which they work, the young men and women who do come to college with more enthusiasm than we suppose. Teachers should know the form which we wish to give this human material. They should know the best techniques and be able to practice their techniques with skill and good will. A teacher at a Catholic college should be "a Knute Rockne of the mind and soul."[11] His work is intensive and not extensive. The worried and harried professor who must "cover the ground" has worried and harried students who will master little of the ground covered.

The third principle of craftsmanship is that the student be given guidance only when he or she feels the need for it. The teacher should almost never "take over" and show the student how to finish or perfect anything. The "trial and error" process requires the student to recognize his errors and learn to correct them. For the teacher, a non-directive, benevolent oversight is required which strains the "normal" parental corrective that most masters use on their apprentices.

Finally, the student should be encouraged to instruct others and thus himself. We all became aware of this principle when we began writing our first talks or lectures. The mind never is required to become as clear and concise in expression than when we have to explain to others what we know. The more students have to explain to others what it is that they know, the more thoroughly they will know it.

This brings up a subject that all teachers agonize over: marks. Here again the perceptions of John Julian Ryan seem both penetrating and devastating.

Nor is anything more ridiculous than the practice of marking a student at the very outset on a skill that he is setting forth to acquire, and then, at the end of the year, averaging in his early marks with his latest 12

John felt that learning requires a sense of leisure. Effective study is always difficult, but never more so than under the pressure of test deadlines. One proposition which again he made a number of times was that every student be required to write a *utopia*, a narrative version of a perfected society, as an entrance requirement. Then as a senior, be required to write a *utopia* informed by four years of intellectual and skills development. The faculty would then be asked to judge the first effort and compare it with the student's senior thesis. This comparison if favorable would be all that he needed to qualify one for graduation. Are marks that culminate in course credits, collected like green stamps until sufficient credits are accumulated for certification a better means for producing educated students?

In conclusion, please be aware that John Julian Ryan's ideas were never merely instrumental in nature. His reforms were all developed to fulfill the purpose of Catholic higher education:

With the Fall man lost the Wisdom that can only be gained again through Faith; hence the teacher's task is to teach all things as ancillary to Faith.13

He then went on to say:

For in a sense the Catholic College is another Seat of Wisdom and he (the teacher) is another St. Joseph in whose care has been put another Christ.14

The reason that John Ryan's vision of the Catholic college should not be forgotten is because it constantly calls us back to first principles.

NOTES

1. John Julian Ryan, "Notre Dame Talk on Humanistic Work: Its Philosophical and Cultural Implications" (Unpublished typescript, 1975).
2. John Julian Ryan, "Introductory Note," in *The Humanization of Man* (New York: Newman Press, 1972).
3. John Julian Ryan *et al*, "Why A *Catholic* College?" *Ave Maria* (October 19, 1968): 9.
4. *Ibid.*
5. *Ibid.*
6. John Julian Ryan, *Beyond Humanism* (New York: Sheed and Ward, 1950), 77-95.
7. Ryan, "Why A *Catholic* College?" 9.
8. John Julian Ryan, *The Idea of A Catholic College* (New York: Sheed and Ward, 1945), 12-13.
9. *Ibid.*, 101.
10. Ryan, *Beyond Humanism*, 30-31.
11. Ryan, *The Idea of A Catholic College*, 83.
12. *Ibid*, 85.
13. *Ibid*, 115.
14. *Ibid*, 116.

PART FOUR

Philosophy and Theology

THE DIVINE LIGHT WITHIN: REFLECTIONS ON THE EDUCATION OF THE MIND TO GOD IN AUGUSTINE, ANSELM, BONAVENTURE AND NEWMAN

Robert L. Fastiggi

Introduction: The Inward Approach to God

In the history of Catholic theology, two basic approaches have developed in regard to the demonstration of God's existence. The more familiar approach is the cosmological. This approach, which is usually introduced to students through a study of the "five ways" of St. Thomas Aquinas, concentrates on the proof of God's existence via sensible experience. It begins with effects of God found within the cosmos and moves towards God as the cause or the necessary condition for what we experience around us. The immense popularity of the cosmological approach, though, has obscured (at least to some extent) the equally important approach to the knowledge of God through subjectivity. The four thinkers I have chosen all follow this inward approach to the knowledge of God. In other words, they don't begin with the senses but instead with the inner depths of the human soul, mind or consciousness.

I think it is vitally important that we introduce our students to both these approaches: the cosmological as well as the inward. Some students might be more persuaded by the cosmological approach since it appears to have its foundations in what all human beings can verify: namely, the experiences of the senses. However, thinkers as important as Augustine, Anselm, Bonaventure and

Newman all felt an attraction to the knowledge of God through subjectivity. Perhaps there are some minds which are more sensitive to the dynamics of interior reflection. Thus, I propose to accomplish two tasks in this brief paper. First, I will trace the historical and metaphysical development of the inner-way tradition in the four seminal thinkers I have chosen. Secondly, I will reflect upon the potential value of this interior approach for the education of the mind to God within the tradition of Catholic learning.

Augustine

One of the most significant contributions of Augustine to western Christian thought is his approach to the knowledge of God through subjectivity. So profound is the influence of Augustine in this regard that Etienne Gilson believes that it is fitting to speak of "the Augustinian doctrine of divine illumination."[1] Two fundamental characteristics of the Augustinian doctrine of divine illumination are introspection and the imagery of the inner light which illumines the mind. Both of these archetypes are found in Platonism and Neo-platonism. They seem to have made their way to Augustine via Marius Victorinus.[2] Augustine's notion of divine illumination can be found in the underlying logic of four distinct but interconnected ideas: 1) By turning in upon itself, the human mind can discover the immediate presence of God as "unchangeable light." 2) God is the immutable light of the intellect whereby it knows immutable truths. 3) God is the innermost depth of the soul. 4) God is reflected in the human mind which is an image of the Trinity.

In Book VII of *The Confessions*, we have a vivid description of Augustine's discovery of God within his own inner self:

> I was admonished by all this to return to my own self, and with you to guide me, I entered into the innermost part of myself, and I was able to do this because you were my helper. I entered and saw with my soul's eye (such as it was) an unchangeable light shining above this eye of my soul and above my mind. It was not the ordinary light which is visible to all flesh, nor something of the same sort, only bigger, as though it might be the ordinary light shining more brightly and filling everything with greatness. No, it was not that; it was different, entirely different from anything of the kind. Nor was it above my mind as oil floats on water or heaven is above the earth. It was higher than I, because it made me, and I was lower because I

was made by it. He who knows truth knows that light, and he who knows that light knows eternity.[3]

This passage illustrates the immediate presence of the divine light within the inner depths of human consciousness. It is clear that Augustine recognizes that the divine light is the creator and that he is the creature. Yet this distinction does not prevent Augustine from being aware of the immediate presence of the unchangeable light within his own subjectivity. The divine light is encountered as the light of the soul. Since it is a case of spirit being made present to spirit, there is no need for mediation through the senses. Paul Tillich observes that it is this emphasis on "the immediacy of the knowledge of God" which distinguishes this Augustinian epistemology (which he calls the ontological approach) from the Thomistic approach (called cosmological by Tillich) which always emphasizes the mediation of the knowledge of God through the senses.[4]

The second characteristic of Augustine's doctrine of divine illumination is the recognition of the divine light as the norm for judging immutable truths. In Book X of the *Confessions*, Augustine refers to God as "the permanent and abiding light" which he must consult in matters of judgment. Likewise, in his *Literal Commentary on Genesis*, Augustine notes the unique quality of the divine light:

> But distinct from all these objects is the light by which the soul is illumined, in order that it may see and truly understand everything, either in itself or in the light. For the light is God himself whereas the soul is a creature; yet since it is rational and intellectual, it is made in his image. And when it tries to behold the light, it trembles in its weakness and finds itself unable to do so. Yet from this source comes all the understanding it is able to attain. When, therefore, it is carried off and, after being withdrawn from the senses of the body, is made present to the vision in a more perfect manner (not by special revelation, but in a way proper to its being), it also sees above itself that Light in whose illumination it is enabled to see the objects that it sees and understands in itself.[5]

Gilson points out that this sense of divine illumination rests on the idea that scientific truths must be made visible by the divine light before they can be grasped by the intellect:

> ... as the sun is the source of physical light which makes things visible, so God is the source of the spiritual light which makes the

sciences intelligible to the mind. Thus God is to our minds what the sun is to our sight; as the sun is the source of light, so God is the source of truth.[6]

The third characteristic of Augustine's doctrine is that God exists in the innermost depths of the soul. In the deepest recesses of himself, he realizes that there is part of his person that transcends himself. He locates this aspect in the faculty of memory which is not so much a power as it is an inner depth or opening to the boundless reaches of the infinite. Thus, he refers to "the fields and the spacious palaces of memory."[7] Augustine is dazzled by the power and depth of his memory:

> It is like a vast and boundless subterranean shrine. Who has ever reached the bottom of it? Yet it is a faculty of my mind and belongs to my nature; nor can I grasp all that I am. Therefore, my mind is not large enough to contain itself. But where can that uncontained part of it be? Is it outside itself and not inside? In that case, how can it fail to contain itself? At this thought great wonder comes over me; I am struck dumb with astonishment.[8]

These vast and infinite aspects of his own inner-self so amaze Augustine that he realizes that the infinite God can be discovered by this turn inward. The introspection that opens up "the plains, caverns and abysses" of memory reveals an awareness of the transcendent God within the very structure of human consciousness. The mind for Augustine is an abyss which opens up to the infinite light of the divine.

The fourth characteristic of Augustine's doctrine of divine illumination is that the soul is an image of God. Since the divine light shines upon the human soul, we can discover God as the light reflected in the mirror of our interior selves. Augustine's original contribution in this regard is his understanding of the soul as an image of the Trinity. In book XIII of the *Confessions*, Augustine suggests that the mind's threefold reality as existence, understanding and will is a type of "mental exercise" which helps towards the understanding of the Triune God. Augustine develops this theme more in depth in his treatise *On the Trinity* when he meditates on how the inner-life of knowledge and love within the human soul is a mirror of the Trinitarian life of God.

Anselm

In tracing the historical heritage of the Augustinian doctrine of the *illuminatio divina*, we find a profound support given in the ontological argument of Anselm. This argument clearly emerges out of the Augustinian approach since Anselm exhorts us to "enter the inner chamber of thy mind" and "shut out all thoughts save that of God."[9] Since the human mind is created in God's image, it has an innate impression of the idea of God within its very structure. As Tillich points out, Anselm's argument is really "the rational description of the relation of our mind to Being as such."[10] God is present to the mind as an innate idea and as the essential support and ground of all intellectual activity. Thus, when Anselm says that he has in his mind the impression of "that than which nothing greater than he thought," he is not referring to a self-generated concept. Rather, he is referring to what he takes to be an encounter with a true reality.

The key to understanding Anselm's ontological argument is the metaphysical foundation upon which it stands. Anselm, like Augustine, believes that God is the infinite light in which all true knowledge is known. As he writes in the *Proslogion*, chapter XIV:

> For how great is that light from which shines every truth that gives light to the rational mind? How great is that truth in which is everything that is true, and outside of which is only nothingness and the false? How boundless is the truth which sees at one glance whatever has been made, and by whom, and through whom, and how it has been made from nothing? What purity, what certainty, what splendour where it is? Assuredly more than a creature can conceive.[11]

When Anselm refers to this light as "more than a creature can conceive," we clearly see that he is referring to something other than a self-generated concept. Anselm believes that his idea of God is based on an inner experience or encounter with the very light which is the foundation of all knowledge. For Anselm, this experience of God *is* real, and therefore, his idea of that than which nothing greater can be thought emerges out of experience with reality rather than mere theoretical speculation. Whether we call this epistemology Idealist or Platonic is not the central issue. The important point is that we understand the metaphysical presuppositions that are operating in Anselm's mind. For Anselm, the very fact that he can conceive of God demands the light of God as its foundation.

It is very clear that Anselm falls into the tradition of the inner-way since there is no appeal to the mediation of the senses. However, it would be wrong to say that Anselm's argument has no foundation in experience. Anselm, like Augustine, begins with the experience of God as an immediate presence within the inner-structure of the mind. Since what he has encountered is "that than which nothing greater can be thought," his argument really amounts to a way of describing the idea of what he has encountered. If one believes that our understanding of God comes via the mediation of the senses (as does Aquinas) then the idea of God is in no way a proof for the existence of God since it is abstracted from that which is only the effect of God and not God himself. However, if one believes that one's idea of God has come through a direct, unmediated encounter with God, then the idea of God is its own proof since it is an idea that comes from an experience of the reality of God and not from the effects of God.

Bonaventure

Bonaventure is one of the greatest examples of the Augustinian illuminationist tradition in the Middle Ages. In chapter three of *The Soul's Journey into God*, Bonaventure exhorts us to enter into ourselves, that is, into our mind, where the divine image shines forth. Here in this inner sanctuary, "the light of truth, as from a candelabrum, glows upon the face of our mind, in which the image of the most blessed Trinity shines in splendor."[12] Probably no other Christian writer is able to embrace the diverse nuances of the illuminationist tradition in as skilled a manner as Bonaventure. Not only does Bonaventure describe the mind as the image of the Trinity, but he also includes the notion of the unchangeable light as the source of our knowledge of unchangeable truth. As he writes:

> But since our mind itself is changeable, it can see such a truth shining forth unchangeably only by means of some light which shines in an absolutely unchangeable way; and it is impossible for this light to be a changeable creature. Therefore, our intellect knows in that Light...which is the true Light and the Word who was in the beginning with God.[13]

Bonaventure gives an even more detailed explanation of divine illumination in question four of *Disputed Questions Concerning Christ's*

Knowledge. After quoting from authorities like Aristotle, Augustine, Anselm and Isaac of Stella, Bonaventure is able to express the very heart of his argument:

> Everything unchangeable is higher than the changeable; but that which is known with certitude is unchangeable because it is necessary truth. But our mind is changeable; therefore, that by which we know is above our minds. Now there is nothing above our minds save God and eternal truth; therefore, divine truth and eternal reason is that by which knowledge exists.[14]

As with his predecessors, Augustine and Anselm, Bonaventure needs to make no appeal to sensible reality. Instead, his approach to God here is entirely interior. Reflecting upon the nature of human knowledge, he comes to the conclusion that he can only know unchangeable truths by means of the Light which is itself unchangeable: namely, the eternal Word of God.

Newman

The issue of faith and reason was of constant concern for John Henry Newman. Perhaps it was because he was living in the century which was trying to absorb the shock-effects of thinkers like Hume and Kant. Even as a young preacher, Newman began to meditate on the reality of conscience as the inner voice which demands God as its source. In his sermon entitled, "Faith Without Sight," he writes:

> Every religious mind, under every dispensation of Providence, will be in the habit of looking out of and beyond self, as regards all matters connected with its highest good. For a man of religious mind is he who attends to the rule of conscience, which is born with him, which he did not make himself, and to which he feels bound in duty to submit. And conscience immediately directs him to some Being exterior to himself ... and who is evidently superior to himself .... Thus, a man is thrown out of himself by that very voice which speaks within him. He looks forth into the world to seek Him who is not of the world, to find behind the shadows and deceits of this shifting scene of time and sense, Him whose Word is eternal and who is spiritual. He looks out of himself for the Living Word to which he may attribute what has echoed in his heart.[15]

We see in this passage a sensitivity to the echoes of the heart combined with the inner disclosure of God contained in the voice of conscience. Newman is gifted with the ability to discern the impression of the divine in the inner-life of human conscience. In one sense, his argument is new, but in another sense, it stands in the long tradition of the approach to God through interiority. He does not begin with the evidence for God in the sensate world. Rather, he begins "with that very Voice which speaks within him."

Newman always felt that there was a proper domain for faith and a proper domain for reason. However, in his *Essay in Aid of a Grammar of Assent*, he traces what might be called the reasons for faith. This essay is described by one scholar as "the contemplation of mind."[16] It represents an effort of some twenty years of numerous drafts.[17] Newman once related to a friend the main thesis of this book in a conversation:

> Object of the book twofold. In the first part shows that you can believe what you cannot understand. In the second part you can believe what you cannot absolutely prove.[18]

What Newman endeavors to accomplish in this book is to explicate the nature and quality of the human assent to God. Although he does not claim to provide an absolute proof for God's existence, he does believe that he provides a clear and credible explanation of how the human mind assents to the truth of the existence of God.

It is in this context that he applies his famous distinction between notional and real assent. Notional assent is given to various abstract and general propositions like "man is an animal" or "some men are learned."[19] These notional assents are cool, detached acknowledgements of validity. They fail to motivate people to heroic action or commitments. Newman believes that the assent to God must not be merely a notional assent but a real assent. Newman understands real assents as more "vivid and forcible" than notional assents.[20] Real assents excite, motivate and stimulate. They involve the affections and the passions. For Newman, real assents are always given to realities which are concrete and personal. Real assents make a difference in a person's life. They motivate action and create "heroes and saints, great statesmen, preachers and reformers . . . . They kindle sympathies between man and man, and knit together the innumerable units which constitute a race or nation."[21] As Newman sums up the matter: "Many a man will live and die upon a dogma: no man will be a martyr for a conclusion."[22]

For Newman, the assent to God can never be one of detached

logic. Instead, it is a "vivid assent" to a Personal Being who is "the fullness and archetype of every possible excellence, the Truth Itself, Wisdom, Love, Justice, Holiness."[23] Newman then proceeds to compare our interior impression of God to the impressions we have of sensible realities:

> By the law of our nature we associate those sensible phenomena with certain units, individuals, whatever they might be called, which are outside the reach of sense, and we picture them to ourselves in those phenomena.... Therefore, when we speak of having a picture of the things which are perceived through the senses, we mean a certain representation, true as far as it goes, but not adequate.[24]

Newman applies this analogy of sense impressions to the moral sense we discover within ourselves as a sign of God's impression of himself within the depths of human conscience. Just as we gain an impression of the mind and character of a great author by the reading of his books, so also do we attain an inner impression of God within our conscience. As Newman explains:

> Now certainly the thought of God, as Theists entertain it, is not guided by an instinctive association of His presence with any sensible phenomena; but the office which the senses directly fulfill as regards creation that devolves indirectly on certain of our mental phenomena as regards the Creator. These phenomena are found in the sense of moral obligation... so from the perceptive power which identifies the intimations of conscience with the reverberations or echoes (so to say) of an external admonition, we proceed on to the notion of a Supreme Ruler and Judge, and then again we image Him and His attributes in these recurring intimations.[25]

Newman makes it clear that he is not proving the existence of God. Instead, he is only seeking "to explain how we gain an image of God and give a real assent to the proposition that He exists."[26] Newman maintains that it is in our conscience that we gain access to God. He describes conscience in various images as "an authoritative monitor," "a voice, imperative and constraining," and "a Supreme Governor, a Judge, holy, just, powerful, all-seeing."[27] He also speaks of conscience as a type of human instinct concerning the good.[28] Newman also believes that children have within them this developing sense of "an Invisible, Personal Power."[29] As this childhood impression grows, it becomes more concrete and real:

It interprets what it sees around it by this previous inward teaching, as the true key of that maze of vast complicated disorder; and thus it gains a more consistent and luminous vision of God from the most unpromising materials. Thus conscience is a connecting between the creature and its Creator; and the firmest hold of theological truth is gained by habits of personal religion.[30]

It is important to note here that Newman does not look upon conscience as an autonomous power of the human subject. In his *Letter to the Duke of Norfolk*, he actually describes conscience as "the aboriginal Vicar of Christ" and also repeats the familiar Thomistic definition of natural law as "an impression of the Divine Light in us, a participation of the eternal law in a rational creature."[31]

Ultimately, Newman sees the knowledge of God as personal knowledge which is deepened and made more vivid by prayer and spiritual growth. People who nurture their prayer life soon find that "they are brought into His presence as that of a Living Person, and are able to hold converse with Him, and that with a directness and simplicity, with a confidence and intimacy."[32]

Newman shares the emphasis on inwardness and subjectivity with his spiritual forebears: Augustine, Anselm and Bonaventure. He tends to unite the intellectual with the spiritual in the great tradition of "faith seeking understanding." Newman tends to favor the inner moral sense of God rather than the interior illumination of knowledge. He also seems to prefer personal images rather than impersonal images like "unchangeable light." In these respects, he differs from his intellectual ancestors of whom we have spoken. Nevertheless, his basic approach to God is generically Augustinian and Anselmian. He has an immediate, interior sense of the divine presence. For him, that is sufficient proof of the existence of God. What he tries to do in the *Grammar of Assent* is to evoke in the reader an awareness of the depth of our inner-sense of the divine.

Newman also wishes to show that the true assent to God must always be real not notional. This type of reasoning is not the pure reasoning of Kant but rather the exercise of what Newman calls "the illative sense." This type of reason is more elastic and personal than pure, cold logic. It is that illuminative sense that enables us to make personal evaluations and judgments. Although judgments which emerge out of this illative sense lack absolute certitude in terms of demonstrable logic, they nevertheless have the quality of personal certitude. Thus, when a man is certain that his wife loves him, the certainty is based on personal knowledge gained by personal experience. In a similar way, the religious person knows that God exists in the depths of conscience and the inwardness of faith. Since God is a personal loving being, the illative sense allows the human mind to have certitude about God's love through experience and personal knowledge. This is not blind faith but is a rational faith based on a life of inward comfort and interior intimations. For Newman, ultimately, the reasons of the heart are in harmony with the reasons of the mind.

Concluding Reflections

What are the possibilities and implications of this inner-way tradition for Catholic higher education? In the first place, from the mere viewpoint of objective theological history, it is important for educators to make their students aware of this interior tradition of the ascent to God. Some students might be more persuaded by the cosmological arguments, but others might resonate better with the divine illumination tradition of Augustine or the ontological argument of Anselm.

Another implication for Catholic learning is the integration of theology with spirituality. Augustine, Anselm, Bonaventure, and Newman all had a sense of the unity of the spiritual and theological. While the classroom might not be the place for meditation or spiritual formation, it still can be used as an arena for evoking spiritual reflections on the part of the students. Often, the texts of authors like Augustine and Bonaventure are sufficiently rich to inspire profound spiritual emotions. The teacher should learn the art of balancing objectivity with an occasional display of emotional and perhaps even spiritual sentiments. Sometimes, it can be accomplished by a simple phrase like: "I personally find this spiritually moving" or, "There is a deep spiritual wisdom to be found here."

Certainly, we must submit Anselm's ontological argument to critical analysis, and we also must examine the intellectual cogency of the divine illuminationist tradition. Still, there is a need to treat our Catholic heritage with tools which transcend the purely rational. Perhaps we can even learn to teach from the perspective of faith seeking understanding.

NOTES

1. Etienne Gilson, *The Christian Philosophy of St. Augustine* trans. L. E. Lynch (New York, 1960), 77.
2. 7, 10. See Mary Clark's Introduction to *Augustine of Hippo: Selected Writings* (Ramsey, N.J., 1984), 6.
3. Augustine, *The Confessions*, trans. 7, 10; Rex Warner (New York, 1963), 149.
4. Paul Tillich, "Two Types of Philosophy of Religion" in *Theology of Culture* (New York, 1959), 10-29.
5. 12, 31, 59; Vernon Bourke, ed., *The Essential Augustine* (Indianapolis, 1974), 97.
6. Gilson, 77.
7. Conf. 10, 8; Warner, 217.
8. *Ibid.*; Warner, 219.
9. Anselm, *Proslogion* in *Anselm: Basic Writings*, trans. S. N. Deane (La Salle, Illinois, 1962), 3.
10. Tillich, 15.
11. *Proslogion* 13.
12. Bonaventure, *The Soul's Journey into God.* 3, 1; trans. E. Cousins (New York, 1978), 79.
13. *Ibid.*, 3, 3; Cousins, 82.
14. Bonaventure, *Disputed Questions concerning Christ's Knowledge: Question Four in A Scholastic Miscellany: Anselm to Ockham*, ed. Eugene Fairweather (New York, 1970), 383.
15. John Henry Newman, "Faith Without Sight," in *Parochial and Plain Sermons*, vol. II (Westminster, Md., 1966), 18.
16. See Thomas Vargish, *The Contemplation of Mind* (London, 1970).
17. C. S. Dessain, *John Henry Newman* (London, 1966), 148.
18. *Ibid.*
19. John Henry Newman, *Grammar of Assent* (Westminster, Md., 1973), 9.
20. *Ibid.*, 11.
21. *Ibid.*, 87-88.
22. *Ibid.*, 93.
23. *Ibid.*, 101.
24. *Ibid.*, 102-103.
25. *Ibid.*, 103-104.
26. *Ibid.*, 105.
27. *Ibid.*, 106-110.
28. *Ibid.*, 110-111.
29. *Ibid.*, 113.
30. *Ibid.*, 117.
31. John Henry Newman, "Letter to the Duke of Norfolk," in *the Essential Newman*, ed. V. F. Blehl, S.J. (New York, 1963), 262. The citation from Aquinas is from the *Summa Theologica* I-II, Q. 91, a. 2.
32. *Grammar*, 117-118.

EXEMPLUM MEDITANDI:
ANSELM'S MODEL FOR CHRISTIAN LEARNING
K. M. Staley

The young Anselm was a lover of learning. Eadmer remarks that even before he entered the monastery "he gave himself up day and night to the study of letters, not only reading with Lanfranc those things which he wished, but teaching carefully to others the things which they required."[1] Anselm entered the monastery, for he thought there, more than anywhere else, he might flourish, grow in wisdom, and reap its rewards. Indeed, he became something of a shining light. During the fifteen years of his abbacy, his reputation as a teacher and man of learning alone brought more than one hundred and eighty monks to Bec.

Anselm's excitement with the life of the mind was a sign of the times. Europe was experiencing something of a renaissance. As Gordon Leff remarks: "Whatever the subject, and whatever the region, there was a universal sense of discovery."[2]

Christian learning in particular was dramatically affected by a renewed interest in grammar, logic, and dialectic. Commentaries on the Scriptures and the works of the Fathers had served as the staple of Christian learning for nearly a millennium. A more speculative theology became possible. Some Christian scholars began to rely upon the guidance offered by the rules of dialectic rather than upon traditional texts. Others viewed this development with anxiety and suspicion. A brief look at two of Anselm's most famous contemporaries is sufficient to give us some idea of the tensions which developed.

Berengar of Tours (d. 1088) was intoxicated with the wine of the new grammar. He denied, by reason of grammatical propriety, that the bread and wine of the Eucharist could really become the body and blood of Christ. Any sentence in which the predicate destroys the subject is, for Berengar, no sentence at all. But this is precisely what happens when the celebrant of the mass utters the sentence, "This [bread] is my body." As the word "body" is pronounced, the bread ceases to be. Berengar concluded that the bread and wine could be only symbols of Christ.[3]

If this is the sort of speculation the new dialectic would allow, then I think one can understand why another of Anselm's contemporaries, St. Peter Damian, remarked that the devil himself must have been the first grammarian. It was the devil, argues Damian, who first taught Adam to decline the noun "God" in the plural.[4]

In the midst of such tension, it is not surprising that the young monks at Bec should have turned to Anselm for guidance. After their repeated and solicitous entreaties, Anselm tells us, he finally put down in writing some of the familiar themes of their conversations.[5] Anselm initially entitled this work, *exemplum meditandi de ratione fidei* — A Model Meditation Upon The Reason of Faith.[6] This work has come down to us under a more familiar title, *Monologion*. His brethren clearly wanted a working model after which to pattern their own meditation; Anselm remarks that the task was a difficult one because the work had to be adaptable to practical use.[7]

Southern has said of the paradigm which Anselm offers that "it would be hard to imagine a more complete break with the tradition."[8] Anselm does, in certain respects, offer his fellow monks a rather novel model for Christian learning—so novel that Lanfranc was quick to regard his most trusted pupil's work with an uneasy suspicion. Anselm intentionally excludes any reference to the authority of Scripture and any other authority, for that matter.[9] He states that he is confident that he can through reason alone (*sola ratione*) convince any man, even one ignorant of God and the Scriptures, of many doctrines of faith[10] — including the doctrine of the Trinity.

Anselm never qualified his confidence in the capacity of reason to penetrate the truths of faith. At the end of the much later work, *Cur Deus Homo*, for example, Anselm states, in the person of Boso:

> And by the solution of the single question proposed, I now see the truth of all that is contained in the Old and New Testament. For in proving that God became man by necessity, leaving out what was

taken from the Bible . . . you convince both Jews and Pagans by the mere force of reason. And the God-man himself originates the New Testament and approves the Old. And as we must acknowledge him to be true, therefore, no one can dissent from anything contained in these books.[11]

Anselm responds in his own person with characteristic humility. Should any error be contained in the work, he is willing to make a correction; and any truth the work contains he owes to God. Nevertheless, his assessment of the work in the person of Boso is astounding to say the least. Not only the incarnation, but the veracity of the Old and New Testament as well, are here the conclusions of an argument advanced on the basis of reason alone (*sola ratione*).

Because of these, and a number of similar texts, it is common in Anselm scholarship to speak of an Anselmian rationalism. Those who embrace this sort of view tend to see Anselm as, I should think, Peter Damian would have seen him, a dangerous, even if orthodox, upstart. Gilson remarks, for example:

And indeed, Anselm of Canterbury, as well as his immediate disciples, remain famous in the history of theology for their recklessness in giving rational demonstrations of all revealed truths. . . . This bold ambition to procure necessary reasons for revealed dogmas had never entered the mind of Saint Augustine; but it was bound to follow from [Anselm's] merely dialectical treatment of Christian faith.[12]

There are difficulties with this interpretation; for there are at least as many texts placed prominently throughout the Anselmian corpus which seem to affirm that absolute primacy of faith over reason.

There is the rather famous formula from *Proslogion* I: "I do not seek to understand in order that I may believe, but I believe in order that I may understand."[13] In the *Cur Deus Homo*, the very first thing Boso has to say is that "the right order demands that we first believe the deep matters of Christian faith before we presume to examine them by means of reason."[14] He assures Anselm that "even if he were unable to understand what he believes, still nothing could shake his constancy." And in his *Epistle on the Incarnation of the Word*, Anselm compares one who would attempt to reinforce Christian faith through reason to one who would try to stake down Mount Olympus, because he was fearful that it might blow away.

Interpreters who stress these texts paint a rather different portrait of Anselm. Gordon Leff, for example, counters Gilson's assessment on nearly every point. He writes:

> St. Anselm's entire position rests upon the primacy of faith. We must recognize, like St. Augustine, he allowed reason no independent validity. For both, reason was an instrument in demonstrating what was already believed: of itself it could not add to certitude, although it could give additional evidences for truth.[15]

In the face of these conflicting texts, more circumspect interpreters have been content to call Anselm inconsistent, and leave the matter at that.

Joseph Pieper charges Anselm with a practical inconsistency. He argues that "in the abstract he [Anselm] could recognize reason's necessary inadequacy to cope with mystery . . . . But he was unable to grasp it in any real sense, that is existentially."[16]

Charlesworth thinks that Anselm is groping towards "some kind of distinction between the function of reason which brings us to faith and the function of reason which operates within faith," but he contends that Anselm lacks the conceptual sophistication to make this distinction with much success. We must simply recognize that these "two strains in his [Anselm's] thought exist in an unresolved, uncrystallized state."[17]

Of these three interpretations, the position that Anselm is inconsistent seems most consistent with the texts that we have considered. But this means that in formulating his new paradigm of Christian learning, Anselm simply failed to address or completely fumbled the most pressing question facing his confreres: is there, as against one like Peter Damian, any sanction for this newfound interest in grammar and dialectic and, if there is, how, given the excesses of a Berengar, is it related to Christian faith?

I do not think that Anselm leaves these questions unanswered. He addresses them with a good deal more insight and sophistication than many commonly suppose. The *Monologion* in particular is one of the most compelling defenses of grammar and dialectic to be found in the eleventh century. Grammar and dialectic are, for Anselm, simply this: a methodological approach to the study of words and language, and words and language are, in one way or another, Anselm's explicit topic in over twenty-five chapters of the *Monologion*. The universe which Anselm describes in these chapters is a universe in which grammar and dialectic could not help but find a home, for it is quite literally a universe of discourse.

Anselm's God is a God who speaks, and with a single word he says two things. God speaks himself. Christ, the person of the Son, is the Word with which the Supreme Being utters and knows himself.[18] With this same word, Anselm argues, the Supreme Being utters creation.[19] And this is to say, for Anselm the act of creation is a divine speech act. When we speak, we speak words. When God speaks, he speaks things (*locutio rerum*).[20]

God's speech differs from ours. Our speech is true to the extent that it corresponds to the way things are. The truth of God's discourse does not depend on its correspondence to creatures. Anselm argues that it is quite the other way around. Creatures may be said to be more or less true to the extent that they correspond to God's Word. He states in *Monologion* 31:

> It is sufficiently clear, then, that in the Word, through which all things were created, is not their image, but their true and simple essence; while in things created, there is not a simple and absolute essence, but an imperfect image of that true essence. Hence, it necessarily follows that this Word is not more or less true according to its likeness to things created, but every created nature has a higher essence and dignity, the more it is seen to approach this Word.[21]

So the things of the world are more or less perfect images of God's Word. Of these creatures, none approaches God in dignity so closely as man,[22] for man, like God, is a speaker.

Human speech, according to Anselm, is caused by and depends upon the things of the world.[23] Creatures cause images and likenesses of themselves to exist in the human mind. Anselm calls these images in the mind natural words. Unlike the words of conventional languages such as Latin or Greek, natural words are common to all races of men. The meaning of a Latin or Greek word is nothing other than this natural word.[24] Without the presence of natural words, a Latin sentence would be meaningless. The words and expressions of a conventional language such as Latin are invented by men in order to express these natural words. Grammar and dialectic equip one to study these conventional languages.

All of this means that in a simple Latin sentence, as Anselm sees it, there is much more than meets the eye. Anselm is confident that in the logical and dialectical realities of our ordinary ways of speaking there lies hidden a distant reflection of the divine. For a Latin sentence is simply an expression of the natural words in our minds. And natural words are images of the things of our world. And these things are, in turn, images of the Divine Word, God himself. Ordinary discourse, then, is an image of God, though an image thrice removed. Grammar and dialectic are not, therefore, to be feared; for they offer great hope, the hope that we might wrest, from the very way we speak, an image of the substance of our faith. Moreover, nothing of our faith, it would seem, falls outside the scope of dialectic, for our language is a mirror of God's perfect knowledge of Himself, of the inner life of the Trinity, and of the Incarnate life of the Son.

It is this confidence which explains and sanctions the novelty of Anselm's *exemplum meditandi*, i.e., the painstaking dialectical and grammatical analyses of the *Monologion*, which became even more characteristic of his later works. It also explains why Anselm thought it quite legitimate, and even desirable, to forego the analysis of the traditional, authoritative texts — including Scripture — in favor of a fresh analysis of simpler, more colloquial forms of discourse.

But given Anselm's confidence that the truths of Christian faith can be established dialectically, what are we to make of those passages in which he insists that faith must precede understanding? Is Anselm inconsistent? Why does he insist upon the primacy of faith?

Anselm's answer is fairly straightforward: true thinking presupposes right willing. The priority of faith in regard to reason is not a logical priority, as Anselm sees it; it is a moral and practical priority.

Anselm's most complete statement in this regard occurs on the occasion of a response to the heretical teachings of a contemporary. Roscelin, a fellow Christian, denied the substantial unity of the persons of the Trinity on the grounds that the Father and the Spirit were not incarnate with the Son. Anselm replies to Roscelin in his *Letter on the Incarnation of the Word*. He begins by describing, perhaps more carefully than in any other work, the relationship between faith and reason:

> Indeed, no Christian ought to question the truth of what the Catholic Church believes.... Rather, by holding *constantly* and unhesitatingly to this faith, by loving it and living according to it humbly, and as best he is able, one ought to seek to discover why it is true....

> So before we examine and judge the deep things of faith, the heart
> must be first *cleansed* by faith . . . . And the eyes must first be enlight-
> ened through keeping the precepts of the Lord . . . . And through
> *humble obedience* to the testimonies of God, we ought to become as
> little children in order to learn the wisdom which the testimony of
> the Lord gives.[25]

Significantly, faith is not here a matter of a proposition taken from
Scripture to serve as a major premise in a syllogism. Faith refers
instead to a threefold disposition of the will.

Faith is a matter of constancy and stability: one must hold fast to
Christian belief, even if one does not understand that belief. This
stability, which faith provides, is Anselm's foremost concern, for he
recognizes that without such constancy, dialectical difficulties
might lead to a rejection of the faith:

> Let no one plunge rashly into complex questions concerning divine
> things without first striving in firmness of faith . . . lest running
> through a misleading mass of sophistries . . . he be ensnared by some
> persistent falsehood.[26]

Secondly, faith is a matter of obedience. There is a charge laid
upon the Christian: do not question the testimonies of God.
Anselm is convinced that sin, which deprives us of the light of
understanding, is not principally a matter of ignorance. Sin enters
the world by willing simply that one's own will be subordinate to
no other. What was lost, then, through disobedience cannot be
fully regained without an act of obedience.[27]

Finally, faith is a matter of humility, which is presupposed by and
follows upon obedience. Without humility, one runs the risk of
mistaking the limits of human understanding for the limits of reality and the divine. Thus, Anselm condemns those who "judge with
foolish pride that what they are not able to understand is not at all
possible, rather than acknowledging with humble wisdom that
many things are possible which they are not able to comprehend."[28]

According to Anselm, then, the Christian who engages in dialectic because he denies or questions the testimonies of Scripture is
not guilty of a logical or methodological error; the most important
truths of Scripture remain demonstrable by reason alone. Rather,
he is guilty of moral error — pride and injustice. For this reason,
non-believers seem to be in a better position than Roscelin, according to Anselm. They are not bound by the promises of baptism, so

their disbelief is not an injustice. In Epistle 136, Anselm writes of Roscelin and advises:

> Our faith ought to be defended by reason against those who ridicule it, but not those who glory in the name of Christian. Regarding the latter, we may justly demand that they stand by the promise made in baptism; as for the former, they should be shown by rational means how irrationally they spurn us. For a Christian ought (*debet*) to proceed through faith to understanding.... [29]

Though the pagan might ridicule the Christian faith, his error, as Anselm sees it, is a failure to see the reasonableness of Christian faith and therefore can be addressed through rational dialectic. In *Cur Deus Homo*, Boso is quite confident that, "although the [infidels] appeal to reason because they do not believe, and we because we do believe; nevertheless the thing sought for is the same."[30] On the other hand, one cannot, it seems, argue with the Christian who ridicules some elements of his own faith. He breaks a promise made in baptism, and this moral error, this injustice, so clouds his intellect that he can no longer see the truth of the faith, which can otherwise be plainly demonstrated without an appeal to the authority of Scripture.[31] One can only demand what justice requires.

Thus, Anselm is confident in the *Monologion* that he can convince through reason alone one who is ignorant of God and the Scriptures of the reasonableness of many matters pertaining to our faith, and yet is equally certain in the *Letter on the Incarnation of the Word* that the Christian who no longer believes can never understand.

There is no inconsistency here. Unlike Peter Damian, Anselm is confident that the truths of faith are intelligible and accessible to human reason. The pursuit of dialectic is fitting and appropriate in the universe of the Word made flesh. But confidence in the utility of dialectic for laying bare the necessity of these truths is not at all the same as confidence in man's ability to use this tool well. The rectitude of thought, thinking that "what is" is,[32] requires the rectitude of the will, willing what one ought to will.[33] If right thinking is to be secured through the logical rigor of dialectic, then right willing is to be regained through the humility and obedience of living faith.

Anselm's position may strike us an unusual one; for today we are more apt to consider intellectual clarity, good will, and devotion as isolated or, at best, incidentally related achievements of a human person. Perhaps this is the reason that commentators continue to find Anselm's reflections on faith and reason baffling. But in the final analysis, Anselm's paradigm is as consistent as it is challenging: Christian learning, that is, the life of learning as willed and practically pursued by Christians, requires more than the intellectual advances that an occasional renaissance can bring.

NOTES

1. Eadmer, *Vita Sancti Anselmi*, in *The Life of St. Anselm*, trans. R. W. Southern (Thomas Nelson and Sons Ltd, New York, 1962), 8.
2. Gordon Leff, *Medical Thought: St. Augustine to Ockham*, (Baltimore, Penguin Books: 1962), 89.
3. Berengar of Tours, *De Sacra Coena Adversus Lanfrancum*, ed. A. F. and F. Th. Vischer (Berlin, 1834) DHGE, 8, 385-407.
4. St. Peter Damian, *De Sancta Simplicitate Inflanti Anteponenda*, PL 145; 687 BC. See Gilson, *History of Christian Philosophy*, p. 616 (New York: Random House 1954).
5. "Quidam fratres saepe me studioseque precati sunt, ut quaedam, quae illis de meditanda divinitatis essentia et quibusdam aliis hujusmodi meditationi cohaerentibus usitato sermone colloquendo protuleram, sub quodam eis meditationis exemplo describerem." Schmitt edition published by Biblioteca de Autores Cristianos (Madrid, 1952). I have followed, with occasional alterations, Dean's translations for the *Monologion* and *Cur Deus Homo.* I have followed Jasper Hopkins, with occasional alterations, in all other instances.
6. See R. W. Southern, *Saint Anselm and His Biographer* (Cambridge University Press, 1966), 52-53.
7. "Quanto enim id quod petebant usu sibi optabant facilius, tanti illud mihi actu injungebant difficilius." *Monologion, Prologus.*
8. Southern, *Anselm and His Biographer*, 51.
9. "... quatenus auctoritate scripturae penitus nihil in ea persuaderetur, sed quidquid per singulas investigationes finis asseret, id ita esse plano stilo et vulgaribus argumentis simpliceque disputatione et rationis necessitatis breviter cogeret et veritatis claritas patenter ostenderet." *Monologion, Prologus.*
10. "Si quis unam naturam, summum omnium quae sunt ... aliaque perplura quae de Deo sive ejus creatura necessario credimus, aut non audiendo aut non credendo ignorat, puto quia ea ipsa ex magna parte, si vel mediocris ingenii est, potest ipse sibi saltem sola ratione persuadere." *Monologion, Cap. I.*
11. "... per unius quaestionis quam proposuimus solutionem, quidquid in novo veterique Testamento continetur, probatum intelligo. Cum enim sic probes Deum fieri hominem ex necessitate ... non solum judaeis, sed etiam paganis sola ratione satisfacias, et ipse idem Deus homo novum condat Testamentum et Vetus approbet: sicut ipsum veracem esse necesse est confiteri, ita nihil quod in illis continetur verum esse potest aliquis diffiteri." *Cur Deus Homo II, 22.*
12. Etienne Gilson, *Reason and Revelation in the Middle Ages*, (New York: Charles Scribner's Sons 1966), 26.
13. *Neque enim quaero intelligere ut credam, sed credo ut intelligam. Proslogion*, 1.
14. "Sicut rectus ordo exigit ut profunda Christianae fidei prius credamus, quam ea

praesumamus ratione discutere, ita negligentia mihi videtur, si, postquam confirmati sumus in fide, non studemus quod credimus intelligere." *Cur Deus Homo I, 1.*

15. Leff, 99. This interpretation became popular only in this century upon the publication of Karl Barth's *Anselm: Fides Quaerens Intellectum,* trans. Ian W. Robertson, SCM London: Press Ltd., 1960.

16. Josef Pieper, *Scholasticism,* trans. Richard and Clara Winston (New York: Pantheon Books 1960), 64.

17. M. J. Charlesworth, *St. Anselm's Proslogion* (Oxford: Clarendon Press, 1965), 34.

18. See *Monologion,* 29, 30, 32.

19. *Idem.,* 33.

20. *Idem.,* 10, 34, 35, 36.

21. "Satis itaque manifestum est in verbo, per quod facta omnia, non esse ipsorum similitudinem, sed veram simplicemque essentiam; in factis vero non esse simplicem absolutamque essentiam, sed verae illius essentiae vix aliquam imitationem. Unde necesse est non idem verbum secundum rerum creaturam similitudinem magis vel minus esse verum, sed omnem creatam naturam eo altiori gradu essentiae dignitatisque consistere, quo magis illi propinquare videtur." *Monologion.* 31.

22. *Monologion,* 66, 67.

23. *Idem.,* 11.

24. *Idem.,* 10.

25. "Nullus quippe Christianus debet disputare, quomodo quod catholica ecclesia corde credit ... sed semper eandem fidem indubitanter tenendo, amando et secundum illam vivendo humiliter quantum potest quaerere rationem quomodo sit ... Prius ergo fide mundandum est cor ... et prius per praeceptorum domini custodiam illuminandi oculi ... et prius per humilem oboedientiam testimoniorum dei fieri parvuli, ut discamus sapientiam quam dat testimonium domini ... quam profunda fidei diiudicando discutiamus." *Epistola De Incarnatione Verbi,* 1.

26. "Nemo ergo se temere immergat in condensa divinarum quaestionum, nisi prius in soliditate fidei conquisita morum et sapientiae gravitate, ne per multiplicia sophismatum diverticula incauta levitate discurrens, aliqua tenaci illaqueetur falsitate." *Epist. de Incar, Ver.,* 1.

27. See *De Casu Diaboli,* 4; *De Libertate Arbitrii,* 10; and *Cur Deus Homo I,* 9-11.

28. "... potius insipienti superbia judicant nullatenus posse esse quod nequent intelligere, quam humili sapientia fateantur esse multa posse quae ipsi non valeant comprehendere." *Epist. de Incarn. Verb,* 1.

29. "Fides enim contra impios ratione defendenda est, non contra eos qui se christiani nominis honore gaudere fatentur. Ab iis enim juste exigendum est ut cautionem in baptismate factam inconcusse teneant; illis vero rationabiliter ostendum est quam irrationabiliter nos contemnant. Nam Christianus per fidem debet, ad intellectum proficere ... " It is significant that the demand upon the Christian in this text is a matter of justice rather than dialectical acumen. This text appears as Epistle 136 in vol. III of the Schmitt edition (Edinburgh: Thomas Nelson and Sons, Edinburg, 1946), 280-281. It appears as Epistle 73 in the Madrid edition, vol. 2, 626.

30. "Quamvis enim illi [infideles] ideo rationem quaerant, quia non credunt, nos vero, quia credimus: unum idemque tamen est quod quaerimus." *Cur Deus Homo I, 2.* One cannot imagine Anselm making a similar statement about Roscelin or Berengar.

31. Several passages in this text make it clear that Anselm considers that this error is principally a moral fault, rather than logical or theoretical failing, and that he believes that knowledge of truth is dependent directly upon the rightness of willing. He remarks, for example, "Et non solum ad intelligendum altiora prohibetur mens ascendere sine fide et mandatorum Dei obedientia, sed etiam aliquando datus intellectus et subtrahitur et fides ipsa subvertitur neglecta bona conscientia." *Epist. de Incarn. Verb.,* 1.

32. "Si ergo vera est et recta cogitatio non ob aliud quam quia putamus esse quod est, aut non esse quod non est: non est aliud eius veritas quam rectitudo." *De Veritate*, 3.

33. "... non ibi aliud potest intelligi veritas quam rectitudo, quoniam sive veritas sive rectitudo non aliud in ejus voluntate fuit quam velle quod debuit." *De Veritate*, #4. Anselm's argument in the *De Veritate* sheds considerable light on his position on faith and reason, as developed in this essay. He argues that truth is to be had both in thinking and willing, that these two dimensions of truth are ultimately one, and that the unity of truth is ultimately to be understood in terms of rectitude. A discussion of this text, unfortunately, lies beyond the scope of the present essay.

THE PROSLOGION
AND SAINT ANSELM'S AUDIENCE
Richard Law

The epigraph for this talk is from Sir Richard Southern's notable book first published twenty-five years ago, *Saint Anselm and His Biographer* (1963): the *Proslogion* "was written in a state of philosophical excitement which (it is probably safe to say) had never before been experienced so intensely in any Benedictine monastery, and was probably never again to be repeated in Benedictine history."[1] Taken literally, this historical generalization is no less disputable than any other containing the phrases, "never before" and "never again," but undoubtedly it reflects Professor Southern's keen appreciation of the spirit of Saint Anselm's famous treatise. The state of philosophical excitement mentioned by Professor Southern pervades the *Proslogion* beginning with its very first words. The title of Chapter I is, "A Rousing of the mind to the contemplation of God," and Saint Anselm's rhetoric therein is vibrant with short directive phrases and energetic predications, as in the first paragraph: *fly* from your affairs, *escape* from the tumult, *abandon* yourself to God, *shut out* everything else. There are series of questions in rapid succession that denote urgency—as in the second paragraph on page 2: "What have I undertaken? What have I actually done? Where was I going? Where have I come to? To what was I aspiring? For what do I yearn?" Chapter I, in which Anselm addresses God and also reflects on himself—"Come now, insignificant man," he writes — exhibits an ardent dramatic style that registers the emotions of Saint Anselm anxious to find the single proof that God really exists. My thesis is that the *Proslogion*, the vehicle for the imperishable ontological argument, is a vivid and lively document that conveys Saint Anselm's profound personal experience with an expressive power that is sufficient to evoke corresponding feelings from the audience. Sir Richard Southern's enthusiastic response, cited above, serves as prime evidence.

My approach to the *Proslogion* is rhetorical, not philosophical. It does not aim to dissect or interpret the ontological argument *per se*, or to take sides in the centuries-long debate that began with the exchange between Saint Anselm and the first doubter of his proof, Gaunilo of Marmoutier. Saint Anselm's argument or derived versions of it have been defended, rejected, or modified by major figures including Saint Bonaventure and Saint Thomas Aquinas, Duns Scotus, Descartes, Immanuel Kant, Hegel, Royce, Santayana, and Karl Barth. During the last thirty years, several books and important articles in philosophical journals have examined the proof, paralogism, or conundrum some more.

In a compact review of the history and the current state of the debate, Arthur C. McGill states that "the traditional view, that the argument simply analyzes a subjective concept, has fallen out of favor, but no broadly accepted alternative has been found."[2] Professor McGill cites Paul Evdokimov, who likens the ontological argument to "one of those inns in Spain to which each person brings his own food and drink."[3] This wry analogy implies that among the variety of views or impressions in the unending debate, none is elite. From his survey of Christian scholars, among whom there is no consensus on interpretation and evaluation, Professor Anthony Nemetz concludes: "Judgments concerning the validity of [Anselm's] argument are as varied as the interpreters."[4] This is not surprising to those of us who would agree with the learned literary historian, Rene Wellek, that criticism is personal but it aims to discover a "structure of determination" in the text itself.[5] The esteemed M. H. Abrams pronounces as follows on the subjectivity of interpretation: a critical essay reflects or is informed by a critical theory, i.e., "a type of theoretical perspective to which the critic is committed, whether explicitly or implicitly, and whether deliberately or as a matter of habit."[6]

By sustaining the disputation over Saint Anselm's proof for hundreds of years, the philosophers comprise the audience that have been the most instrumental in perpetuating it. I would call them the dialectic audience. Engaged in philosophical discussion and debate, understandably they minimize or disregard the emotiveness of Saint Anselm's presentation in order to concentrate on semantic, grammatical, and logical elements. Regardless of how they perceive or reformulate the argument in the *Proslogion*, the dialectic audience characteristically would aim for dispassionate understanding and reasoning.

Notwithstanding the historic significance of the philosophical debate, my disciplinary interest is in the *Proslogion* and the readers that one could call the sensitive audience, an audience which includes Sir Richard Southern, Professor G. R. Evans, and other persons of note who put a premium on the personal appeal that the treatise exerts by virtue of Saint Anselm's eloquent, imaginative verbal expression. Professor Southern associates the manner of the *Proslogion* with that of Saint Anselm's devotional pieces written a little earlier, including the prayers, which are praiseworthy as "the work of a man with great literary gifts."[7] Professor Southern calls attention to the abundant imagery, figures of speech, and emotional pitch that the prayers display. It is his brief commentary on the prayers that furnished the impetus for me to highlight figurative and dramatic elements in the *Proslogion* which make the text so affective. The ontological argument is contained in a rhetorical discourse that affects or influences the disposition of the sensitive audience.

To appreciate the dramatic imagination of Saint Anselm as he recalls how he felt at the time he was occupied with the ontological argument, let us peruse just the middle of the first paragraph of the preface. Therein he discloses that his diligent search for the argument was frustrating. Sometimes he "almost reached what [he] was seeking"; sometimes it "eluded [him] completely." "Finally, in desperation," Anselm writes, he was about to quit the search, the idea seeming to be "something impossible to find."

But in lines 17-22, the hide-and-seek becomes a personal encounter that includes three reversals in quick succession:

1. "In spite of [his] resistance to it," the idea, which had been tantalizing and eluding Anselm, now on the contrary, "began to force itself upon [him] more and more pressingly."

2. Instead of yielding to or embracing the idea, Anselm got "quite worn out with resisting" it and endured mental conflict, despair, and distraction.

3. For the third reversal, the idea, which had previously been an elusive quarry, finally overcame Anselm's resistance, and he "eagerly grasped the notion which [he] had been rejecting."

Saint Anselm's occupation with the irrepressible idea is depicted as though it were a match or contest between him and a percipient agent. According to his preface, it was forceful; it eluded, importuned, and enlightened Anselm. The figurative overtones which I have stressed augment the vivid dramatic impression of Saint Anselm's perturbing experience trying to formulate the argument. Extremely important, furthermore, is the connection between the idea personified as an active agent and the Creator that it represents. Turning now to the *Proslogion* proper, please observe how the second paragraph of Chapter I begins: "Come then, Lord my God, teach my heart where and how to seek You...and find You." This prayer or petition supports, I trust, my impression that the shifting reactions of Saint Anselm and the idea correspond to the spiritual engagement between Saint Anselm and God, in which Anselm struggled almost to the point of despair, and then was divinely inspired.

Another metaphorical function of this prayer, "Lord my God, teach my heart," is worth pursuing, too. Obviously, the search for the single argument or proof that God really exists is work for a powerful mind. Yet Saint Anselm beseeches God to teach his heart. Also, the first paragraph ends as Saint Anselm directs his "whole heart" to speak to God. And in Chapter IV (in the middle of page 3), he rebukes the Fool for saying "in his heart what he could not think." Indeed, the first assumption in this paragraph is, "to say in one's heart and to think are the same." Here I would suggest that the image of saying in one's heart, which Saint Anselm appropriates from the Psalms, functions as synecdoche. That is, the heart signifies all aspects of human comprehension; it is not the alternative to reasoning. In combining the metaphorical heart with thought or the process of thinking, Saint Anselm is linking faith and reason and is professing that his philosophical quest is not exclusively intellectual or cerebral, but actually engages a person's whole disposition, which inherently involves the emotions. (Early in this century, T. S. Eliot explained that during the Age of Reason poets were impaired by "dissociation of sensibility." Mr. Eliot's famous term surely does not pertain to Saint Anselm.)

Chapter I is predominantly a supplication to God, whose presence is so utterly certain that searching for proof of his real being is an unequivocal demonstration of Saint Anselm's faith. Please observe lines 18-23 in Chapter I (near the bottom of the first page).

"What shall your servant do?" Saint Anselm asks, and then describes himself as "tormented by love" of God, yearning to see God, desiring to come close to God, and longing to find God. The predication here signifies that for Saint Anselm this is a personal mission — as distinct from a theoretical exercise. That it is not abstract, but substantial, is signified by another image from the Psalms that Anselm reiterates: "I seek your countenance," he pleads; "I do not know your face"; I am "cast off from your face." Over on page 2, the third paragraph pursues a lament comprised of phrases from the Psalms: "O Lord, how long, how long will you turn your countenance from us? When will you look upon us?" and so on.

The forlorn tone is intensified by Saint Anselm's naming himself "this exile" and grieving over the sad condition of humanity since the Fall. Anselm states that he was made in order to see God, but cannot do so. The next paragraph focuses on all mankind, and the first sentence exclaims that everyone has lost what he was made for. Thus Saint Anselm individually and man collectively or universally suffers the same anguish, being unable to see God. (Parenthetically, I should acknowledge here Father Anselm Stolz's cogent thesis [published in 1933] that the *Proslogion* "is essentially a piece of mystical theology," "a quest by faith for a vision of God.")[8]

The imagery in the first paragraph on page 2 is striking, and the rhythmic series of antithetical clauses and phrases is arresting. "Once man ate the bread of angels; now he eats the bread of sorrow," and so on. In the couplet, "He groaned with fullness; we sigh with hunger," just as the concepts of well-being and misery are contrasted, so also are the tonal impressions. To groan is to utter a low or deep sound of strain, perhaps indicative here of Adam's reaction to the incredible immensity of his blessings; whereas to sigh is to breathe somewhat audibly, a faint sound indicative here of weakness and depression. The paragraph is replete with tell-and-show expressions, such as "[Adam] was prosperous; we go begging." The rhetorical questions in lines 9-11 underscore how unbelievable it seems that Adam lost Paradise. "Why," Saint Anselm asks, "since it was easy for him, did he not keep for us that which we lack so much?"

The first sentence in the second paragraph on page 2 completes the bond between the anguished speaker, Saint Anselm, and all "the miserable children of Eve." Then comes the series of rapid rhetorical questions that convey his sense of dismay, perhaps even incomprehension, that he is possessed of this desire to see God. Lines 15ff. contain a list of stark reversals for Anselm. His endeavors have resulted in confusion, not goodness; tribulation, not peace; sobbing, not happiness; sighs, not gladness. Following the paragraphs depicting his and all humanity's exile and anguish, and also the frustration or futility of his immediate strivings, the final paragraphs of Chapter I emphasize Saint Anselm's reliance on God. With this faith he proceeds into Chapter II, beginning with the friendly greeting, "Well then, Lord," and expresses confidence that God will grant him the understanding for which he yearns.

In the brief context of the ontological argument, Saint Anselm borrows from the Psalms the familiar figure of the Fool who said in his heart, there is no God. Anselm then posits the Fool as the individual who must be convinced by the proof. He uses the Fool to stress the point that obviously any sensible or intelligent person would acknowledge the validity of the proof. "Even the Fool, then, is forced to agree," Anselm declares in line 18 (near the bottom of page 2). Over on page 3, Saint Anselm concludes Chapter III by separating the Fool from anyone with a "rational mind" — thus implying that the Fool is irrational. Then he dismisses the Fool by means of a rhetorical question containing a redundancy that is at once amusing and decisive: Why did the Fool deny God's existence? is the question. "Why indeed, unless because he was stupid and a fool?" The Fool functions as the atheist *via* the scriptural allusion and also as a straw man whose position is confuted with such ease that no reasonable person ought to consider it seriously. Apparently, the monk Gaunilo appreciated Saint Anselm's tactic, for his criticism of Anselm's proof is entitled, "A Reply by a Certain Writer on Behalf of the Fool."

It is most likely that Saint Anselm's first audience, the monks at Bec (that Professor Southern names "eager pupils")[9] were especially edified by the *Proslogion* because they knew it was a true account of their Prior's recent endeavor and achievement. The ontological argument proper occupies Chapters II, III, and part of IV. Chapter I and most of the text after Chapter IV comprise a devotional context for the argument which enhances its appeal to the faithful. By and large, the *Proslogion* is a profound meditation rife with biblical allusions and also a recollection capable of eliciting the fervent response of the faithful and fostering their personal involvement in meditating God.

At the beginning of the second paragraph in the preface (on the first page again), Saint Anselm reveals that he wrote the *Proslogion* because he judged "that what had given [him] such joy to discover would afford pleasure . . . to anyone who might read it." Professor G. R. Evans comments on this objective as follows: "A little Wordsworth, [Anselm] wanted to be able to recollect emotion in tranquillity, to be able, in times of meditation, to feel that first sensation again . . . . He [also] tries to help the reader by a shorter route into that state of preparedness which he himself had had to reach before the argument became clear to him."[10]

For its first audience at Bec, the *Proslogion* afforded the pleasure that Saint Anselm intended, no doubt, just as it has done for so many readers since then, especially those with religious inclination. That pleasure derives, not only from the proof whose discovery gave him such joy, but also from his account of his search, discovery, and exaltation, and because it is written so expressively. The words *joy* and *happiness* occur often in the later chapters of the work. Naturally this is so because these are Saint Anselm's feelings while he continually thanks God and celebrates His divine attributes. The gratitude and praise begin as soon as the compact proof is completed, that is, with the vigorous one-sentence paragraph that concludes Chapter IV: "I give thanks, good Lord, I give thanks to You," and so on. The joy that Anselm got through discovering the proof outweighs the despondence he felt beforehand. Chapter V exhibits the spirit that prevails through the succeeding twenty-one chapters. It is noteworthy that among the first attributes of the Supreme Being, Saint Anselm designates happiness. He tells God, "You are . . . whatever it is better to be than not to be," and this includes being "happy rather than unhappy." Small wonder that the *Proslogion* still gratifies the minds and hearts of Saint Anselm's audience.

NOTES

All citations of the *Proslogion* are to the reprinted edition by M. J. Charlesworth (Notre Dame: University of Notre Dame Press, 1979).

1. R. W. Southern, *Saint Anselm and His Biographer* (Cambridge: Cambridge University Press, 1963), 57.

2. Arthur C. McGill, "Recent Discussions of Anselm's Argument," in *The Many-Faced Argument*, ed. John Hick and Arthur C. McGill (New York: The Macmillan Co., 1967), 104.

3. Paul Evdokimov, *Spicilegium Beccense*, 234, cited in McGill, n. 230, 104.

4. Anthony Nemetz, "Ontological Argument," *New Catholic Encyclopedia*, 10 (New York: McGraw-Hill Book Co., 1967), 701.

5. Rene Wellek, *A History of Modern Criticism: 1750-1950*, (New Haven: Yale University Press, 1986), 76:296.

6. M. H. Abrams, "What's the Use of Theorizing about the Arts?" in *In Search of Literary Theory*, ed. Morton W. Bloomfield (Ithaca, N.Y.: Cornell University Press, 1972), 37.

7. Southern, 46.

8. Anselm Stolz, "Anselm's Theology in the *Proslogion*," in *The Many-Faced Argument*, 183-206.

9. Southern, 51.

10. G. R. Evans, *Anselm and Talking About God* (Oxford: Clarendon Press, 1978), 41.

SAINT ANSELM AND THE FILIOQUE

George C. Berthold

It is through a providential accident that we have as clear and reasoned a treatise as we do on the procession of the Holy Spirit from both Father and Son from the pen of Anselm of Canterbury. His presence at the council of Bari in southeast Italy, occasioned by matters of a completely different nature, brought him into direct contact with the major theological question which had exploded in the major split of eastern and western churches in 1054.

Anselm, it has been said,[1] had much more success in the realm of ideas than in that of public life and diocesan administration. His confrontations with two successive kings of England, William Rufus and Henry, showed him to be an intrepid defender of the rights of the church but they were exasperating encounters for the scholarly abbot now thrust into the maelstrom of court intrigues. Jousting with these two fearsome and ambitious sons of William the Conqueror was a far cry from the scholarly peace of monastic contemplation and Anselm yearned to be rid of his burden.[2]

He saw a chance of unburdening himself of episcopal office on his first trip to Rome in bringing the state of the English church to the attention of Pope Urban II. It was this trip that would bring Anselm into the orbit of the Greco-Latin dispute. Urban would not accept his resignation but rather praised him "almost as our equal, for he is the apostolic patriarch of that other world."[3] He promised his support in his struggle with the king. For Anselm, however, support did not spell relief; resignation would have been much closer to his mind, and so he continued his entreaties.[4] But the pope was not inclined to lose for the service of the church a man of such manifest gifts and international reputation. He invited him to the council he had called at Bari (October 1098) to effect a reconciliation with the Greek Christians who were of course very numerous in Norman Italy. The Crusades had exacerbated the frictions between Greeks and Latins. As a crossroads of both cultures southern Italy seemed a fertile place for a rapprochement. Anselm's providential presence in Italy at this time, due to his defense of the church's freedom, makes him available for this important ecumenical encounter.

At Bari and with great frankness the major theological questions dividing the churches of east and west since the solemn mutual excommunications forty-four years before were brought up.[5] One question, however, proved to be of great doctrinal moment, that of the role of the Son in the procession of the Holy Spirit from the Father, and the addition of the term *filioque* to the western version of the universal creed. This had been of concern for some centuries preceding the actual break but it became a primary cause of the schism between the churches at the climactic moment in July 1054 at Constantinople.

And so in Bari, Anselm, archbishop of that far-off see in Canterbury, was asked by Pope Urban to present the western arguments in favor of the *filioque* and the addition of this word to the creed. This he did so successfully that the Greek bishops present declared their assent to the acceptability of the western formula and Anselm's ecumenical reputation was greatly enhanced. The success of this discourse led to the publication in 1102 of a reworked treatment of it in the *De Processione Spiritus Sancti*. It is this work that we propose to analyze.[6]

At the outset of his treatise Anselm explains his method and purpose. The Greeks do not accept the western explanation of the origin of the Holy Spirit, that he proceeds eternally from the Father *and the Son (filioque)*, and object to the term's inclusion in the creed. Since they do accept the gospels and church councils as authoritative Anselm wants to proceed on the basis of these to persuade them rationally (*rationabiliter*) "from that which they confess without question to that which they do not accept."[7] The premises, then, are divinely guaranteed truths of Holy Scripture. By reason (*rationabiliter*) Anselm will draw out what he regards as necessary deductions from the inspired premises which will necessitate the inevitable truth of the *filioque*.

It is essential to understand the Christian doctrine of the Trinity as stating that God is one in nature but three in persons. Because of the divine unity whatever is said about the one God is said about Father, Son, and Holy Spirit. However the Father, the Son, and the Holy Spirit are distinct and real persons who may not be called by each other's personal names since these names are based on the *opposition of relation* among them.[8] That God is eternal, immortal, creator, etc. does not imply a relation and thus can be applied to all three.

A preliminary distinction which does not apply to all three is that between a) God from whom God exists and b) God from God. In accordance with the understanding of opposition of relation Anselm will argue that the Father is *a* but not *b*, the Son is *a* and *b*, the Holy Spirit is *b* but not *a*. Clearly for both east and west, the Father is the source of the Trinity; he is God from whom God exists. There is no dispute over that point.

As to the Son, he exists from the Father's essence, as does the Holy Spirit. In order not to compromise their divinity or the divine unity or the principle that God exists from God, Anselm argues that either the Son exists from the Holy Spirit or the Holy Spirit from the Son. One of these assertions must be true and the other false.

Now it is not possible for the Son to exist from the Holy Spirit since then the Holy Spirit would be the father of the Son if begotten from him or the Son would be spirit of the Holy Spirit if he proceeds from him. Since neither of these propositions is acceptable, the Son cannot be from the Holy Spirit but rather the Holy Spirit must be from the Son.

If you look at the Holy Spirit, it is clear that he can have his existence from another or from no one. If the latter is the case, then he must exist as the Father exists. If this is true then either there are two Gods or the Father is the Holy Spirit. Of course since both of these are absurd then he does not have his existence from no one (as the Father) but rather exists from another. Certainly this must be the Father (at least). At the discussion in Bari this was brought up as a difficulty. The bishop of Bari, while agreeing that the Holy Spirit differs from the Father by proceeding from him, denied that he has his existence from the Father. But, Anselm explains, to proceed means either to be sent or given by the Father or to exist from him. If the former then the Holy Spirit proceeds as much from the Son as from the Father [i.e., economically]. But the

Holy Spirit is always different from the Father even before creation. He proceeds eternally. Thus he must have his existence from the Father. As existing from the Father he is God from God, thus he is from the Son. Even though the creed does not say that he is God from God the Greeks believe it as we do.

Now he does not have his existence from God as Father but as God. Anselm reasons in this way: "... if the Holy Spirit exists from the Father because he exists from God who is the Father, then it cannot be denied that he also exists from the Son since he exists from God who is the Son."[9]

Let us look at the scriptural passages addressed by Anselm. In John 17:3 ("Eternal life is this: to know you, the only true God, and him whom you have sent, Jesus Christ"), the one true God can mean either Father and Son, or Father alone or Son alone. But if we name Father alone or Son alone we do not mean one true God then neither person is perfect God. So except for the opposition of relation the one true God is the same by both names. Had the evangelist added, "and the Holy Spirit proceeds from this one true God," he would clearly have included the Son since the Son is included in the term one true God.

Consider John 14:26, "the Paraclete, the Holy Spirit whom the Father will send *in my name* will instruct you in everything." Anselm sees this as meaning that the one whom the Father will send the Son will also send. Likewise in 15:26, "when the Paraclete comes, the Spirit of truth who comes from the Father and whom I myself will send from the Father." This text makes clear that Son and Father will both send the Holy Spirit. There is only one sending; both send together. He is not more the Spirit of one than the other.

But doesn't the Holy Spirit send the Son as prophesied in Isaiah 48:16? "Now the Lord God has sent me and his Spirit." Yes, this is true but it refers to the humanity of Christ, to the incarnate mission of the Son. It pertains to the "economy" of salvation.[10]

John 20:22: After the resurrection we are told that Jesus breathed on his disciples and said, "Receive the Holy Spirit." It is not that his breath was the Holy Spirit but rather it symbolized the third person of the Trinity. "This he did so that we might understand that the Holy Spirit proceeds from him."[11] It is as if he had said, just as my breath proceeds from me the Holy Spirit proceeds from my person. This striking analogy comparing the conferral of the Holy Spirit on the apostles by Christ with the eternal procession of the Holy Spirit from the Son in the bosom of the Holy Trinity is precisely the image and even the words used seven centuries before by St. Cyril of Alexandria, one of the great eastern doctors, in his commentary on John.[12] I do not know if Anselm had any access to this work but the doctrine and even the language are strikingly close. The Greeks would certainly listen to St. Cyril.

In Psalm 33:6: "By the word of the Lord the heavens were made; by the breath [spirit] of his mouth all their host." This breath or spirit is the Holy Spirit come from the divine essence, so as Christ's spirit he comes from the essence of the Son.[13]

John 16:13: "[The Holy Spirit] will not speak on his own but will speak only what he hears...he will have received from me what he will announce to you" (14). Here Christ shows clearly that it is from him as well as from the Father that the Holy Spirit receives his knowledge or essence (since these two are not different.) Therefore the Holy Spirit proceeds also from the Son.[14]

Matthew 11:27: "No one knows the Son except the Father, and no one knows the Father but the Son — and anyone to whom the Son wishes to reveal him." Either the Holy Spirit doesn't know the Father and the Son or the Son reveals to the Holy Spirit knowledge of the Father and of himself. "This knowledge is nothing other than the essence of the same Holy Spirit."[15] If you do not accept the *filioque* you have two alternatives: 1) the Holy Spirit does not know the Father and the Son unless the Son reveals this knowledge; or 2) since the Father and the Son are one with the Holy Spirit in knowing one another, the Holy Spirit must share in the same knowledge. If the first alternative, then the Holy Spirit has his knowledge = existence from the Son. If the second alternative, then the Father and the Son know themselves through the divine essence, which is also the Holy Spirit's. So when the Greeks say that the Holy Spirit proceeds from the Father and, "I and Father are one" (Jn 10:30) it must be that "because of the essential identity of Father and Son the Holy Spirit without a doubt proceeds also from the Son."[16]

To the objection raised by the Greeks that we are allowed to speak of the Holy Spirit's procession only *through* the Son not *from* him, Anselm points to Romans 11:36: "all things are from him, through him, and in him." But this passage, he admits, refers only to created things. Rather, Anselm wants to examine what procession through the Son means. There is no other way for the Greeks to show that the Holy Spirit proceeds from the Father *through* the

Son than to affirm that he proceeds also *from* the Son. For the Holy Spirit proceeds from the Father's deity. But Father and Son have the same deity . . . it is impossible to understand how the Holy Spirit proceeds from the deity of the Father *through* the deity of the Son but not *from* the deity of the Son, since it is absurd to say that the Holy Spirit proceeds from the Father's paternity or the Son's sonship.

The Greeks continue: since the Father creates through his Word, why not say that the Holy Spirit proceeds through the Word since the essence is the same? Anselm responds by pointing to John 5:19: "whatever the Father does the Son does likewise." Since the Holy Spirit proceeds from the Father *through* the Son he also proceeds *from* the Son just as what was created through the Word was also created by the Word.[17] The celebrated example of the spring, river and lake is brought in. They are distinct even though they contain the same waters.

> Therefore just as the lake does not come about from the fact that the spring and river are different from each other but from the water which they have in common, so the Holy Spirit does not exist from the fact that the Father and Son are different from each other but from the divine essence in which they are one. So if the Father is no more than the Son what the Holy Spririt proceeds from, then it cannot be understood why he exists more from the Father than the Son.[18]

What has dialectics allowed Anselm to do in this treatise? How does he understand *rationabiliter*? To quote Anselm:

> . . . through those things which are said we are taught to understand in a similar way those things which lie hid in parallel statements, especially when we see that these things which are left unsaid clearly follow by rational necessity (*rationabili necessitate*) from those things which are said, and that there is no reason to the contrary.[19]

Thus we are to read the Holy Spirit in John 17:3; 5:26; 14:10-11; 14:9.

Where in Scripture do we read *his verbis* that one God exists in three persons, or that God is a trinity, or that God is from God? Neither do we see the words *person* and *trinity* in the creed. But since these things clearly follow from what is stated, we believe them. The *filoque* is "new" only in the sense that these are new, not as added to Holy Writ but as deduced from it. Thus Anselm can conclude: "Therefore we ought to accept with certainty not only the facts we read in Holy Scripture but also whatever follows from them by rational necessity — provided there is no reason against this."[20]

The vexing problem of the *filioque* is with us still as a contemporary ecumenical problem. Honesty compels us to take seriously the reflections of this giant of early medieval theology in the west and his penetrating analyses of this greatest mystery of the Christian faith. At the beginning of the work he tells us he has written this treatise on the Holy Spirit relying on the Spirit himself. He calls on the Holy Spirit to lead opponents *rationabiliter* to accept what he saw was the reasonable deduction from scriptural truth. The dialectical method in which he was engaged was no dry exercise in human reasoning but rather it was demanded by God's addressing his word to us reasonable human beings, challenging us to respond in a way characteristic of our nature. We believe in order to understand.

NOTES

1. R. W. Southern, *St. Anselm and his Biographer* (Cambridge University Press, 1963), 179-180.

2. Eadmer, *Historia Novorum in Anglia* (hereafter cited as *HN*), 2 ed. Martin Rule (Kraus Reprint, 1965), 99.

3. Eadmer, *Vita Sancti Anselmi* (hereafter cited as *VA*), ed. R.W. Southern, 2, 29 (Oxford: Clarendon, 1962), 105.

4. *HN*, 99-103; *VA* 2, 34.

5. *HN*, 105-106. As the conciliar proceedings have not otherwise survived we are fortunate in having this eyewitness account by Eadmer: *Inter haec ego patri per omnia praesens aderam . . . .* (107).

6. In his *Letters on the Sacraments*, Anselm turns to other matters of Greek concern, e.g., to the western use of unfermented bread in the eucharist, and to marriage questions. After the present volume had been given to the printers I came across the study of Paul Gilbert, "La Confession de Foi dans le *De Processione Spiritus Sancti* de Saint Anselme," in Maternus Hoegen, (ed.), *L'Attualita Filosofica di Anselmo D'Aosta* (Rome, 1990), 229-262.

7. Anselm, *De Processione Spiritus Sancti, Opera Omnia* vol. 2, 177. References are to the edition of F. Schmitt (Edinburgh: Thomas Nelson and Sons, 1946).

8. "Nam quoniam filius existit de deo nascendo et spiritus sanctus procedendo, ipsa diversitate nativitatis et processionis referuntur ad invicem, ut diversi et alii ab invicem; et quando substantia habet esse de substantia, duae fiunt ibi relationes insociabiles, si secundum illa nomina ponantur substantiae," *ibid*, 179; "Supradicta vero relationis oppositiò, quae ex hoc nascitur, quia supradictis duobus modis Deus est de Deo, prohibet patrem, et filium, et spiritum sanctum de invicem dici, et propria singulorum aliis attribui," *ibid.*, 180. Cf. Augustine, Ep. 238,2,14: "Fides

autem nostra est Patrem et Filium et Spiritum Sanctum unum Deum credere et confiteri; nec autem eum, qui Filius est, Patrem dicere, nec eum qui Pater est, Filium, nec eum qui Spiritus Patris et Filii est, aut Patrem aut Filium nuncupare. His enim appellationibus hoc significatur, quo ad se invicem referuntur, non ipsa substantia, qua unum sunt" (PL 33, 1043). Numerous instances of this position can be found in the Greek Fathers, e.g. Basil, *Adv. Eun.* 2, 28; Gregory of Nazianzus, Or. 25, 16; 29 (3rd Theol.), 16; 31 (5th Theol.), 8; Cyril of Alexandria, *Thesaurus*, 11; *Dialogues on the Holy and Consubstantial Trinity*, 4.

The term "opposition" will become celebrated and official in the *Decretum pro Iacobitis* of the Council of Florence: Denz.-Schönmetzer (ed. 36) 1330. Anselm may have gotten this from Boethius: Quocirca, si Patre ac Filius ad aliquid dicuntur, nihilque aliud . . . differunt nisi sola relatione, relatio vero non predicatur ad id de quo praedicatur quasi ipsa sit et secundum rem de qua dicitur, sed, si dici potest, quo quidem modo id quod vix intelligi potuit, interpretatum est personarum (*De Trinitate* 5, PL 64, 1254 BC).

9. *De Processione Spiritus Sancti*, 2, 190.
10. ". . . hoc secundum hominem quem gerebat intelligendum est, qui patris et spiritus sancti una voluntate et dispositione mundum redempturus in mundo apparuit," 4, 192.
11. 5, 194.
12. Jo. 9, 810, PG 74, 257CD. cf. G. C. Berthold, "Cyril of Alexandria and the *Filioque*," *Studia Patristica* 19 (Leuven: Peeters, 1989), 143-147.
13. *De Processione*, 5, 195.
14. 6, 197.
15. 7, 198.
16. 199.
17. 9, 203.
18. 205; cf. 209. Anselm had used this image (the Nile) in his *Epistola de Incarnatione Verbi*, 13.
19. 11, 208.
20. 11, 209.

JOSEF FUCHS AND THE QUESTION OF A DISTINCTIVELY CHRISTIAN MORALITY

Kevin A. McMahon

The debate over whether Christianity has a truly unique contribution to make to our understanding of what human beings ought and ought not to do has heated up in recent years, especially with the publication by the American Catholic bishops of their pastoral letters on the issues of peace and economic justice. Although the bishops were motivated primarily by their duty to inform the consciences of American Catholics, they also expressed the hope that their words might help in the formation of a national "moral vision."[1] Just how much help could, or should, one expect from the American bishops, or from the church as a whole for what matter? Does Christianity have access to moral truths that are unavailable to non-Christians? The German theologian, Josef Fuchs, has long been at the forefront of this debate. What can be called his signature article on the question entitled, "Is There a Distinctively Christian Morality?" was published in 1970, but really he has grappled with the issue under one form or another in much of his work for the past thirty years.

Fuchs has taken as his point of departure the idea, foundational in the Catholic moral tradition, that morality is a matter of living one's life in accordance with reason, human reason. The moral act is that which promotes one's humanity, one's dignity as a person. Morality, then, concerns the *humanum*, the human, so that to speak of Christian morality is to speak of the *humanum Christianum*, the Christian-human; or as Fuchs puts it, "Christian morality is the morality of men and women who believe in Christ."[2] The Christian, inasmuch as he or she is a human person, shares a common moral life with all other men and women. What the Christian's faith adds is a new intentionality, new attitudes, new virtues like faith, hope and charity, new reasons why one does what he or she does. Christian intentionality permeates the believer's entire life, making that life a following after Christ. But *what* the believer does, the content of his or her behavior, at least as it concerns other men and women, is not new. Believer and unbeliever have the same moral task: to discover and put into practice whatever it is that fosters the human. To the question, "Is there a distinctively Christian morality," Fuchs thus has an unwavering answer: "No." There is not a distinctively Christian morality, not a different morality, not a higher morality for Christians than for non-Christians. There is only one morality, the morality of human beings, Christian and non-Christian. And it is as human beings that all of us must join in a combined effort to determine what the authentically human life demands.

Now it must be remembered that Fuchs is not denying that the Christian, by virtue of his or her faith, has privileged knowledge of the nature and activity of God the Father who has sent his Son to give the Spirit. Nor is he denying that the activity of following after Christ gives rise to specific patterns of life within the church, such as Christian virginity, and to specific obligations, such as loving God and submitting one's will to the Father, and even to specific obligations that only the church has determined, such as worshiping God with the ecclesial community on the Sabbath. His point is that the very things we expect of the moral Christian as moral —truthfulness, justice, fidelity, honesty, etc.—are to be expected of any person who is called moral. And the personal actions we consider right or wrong for Christians are no less right or wrong for everyone else as well. Christians do not have a separate moral code. "It follows from this," Fuchs writes,

> that Christians and non-Christians face the same moral questions, and that both must seek their solution in genuinely human reflection and according to the same norms; e.g., whether adultery and premarital intercourse are morally right or can be so, whether the wealthy nations of the world must help the poor nations and to what extent, whether birth control is justified and should be provided, and what types of birth control are worthy of the dignity of the human person. Such questions are questions for all of humanity;

if, therefore, our church and other human communities do not always reach the same conclusions, this is not because there exists a different morality for Christians and non-Christians.[3]

To the question "What ought I to do," there is the same answer for both believer and unbeliever: "foster the human." But precisely what it means in the concrete to foster the human, what the conduct of the person ought to be, what the norms of human morality are, these are questions that cannot be answered so easily. For morality, Fuchs states, is a matter of realizing one's own individual humanity, not humanity in the abstract. And each of us is individuated, so to speak, by the particular circumstances in which we find ourselves. Some of these circumstances are common to all men and women. We were all created as part of a divine plan of salvation, and we all live in a world conditioned by human sin. Some of these circumstances, however, are quite specific: each of us lives in a particular culture and a particular time period; we live in a particular society, even a particular community within that society. Furthermore, Fuchs notes that to realize or "unfold" one's humanity means to develop, through one's activity, the truly human aspects of one's being. But these aspects are known only through reflection on experience—individual experience, of course, but more importantly, communal experience. It is through shared, social reflection that you will most consistently arrive at genuinely human values, and also come to know the kind of acts that will promote these values, and the kind of acts that will harm them. There are a number of human aspects that presumably every community will value, such as personhood itself, and our inner orientation to other persons. But there are other, perhaps less fundamental, aspects, such as the social equality of men and women, that not every community will value, or will come to value over time. Nor can it be expected that every society will agree about what pattern of behavior best promotes a set of values, say, what pattern of marriage best fosters the value of offspring, of man and woman in their social roles, etc. Although theoretically there may be an ideal pattern of marriage, what Fuchs might call a "most human" pattern of marriage, still insofar as the pattern that a community has adopted is in fact human and does promote human values, even if incompletely, then it must be regarded as a morally correct form of behavior, and one should be very wary of the suggestion that it be replaced by some other pattern, developed in some other culture, that more closely approximates the ideal. Thus, European monogamy and African polygamy are properly regarded as two equally correct (that is, morally correct) forms of marriage. In this way Fuchs can defend the idea of a moral pluralism.[4]

From his analysis Fuchs concludes that there can be no such thing as a priori, universal moral norms, rules that one can be certain ought to be arrived at and followed by all people, at all times, in every culture, and under every set of circumstances. What he accepts are absolute, meaning objective, norms, non-arbitrary norms that reflect the values of a community and its understanding of how best to promote them. Such norms can, of course, change as the thinking of the community changes; and beyond this, they must be applied by each individual to his or her own moral situation. An example he gives is the moral precept "Do not kill" which, as he says, is better stated "Do not murder," meaning that one should never take a human life unjustly or wrongfully. But now the question is, under what circumstances is taking a human life a wrongful act? Is it always wrong to take a human life for any reason? Is war always wrong? Is capital punishment always wrong? Is suicide always wrong, even if it is necessary to protect a state secret?[5] What is of universal validity in the precept "Do not murder" is its claim about the value of human life. But just pointing to this value is not going to provide answers to every moral question, especially when, in a particular situation, a number of human values are in conflict with each other. In the end, it is the individual who must determine for himself, using what Fuchs refers to as his "evaluating reason," what act he ought to perform in order to realize best the aspects or values of his and others' humanity. Only then can the act be said to be fully objective, conforming to his concrete reality as a person.[6]

It is because of the requirement to maximize human values in the situation, Fuchs writes, that some actions proscribed by moral norms in the abstract may in the concrete be the morally right things to do. Usually it would be because, as we just noted, values come into conflict with each other. But these conflicts are often the consequence of sin in the world, as when there is a choice between taking one's own life or betraying one's country. And the presence of sin reveals itself in still another way: in the inability of the person to control his or her actions fully. Although in the beginning God made man an integral whole, with our desires and emotions united in concert with our reason and will, this order was disrupted by original sin. We exist now as persons in a fallen world, fallen in our very selves. And this inner fallenness, which Fuchs refers to as concupiscence, is thus part of our circumstances, part of the reality to which our moral decisions must conform. If it happens that the protection of a particular human value (a value of human well-being, as opposed to a value of the person as such, e.g., personhood, which must always be protected) would demand too much of the person, then it cannot be a moral requirement that the person protect it. Even if we take into consideration the grace won for us by Christ, still that grace will not be fully effective until the time of eschatological glory. Until then, Fuchs warns, we must be careful not to make "life an unbearable burden."[7] The particular example he uses is that of artificial contraception. Granted, he writes, that contraceptive intercourse always involves an "evil for man," it is nonetheless a non-moral evil, a physical or pre-moral evil. It could be regarded as a moral evil only if the individual realized this disvalue without any justification, without at the same time realizing an equivalent or greater value to counterbalance it. But if in fact there are other values, such as the value of marital intimacy, and if the periodic abstinence required by other forms of birth control involves too great a burden for the person, then the judgment to use artificial contraception is the morally right decision, and their use is morally correct. One might "regret" that the situation involves the realization of a disvalue, but there is no need to "repent" in any sense, for the act is morally good.[8] Fuchs explains,

> This is not a matter of detracting from an ideal solution because of difficulties encountered, but of seeking, finding, and living in radical uprightness that which is really right in the context of concrete human reality *with* its limitations. In other words, that which is radically right is not to be sought in an abstract ideal nor in a goal that seems obligatory but turns out to be unattainable, but in the best possible development of reality as it is encountered.[9]

Even in so brief a review as this, one cannot help but see and admire in Fuchs' work its qualities of unity, consistency, and perhaps most importantly, its abiding regard for the human moral agent as one entrusted with the responsibility of molding his own existence. Certainly, too, Fuchs is right when he states that Christians are not in possession of a separate, sectarian moral standard that is binding on Christians alone. Yet his exclusion at the outset of even the possibility of the content of morality being shaped by our relation to God in Christ, which the Christian knows of in faith, is a serious flaw. For in faith the Christian knows that it has been the intention of our Creator from the very beginning that every member of our race participate, whether implicitly or explicitly, in the transformation that the Greek Fathers called our "divinization"; that in the grace of Christ, having put off the old man (Rom. 6:11) we might grow into the complete man, Christ come to fullness (Eph. 4:13-15). The unity for which we are destined is a unity in Christ, and the human unity which we possess, broken though it is, had its origin in Christ, in whom all things were made (Col. 1:15-18). All things were made in Jesus Christ, the passage states, the God-man; thus St. Paul implies that humanity is the locus, through Christ, in which the Father who has made all things is now drawing all things back to himself. It is indeed true that the moral act perfects us. But we in our existential and essential reality bear the mark of this relation to Christ. How can it be expected that the moral act in its content be untouched by our primordial conformity to Christ?

It is of particular significance that of all the existential conditions that affect our being as humans, the condition that, according to Fuchs, has the least influence on us is our existential relation to God in Christ. We see this, for example, in his view of our situation in human history. Our fallenness continues to have a considerably greater effect on us than does our redemption in Christ. Our moral weakness is more real here and now than is the saving grace whose true effectiveness lies in the eschaton. Furthermore, in grappling with the conflicts of morality, it is not on the Lord of history—who is at work drawing us to our final end through and in every human good—that Fuchs advises concentration, but on the object of minimizing the occurrence of human disvalues, even if that involves the direct violation of some human good.

It is not that Fuchs is unaware of such passages as the one we cited from the first chapter of Colossians. In fact he refers to that passage, and others like it, several times in his earlier work. But he interprets them as providing a warrant for relying solely upon reason to understand our being and direct our actions. In his Latin textbook on moral theology, entitled *Theologia moralis generalis* and published in 1963, Fuchs stated,

> as in Christ human nature was intended as a vessel of the Word, so our nature seems to be meant to be a receptacle of the supernatural life: the consequence on the moral level being that the natural order, moral in itself, is directed toward the supernatural; more, it is part of it, since grace is the final perfection of man as created in Christ.[10]

The natural order might be part of the supernatural order, but it is evident in what Fuchs says elsewhere that our having been created in Christ makes no more intrinsic difference to our nature than does frosting to a cake. For example, in his book called *Natural Law*, Fuchs asks,

> But is nature, as it is *de facto* created, not in reality *nature* in the sense of the *substratum* of the supernatural? And has not this nature truly in itself a *proper* meaning and a *proper* order, although this meaning and this order are not defined in all their details?[11]

And a bit later on he writes that Jesus' significance for the Christian moral life lies "in his absolute surrender to the Father and consequently in his faithfulness to what is called nature . . . . In the God-man the Father has given us the prototype of the Christian . . . . He is our prototype because he is truly man and realizes in himself the essence of man's natural being, no more and no less than we do."[12]

It is because he regards Christ as prototypical inasmuch as he is, so to speak, the perfect natural man, that Fuchs can maintain that the faith adds nothing to the substance of the moral life. From this several other positions follow, such as the claim that there can be no normative moral teaching in the Scriptures, and the denial that the episcopal magisterium can have any unique authority to teach on moral questions.[13] Moral content is determined, by definition, through human reflection on human experience and through the individual's evaluation of the concrete situation. To say, however, that Christian faith does shape one's understanding of the moral right and wrong is not to assign Christians a peculiar ethic all their own. It is to state that the one human morality by which all individuals are perfected is most fully understood only in the light of Christian faith. What today has become the particularly neuralgic area of sexual morality offers the clearest example of this. The

Catholic Church's teachings on issues ranging from artificial contraception to the indissolubility of marriage increasingly strike the modern mind as entirely untenable. Yet theologically they flow with complete consistency from the insight, asserted in faith, that marriage is the fullest expression of how we as male and female image God in the temporal order, and that human marriage exists as an image of the *mysterion* to which St. Paul refers (Eph. 5:32), the mystery of Christ's primordial union with his creation, and the even deeper unity of Christ with his church effected in the Incarnation.

Fuchs often speaks of us in his work as if we had been merely inserted by God into the salvific order.[14] And the human dimension that demonstrates this idea of "insertion" most clearly in his writings is the sexual. Speaking of marriage in the book *Natural Law* he states,

> It cannot be denied that the analysis of the physical and spiritual being of man and woman yields a fundamental knowledge of the sexual life and of the state of marriage which retains its validity in any and every situation of the history of salvation and in any supernatural mode of realization.[15]

In other words, Fuchs is claiming that we are able, through a rational analysis of human sexuality, including of course analyses based on our human experiences, to unveil the fundamental structure of this human dimension, a structure that remains unchanged no matter what the condition in which human beings exist, created in Christ or not created in Christ, ordered to the beatific vision or ordered to a natural end, in a state of human integrity or in a state of fallen nature. The implication is that the deepest part of our sexuality, and so the proper modes of living out our sexuality, remain unshaped by God's salvific intent. As it is, we have been created in the order of salvation, and Fuchs writes that we participate in this order through the virtues of faith and love.[16] So he observes that the exercise of these virtues pertains to our salvation. Our sexual patterns, as such, do not. The difference between polygamy and monogamy, he remarks, is "surely not an unimportant cultural and ethical question, but not in itself determinative of salvation." And he continues,

> the materiality of culturally and ethically right mastery of the concrete reality of life — education, technology, sexuality, etc. — are not

directly concerned with salvation, or union with God; only faith and love, *together with the effort* to incarnate this materiality in the "true" way in the reality of life are thus concerned.... The material mode of this Incarnation can represent only a *secundarium*.[17]

The fact that Fuchs capitalizes the word "Incarnation" immediately suggests to the reader that an analogy is being drawn between the relation of Christ's divine to his human nature, and the relation of faith and love to the content of morality. If so, then Fuchs is providing a unique illumination of what we have been criticizing in his work. For the description of Christ's human nature as a material *secundarium* to the divine is precisely the kind of thinking that underlies Fuchs' claim that there would be no essential difference between the human being as he actually exists, created within the order of salvation, and some hypothetical human being who had been created apart from such an order. It is also behind the conclusion that the pattern of human action remains unchanged whether or not there is an existential ordination to the divine; in other words, that faith and love transform a human act into something that directs one to the saving God, but on the level of intentionality alone, without changing the content of the act.

Yet the Incarnation was not a matter of the divine Word joining himself to an already constituted human being. And if the Word, in the power of the *Spiritus Creator*, was able to receive the flesh of his body from Mary's womb, if she was able to serve as the new Eve, it is only because the first Eve was in her very nature and being, together with the first man, created to be the mother of a humanity which could provide the womb for the birth of God. The Word could become joined with the human in Jesus only because the human in the beginning had been created in Christ. We bear the mark of this creation in our human nature. Our rationality is a kind of material rationality that is driven by the desire to be completed by what we know. Our sexuality and our sexual lives are expressive of an inner orientation to some fundamental union outside ourselves. It is grace, faith and love, that perfects these activities, consciously and existentially directing them to God himself. But they are already the kind of activities whose structure is a sort of anticipation of the reception of grace. That is why the pattern of marriage, for example, is not something to be determined entirely by individuals in view of their own self-concepts (to use an expression of Fuchs), or through reflection on their experiences, or in light of the aspects of the human that they value and wish to promote. Certainly it is true that polygamous tribesmen, as polygamous, no less than monogamous grocers, have been redeemed. But it is only the monogamous union, in its one flesh joining of man and woman, that adequately images the one flesh union of Christ with humanity, and which allows for a direct participation of the marital love in the singular, entire, and irrevocable gift of self to God which is our human perfection — a self-giving that is focused and completed by grace, but that is present and active in our nature.

If there were ever a time in which moral theology was in need of renewal, it is our own. Josef Fuchs has done much to show that such a renewal can benefit greatly from the human sciences, and to remind us that any renewal must recognize that morality is finally a universally human affair. But we must bear in mind, too, that all the richness moral theology can hope to possess will come to it only when it draws its life from meditation upon the revelation of the mystery of our being in Christ. It is only as Christocentric that moral theology can thrive as theology, and only as Christocentric that it can offer the full illumination of our selves, unavailable from any other source, that is sought by all persons in their common quest for the end of human completion.

NOTES

1. National Conference of Catholic Bishops, *Economic Justice for All: Catholic Social Teaching and the U.S. Economy*, no. 27; quoted by John Langan, S.J., "Notes on Moral Theology: The Christian Difference in Ethics," *Theological Studies* 49 (1988): 131-32.
2. Josef Fuchs, S.J., "Is there a Distinctively Christian Morality?" in *Personal Responsibility and Christian Morality*, trans. William Cleves et al. (Washington: Georgetown University Press, 1983; Dublin: Gill and Macmillan, 1983), 54. This essay was first delivered as a lecture in Zurich in 1968, and was published under the title "Gibt es eine spezifisch christliche Moral?" *Stimmen der Zeit* 95 (1970): 99-112.
3. *Ibid.*, 60.
4. Josef Fuchs, S.J., "The Absoluteness of Moral Terms," *Gregorianum* 52 (1971): 423.
5. *Ibid.*, 450. See also "Christian Faith and the Disposing of Human Life," *Theological Studies* 46 (1985): 678.
6. Fuchs, "Absoluteness," 448-51.
7. Josef Fuchs, S.J., "The 'Sin of the World' and Normative Morality," *Gregorianum* 61 (1980): 52.
8. *Ibid.*, 66-7.
9. *Ibid.*, 71.

10. Quoted in Josef Fuchs, S.J., *Natural Law, A Theological Investigation*, trans. Helmut Reckter, S.J., and John A. Dowling (New York: Sheed and Ward, 1965), n. 20:75. This work was first published as *Lex Naturae: Zur Theologie des Naturrechts* (Dusseldorf: Patmos Verlag, 1956).
11. Fuchs, *Natural Law*, n. 22: 55.
12. *Ibid.*, 75.
13. Fuchs, "Absoluteness"; 418-28; "Is there a Distinctively Christian Morality?" n. 1: 67; "Sittliche Wahrheit—zwischen Objektivismus und Subjektivismus," *Gregorianum* 63 (1982): 633ff.
14. Fuchs, *Natural Law*, n. 6: 67; 43. "Morale théologique et morale de situation," *Nouvelle Révue Théologique* (1954): 1076; "Esiste una morale non-cristiana?" *Rassegna di Teologia* 14 (1973): "Is there a normative Non-Christian Morality?" in *Personal Responsibility and Christian Morality*, n. 5: 80.
15. Fuchs, *Natural Law*, n. 23: 56.
16. Fuchs, "Absoluteness;" 423.
17. *Ibid.* It must be pointed out that in a later collection of Fuchs' writings, the word "Incarnation" in this passage is not capitalized. See "The Absoluteness of Behavioral Moral Norms," in *Personal Responsibility and Christian Morality*, 122. The authors note on p. 230 of their collection that they have "slightly changed" the content of this and a second article in the book, although they do not say whether these changes were authorized by Fuchs himself.

FROM "SOCIAL JUSTICE" TO "READING THE SIGNS OF THE TIMES": THE HERMENEUTICAL CRISIS OF CATHOLIC SOCIAL TEACHING

Stephen F. Torraco

One night, when I was just a lad, I was watching a television variety show; and by that fascinating faculty called memory, I can still "hear" and "see" a particular number that featured a refrain and intervening clips of comical scenes. The lyrics of the refrain were: "It's a sign of the times." Following the refrain each time was a scene depicting an event or situation characteristic of modern society. The scenes dealt with family life, marriage, work, religion, politics, and other themes. The refrain obviously meant that each of these scenes was an accurate sample of modern life that could be easily recognized, appreciated, and laughed at by the audience.

In the course of the performance there was not the slightest hint of what today is called a "value judgment." There was no suggestion that these "signs of the times" were either good or bad, that they were pointing to better or worse times, or even that they were indications of the presence of the Kingdom of God in our midst. Rather, and to quote the only words of Walter Cronkite that I will ever remember, the message simply was, "And that's the way it is."

Little did I realize while watching that show that at approximately the same point in time Pope John XXIII, in his formal convocation to the Second Vatican Council, introduced the notion of discerning the "signs of the times" to Catholic social thought.

As we make our own the recommendation of Jesus that we learn how to discern the 'signs of the times' (Mt. 16:3), we seem to see amid so much darkness not a few indications that give hope for the future of the Church and the human race.[1]

Less than two years later, Pope John employed the notion in a sustained and thematic way in *Pacem in Terris*. At the conclusion of each of the four parts of that encyclical Pope John enumerated specific "signs of the times" as manifestations of the gospel at work in the movement of history. For example: socialization, the improvement of the condition of the working classes, the entry of women into public life, the increasing concern in the world for human dignity and human rights, the emancipation of colonized peoples, and so on.[2] Clearly, Pope John's message was not simply "And that's the way it is."

Twenty-five years have passed since the official publication of *Pacem in Terris* and, in the spirit of both Cardinal Ratzinger's claim that the social doctrine of the church is by no means closed and his invitation to scholars to continue to work in this area,[3] I am still wondering what Pope John thought he was saying; and I am not the only one. In the fifteenth anniversary edition of his *A Theology of Liberation*, Gustavo Gutierrez himself notes that the notion of reading the "signs of the times" is still ambiguous, even though Gutierrez does not allow this ambiguity to deter him from re-publishing his book which presents his liberation theology as a reading of the signs of the times.[4]

Not only is it ironic that the meaning of "reading the signs of the times" is ambiguous; this proposed principle for understanding social and political things seems to have obscured rather than illumined Catholic social teaching in our time. Pluralism would be too kind a word to use to describe the conflicting interpretations of Catholic social teaching that claim to be reading the "signs of the times." Witness the recent response to Cardinal Ratzinger by Juan Luis Segundo. In his *Theology and the Church: A Response to Cardinal Ratzinger and a Warning to the Whole Church*, Segundo puts it quite bluntly: either Ratzinger or he is right about "reading the signs of the times." But only one of them can be right.[5] Not only is it appropriate to ask how there can be so many different interpretations of a single teaching, but also what kind of a teaching is it that can be understood in so many different ways? Quite bluntly, what good is such a teaching?[6]

The introduction of reading the "signs of the times" in the light of the Gospel as the principle for understanding the relationship between Christianity and civil society is itself a sign of a hermeneutical crisis, both theological and political.

In order to understand the breadth and depth of this crisis, I think it is helpful to re-examine Pope Pius XI's *Quadragesimo Anno*. That encyclical is important, not only because of its review of and development of *Rerum Novarum*, but also because Pope Pius XI provides a second order or hermeneutical reflection upon Pope Leo XIII's message. Pope Pius steps back, as it were, from the content of *Rerum Novarum*. He attempts to make sense of the way in which Pope Leo had made sense of the social problems of his own time. What was Pope Leo doing when he taught what he taught? Was he simply repeating the teaching of St. Thomas Aquinas? Was he deviating from that teaching? Was he providing a coherent message consistently based on a set of principles? Or was *Rerum Novarum* simply an exercise in patchwork? In response, Pope Pius tells us that in *Rerum Novarum* he finds and he himself continues in *Quadragesimo Anno* what he calls a teaching about "social justice" for the modern era, a "new social philosophy."[7]

Like *Pacem in Terris*, *Quadragesimo Anno* is famous for introducing a term ("social justice") without ever fully explaining it. However, on this point there are differences between the two encyclicals. In *Pacem in Terris* Pope John introduces a phrase taken from a saying attributed to Jesus in the Gospel of Matthew. In *Quadragesimo Anno* Pope Pius introduces a term coined by a nineteenth century Italian philosopher.[8] Pope John never defines what he means by reading the "signs of the times." Unlike Pius, John never steps back to offer a second order or hermeneutical explanation. Perhaps John thought that the Scriptural citation and his actual employment of this principle in *Pacem in Terris* would be sufficient. Likewise, Pope Pius XI never provides us with a full definition of "social justice." Consequently, up to the present day the term has spun a history as ambiguous as that of "reading the signs of the times." However, at least Pope Pius hinted at what he meant. In certain passages of *Quadragesimo Anno* the terms "social justice" and the "common good" are spoken of together and in some instances even equated.[9]

I agree with those who have argued that by "social justice" Pope Pius is referring to Saint Thomas Aquinas' notion of legal or general justice, a notion misunderstood as much today as at the time in which Pope Pius wrote.[10] Many have understood general or legal justice to mean a narrow or legalistic devotion to the laws of one's society. This interpretation does not recognize Thomas' deeper and wider notion of devotion to the common good. It was precisely to avoid this misunderstanding that Pope Pius adopted the term "social justice."[11]

Moreover, there seems to be a deeper significance to Pius' choice. Anyone who has studied political philosophers like Aristotle, Plato, Thomas Aquinas, Marsilius of Padua, and others immediately recognizes that the term "social justice" is odd. Doesn't justice already imply "social"? Is there a "nonsocial" justice? In fact, isn't justice the only social virtue, strictly speaking? Isn't it the virtue that directs all the other virtues outward to the common good of society?[12]

Pope Pius' use of "social justice" instead of legal or general justice suggests to me that he was trying to respond to the crisis of modern political understanding made visible by the social, political, and economic ills of the late nineteenth and early twentieth centuries. More specifically and in terms of the history of political understanding, following the rejection of the classical natural law teaching by Machiavelli, Hobbes and Locke in favor of the modern natural right theory, Rousseau's critique of the "bourgeois" modern rights theory signaled the crisis of any political or social teaching that drew its guidance from nature, as a result of Rousseau's shift from the classical approach to politics within the framework of the duality of body and soul to his own approach within his newly defined duality of nature and history. While for Thomas Aquinas it went without saying that humans are social by nature, for Hobbes and Locke the very opposite view became the starting point. But in Rousseau's view, no one had ever really uncovered the full truth about human nature until, of course, he did in his *Discourse on the Origins of Inequality*. Rousseau teaches us that the fundamental problem is society as such; that human and social are in principle contradictory and can be reconciled only to the extent that human nature can be transformed by history.[13] It was as a response to this first serious modern hermeneutical crisis, manifested in the problems of the late nineteenth and early twentieth century, that I understand Pope Pius' use of the term "social justice."

This may be a correct interpretation of Pope Pius' thinking; or maybe it is simply a "kinder, gentler" approach to *Quadragesimo Anno*;

even wishful thinking on my part. In any case, my point in re-examining this encyclical is made clear. Even if my interpretation of Pope Pius' intention is correct, Pope Pius did not make his intention clear. Even if he did understand the hermeneutical crisis of modern social thought, he did not make this clear to the many readers of *Quadragesimo Anno* whose minds were already and unwittingly formed in the "seminary" of Rousseau's thought. Thus, and ironically, if Pope Pius resorted to the term "social justice" in the effort to respond to the modern hermeneutical crisis in social and political thinking, it only led to a crisis in Catholic social thinking itself. Indeed although Rousseau never used the term "social justice," he could easily have used it to summarize the political transformation of human nature that he proposed, what one scholar has called Rousseau's doctrine of transubstantiation.[14] It could equally be used to summarize Immanuel Kant's famous statement: "the problem of organizing a state, however hard it may seem, can be solved even for a race of devils, if only they are intelligent."[15] Today, the word is in the spontaneous vocabulary, not only of every member of every justice and peace committee of every parish and diocese, but even of presidential candidates, housewives, and high school students of every race, color, and creed; and for the most part, the term is used by Catholics and non-Catholics alike in the way that Rousseau and Kant would have meant it.

In short, Pope Pius unwittingly opened the door of Catholic social teaching to modern historical consciousness, rooted ultimately in the political philosophy of Rousseau. This crisis in Catholic social thinking came to full blossom in Pope John's "reading the signs of the times," a phrase equally appropriate to describe Rousseau's political philosophy.

How and why, only after several centuries of dormancy, did Matthew 16:3 pop out at Pope John from the pages of Scripture? How and why could he presume that the meaning of Jesus' words was so clear? How and why could Pope John so easily take the phrase, "reading the signs of the times," to be a principle for understanding social and political things? Apparently, Saint John Chrysostom did not understand these words in the same way at all:

> What then saith He to all this? "Ye can discern the face of the sky, but can ye not discern the signs of the times?"

> See His meekness and moderation. For not even as before did He refuse merely, and say, "There shall none be given them." But He

states also the cause why He gives it not, even though they were not asking for that information.

What then was the cause? "Much as in the sky," saith He, "one thing is a sign of a storm, another of fair weather, and no one when he saw the sign of foul weather would seek for a calm, neither in calm and fair weather for a storm; so should you reckon with regard to Me also. For this present time of My Coming is different from that which is to come. Now there is need of these signs which are on earth, but those in Heaven are stored up against that time. Now as a Physician am I come; then I shall be here as a Judge; now to seek that which is gone astray, then to demand an account. Therefore in a hidden manner am I come, but then with much publicity, folding up the heaven, hiding the sun, not suffering the moon to give her light. Then the 'very powers of the heavens shall be shaken,' and the manifestation of My Coming shall imitate lightning that appears at once to all. But not now is the time for these signs; for I am come to die, and to suffer all extremities."[16]

Clearly Saint John Chrysostom understands the "signs of the times" at issue to refer only to the first coming of Christ, and not to the second coming. According to Chrysostom, the signs associated with the second coming of Christ, or with the final coming of God's Kingdom, are emphatically nonearthly, much less nonsocial.

Interestingly enough, during the debates preceding the publication of *Gaudium et Spes*, a number of participants objected to the meaning given by that document (the same meaning given by Pope John) to "reading the signs of the times" and emphasized, like Chrysostom, that in Scripture the phrase has an exclusively Christological meaning. In response to this objection, in the final draft of *Gaudium et Spes* the reference to Matthew 16:3 was omitted; but the phrase was retained![17]

How is this to be interpreted? Does this mean that the Council is admitting that the meaning given to "reading the signs of the times" in *Gaudium et Spes* does not have a basis in Scripture? If "reading the signs of the times" does not have a basis in Scripture, then what is its basis? What meaning are we to give to this phrase once it is no longer claimed that the signs in question are the ones to which Jesus refers in Matthew 16:3? How does one read the signs of the times if, contrary to what Pope John suggested in his formal convocation to the Council, the "advice of Jesus" on this matter is not applicable?

Since the introduction of "reading the signs of the times" by Pope John, this phrase has appeared in several official documents, beginning with *Gaudium et Spes*. In paragraph 11 of this document, the Council Fathers described it as "deciphering authentic signs of God's presence and purpose in the happiness, needs, and desires in which this people (the church) has a part along with other men of our age." In paragraph 44, it is called an "accommodated preaching of the revealed Word." Moreover, "reading the signs of the times" is said to be the task of the entire people of God. Yet in the same document the church's task is described as "imparting knowledge of the divine and natural law."[18]

By reading these passages alone, one is confronted with an ambiguity. On the one hand, "reading the signs of the times" is said to involve the discernment of the way in which God is at work in history. The implication is that there is something intelligible in history — a truth that one can perceive. Moreover, the suggestion is that there is the possibility of access to specific knowledge of the way in which God is at work in history. On the other hand, imparting the knowledge of the divine and natural law would suggest that "reading the signs of the times" involves examining the events and features that characterize a given era and applying the divine and natural law to these events and features. In this case, there is no implication that there is a way of perceiving how God is at work in history.

Both of these interpretations of "reading the signs of the times" appear to have a basis in *Gaudium et Spes* and in other documents published since then. Both interpretations suggest that "reading the signs of the times" is an inductive approach to the relationship between Christianity and civil society. However, the difference between these two interpretations should not be overlooked. The former proposes the discerning of truth *in history; the latter, discerning history in the light of the truth*. This second approach is no different from the attempt of Pope Pius XI to address the social ills of his day in the light of the teaching of Saint Thomas Aquinas.

In his reflections on the occasion of the tenth anniversary of *Pacem in Terris* in 1973, Cardinal Maurice Roy of the Pontifical Commission on Justice and Peace claimed that the full explanation of "reading the signs of the times" is provided by Pope Paul VI.[19] Cardinal Roy refers to Pope Paul's calling it a "theological interpretation of contemporary history" and "not merely a matter of posthumous reading of the past," and an effort to "discover in time, signs . . . indications of a relationship with the Kingdom of God."[20] Here we have the first of the two possible interpretations described a moment ago.

According to Cardinal Roy, it is only in *Octogesima Adveniens* that Pope Paul finally completes the explanation.[21] In that document, the Cardinal points out, we learn that every man must discern *between events* and the *moral good* they *know* through their *consciences*. Moreover, and virtually in the same breath, the Cardinal points to the document's teaching that Christians have something specific to say and do in interpreting and accomplishing history. Theirs is the task of discovering "correspondences" or "resemblances" between the movement of history and the Kingdom of God.[22]

Not only do I not find in *Octogesima Adveniens* the clarity about "reading the signs of the times" that Cardinal Roy claims is there (there is as much a difference between "discovering 'resemblances' between the movement of history and the Kingdom of God" and "discerning between events and the moral good they know through their consciences" as there is between discovering truth in history and reading history in the light of the truth); it seems to me that the thoughtful reader of *Octogesima Adveniens* must reasonably suspect, if not conclude, that Paul VI has led the entire business of "reading the signs of the times" (in the sense of reading truth *in* history) to the end of a dead-end road:

> In the face of such widely varying situations it is difficult for us to utter a *unified message* and to put forward a solution which has *universal validity*. Such is not our ambition, nor is it our mission. . . . It is up to the Christian communities to analyze with objectivity the situation which is proper to their own country, to shed on it the light of the Gospel's unalterable words and to draw principles of reflection, norms of judgment, and directives for action from the *social teaching* of the Church. This *social teaching* has been worked out in the course of history . . . [emphasis added].[23]

So there is no unified message with universal validity; but there is a social teaching of the church that has been worked out in the course of history. Is this to suggest that the social teaching of the church is not a message that has universal validity? Are we to conclude that the church's social teaching is, as Clodovis Boff puts it, "a box of spare parts"?[24] Did Pope Pius XI think that his message in *Quadragesimo Anno* was not universally valid? If Pius thought that such a message was not possible, there would have been no "social teaching of the church" for Pope Paul to refer to.

It seems that Pope Paul was aware of this problem. In other sections of *Octogesima Adveniens* he says that ". . . the church has a specific message to proclaim" and ". . . man nevertheless needs to have light shed upon his future . . . by *permanent eternal truths.*"[25]

It is ironic that *Octogesima Adveniens* is the letter in which Pope Paul teaches that the "Christian faith is above and is sometimes opposed to the ideologies . . . ";[26] for ideological imprisonment is precisely what "reading the signs of the times" (in the sense of discerning truth in history) cannot in principle overcome.

Earlier I suggested that the introduction of "reading the signs of the times" into official Catholic social teaching is itself a sign of a hermeneutical crisis of a political and theological nature. The political nature of the crisis lies in the fact that "reading the signs of the times" is not and cannot be an adequate principle for understanding social and political things. It adds no light on political things. It begs the question of hermeneutics. It has no backbone of its own; it has no content; it is hollow. It is a free ride for any ideology that wants a ride, whether its proponent is Paulo Evaristo Cardinal Arns of Sao Paulo, who reads the signs of God's Kingdom in Fidel Castro's atheistic and socialist police state,[27] or Bishop Eusebius of Caesarea, who read the signs of the same Kingdom in the reign of Emperor Constantine.[28]

Rousseau consciously introduced the shift from reading history in the light of the truth to reading the truth in history or from nonhistoricism to historicism. He knew what he was choosing; he knew what he was rejecting. In contrast, that both approaches to political things are to be found in the recent literature of Catholic social teaching manifests a serious neglect of the history of political understanding. Moreover, while Rousseau clearly understood that his reformulation of the human political problem implies, not only the rejection of the classical natural law and the modern natural right teaching, but also the redefinition of political thinking itself, recent Catholic social teaching presumes that the task of "reading the signs of the times" is not only self-evident but also a task that all members of the church can and must readily do, as if political prudence were within the reach of the many. But the result has been that, instead of the people of God, the "readers" of the signs of the times have been Francis Bacon, Thomas Hobbes, John Locke, Rousseau, quite uneasily along with St. Augustine and St. Thomas Aquinas.

More than anything else, "reading the signs of the times" is unwittingly but inevitably informed by inconsistent and even contradictory anthropological and political premises. Parts of *Mater et Magistra* and *Gaudium et Spes* would harmonize quite nicely with Francis Bacon's intentions in his *New Atlantis*; other parts of these documents, with St. Augustine's *City of God*. Hobbes' and Locke's natural right teaching finds a home in *Pacem in Terris*; but so does Thomas Aquinas' natural law doctrine.[29] "Reading the signs of the times," and even "in the light of the Gospel" has yielded only a cacophany of rhetoric, like the political rhetoric reviewed by Aristotle in the *Politics*. However, following his review, Aristotle is led to a conclusion that seems the only appropriate one for Catholic social teaching: "This must be made clear, since this too raises a difficulty, and calls for political philosophy."[30]

Earlier, I mentioned Eusebius of Caesarea and Paulo Evaristo Cardinal Arns in the same breath; and I did so by design. Their political intentions are quite different, but their theological premises are identical. Perhaps the best way to introduce the explanation of the meaning and significance of this theological premise is by reviewing M. D. Chenu's description of the different kinds of signs. He lists three: *natural* (proceeding from the nature of things in their immediate and spontaneous givenness); *conventional* (proceeding from human initiative and with recourse to a gesture, a word, or a figure with a view to communicating with other humans); and *historical* (an "event" accomplished by humans, and which, beyond its own immediate content, has the value of expressing another reality). As an example of a historical sign, Chenu refers to the taking of the Bastille in 1789.[31]

It is interesting to note, and I presume that Chenu noted, that Saint Augustine wrote a little book about signs. In Book 2 of his *De Doctrina Christina*, Augustine also speaks of natural and conventional signs, but not of historical signs. In fact, he defines history in the traditional or nonhistoricist terms of the accurate and useful narration of past events; and he contrasts it to the pseudo-art of soothsaying that claims to tell us what ought to be done.[32]

From Augustine's vantage point, it would appear that Pope Paul VI's claim that "reading the signs of the times" is "not merely a posthumous reading of the past" but an effort to "discover in time signs... of a relationship with the Kingdom of God" is a description of the historical soothsaying that *De Doctrina Christiana* rejects. The key theological reason for Augustine's rejection of this kind of "reading" is developed in the later books of the *City of God*. Augustine wrote these later books precisely to refute the theological premise of Eusebius of Caesarea, championed by Orosius in his *Seven Books of History Against the Pagans* at the time of Augustine. Basically, Augustine argues that while Christians do believe that God is present and active in guiding history to its divinely established end, there is no way of knowing exactly how God is bringing this about. The design of God's Providence in history remains completely cloaked in mystery for believers as well as nonbelievers. Even with the presence and activity of God in history, history itself still appears as a succession of ups and downs, or as a teacher of mine once put it, one damn thing after another. To think otherwise would jeopardize the divine causality of the coming of God's Kingdom and to risk replacing the Holy Spirit with the human spirit.[33]

The theological nature of the present hermeneutical crisis of Catholic social teaching is manifested in the presence, side by side with one another at times, of both the Eusebian or Orosian and the Augustinian views of history in various recent ecclesiastical documents. So if *Gaudium et Spes* calls for and actually employs the principle of "reading the signs of the times in the light of the Gospel," it also insists that earthly progress must be carefully distinguished from the growth of God's Kingdom.[34] The point is that one cannot have it both ways; and this is the valuable and significant point made by Segundo in his response to Cardinal Ratzinger that I referred to previously. Segundo is absolutely right in saying that he and Ratzinger cannot both be correct. And if we take our bearings from Augustine, it follows that Segundo is wrong and Ratzinger is right.

In the encyclicals and letters of Pope John Paul II and in the recent instructions on liberation theology by Cardinal Ratzinger, a new theme has emerged, and the new theme appears to subvert the possibility that "reading the signs of the times" could ever mean reading the truth in history. When he addressed the Latin American bishops at Puebla in 1979, Pope John Paul II emphasized, not "reading the signs of the times," but "the truth:" the truth about humanity, about Christ, and about the church; a truth to which we have access, not by the "reading of the signs of the times" by the whole people of God, but through the teaching magisterium of the church.[35]

However, the connection between "the truth" and "reading the signs of the times" has not yet been made entirely clear in official church documents. For example, even as Cardinal Ratzinger, in his recent instructions of liberation theology, continues Pope John Paul's theme of the "truth about humanity, about Christ, and about the church," in the same documents are to be found several references to the signs of the times without any clear indication that these signs are to be understood as features of modern society rather than as manifestations of the presence and activity of God's Kingdom in history.[36]

The significance of the social teaching of Pope John Paul II is that it has apparently unwittingly undone what Pope John and Vatican II unwittingly did. Pope John Paul has introduced the possibility of eliminating the historicist and Eusebian approach of reading truth *in* history in favor of reading history in the light of the truth. However, the latter approach, equally the approach of Pope Pius XI, does not excuse the church from the discipline that would have spared us from this hermeneutical crisis in the first place and will be necessary ultimately to resolve it. Even if, as in the case of Pope Pius XI or even Pope John Paul himself, one is clear about *what* one is doing when one reads history in the light of the truth, this does not necessarily mean that one knows *how* to do it. Meaning well must be supplemented by meaning correctly; and with a view to the correct understanding of politics and the problems of civil society, there is no substitute for the discipline of political philosophy. The cost of neglecting this discipline is currently being paid in three ways: 1) the demise of the fundamentally spiritual and transpolitical character of Catholic social teaching; 2) the blurring, if not the forfeiture, of Catholicism's principled rejection of the Machiavellian redefinition of politics; 3) the failure to preserve in modern times the classical view of the indispensable unity of morality and politics.

In our time the road back to the recovery of political philosophy begins with the study of the history of political philosophy.[37] The aim of such a study is to retrieve the wider and deeper framework of political understanding and to transcend the narrow confines of the tension between egalitarianism and technocracy, the confines in which Catholic social teaching and its interpreters appear to be imprisoned.

Perhaps one could say that this is one of the "signs of the time." By which, of course, I mean: "And that's the way it is."

NOTES

1. *Humanae Salutis* (December, 1961).
2. *Pacem in Terris*, nn.39-45, 75-79, 126-129, 142-145.
3. See *Instruction on Certain Aspects of the "Theology of Liberation"*, 12; *Instruction on Christian Freedom and Liberation*, 72.
4. Gustavo Gutierrez, *A Theology of Liberation* (New York, 1988), n.29:180. See also his new Introduction, xx.
5. Juan Luis Segundo, *Theology and the Church: A Response to Cardinal Ratzinger and a Warning to the Whole Church* (San Francisco, 1987), 14, 65-66.
6. See Philip Berryman, *Liberation Theology* (Oak Park, Ill., 1987), 199-200.
7. For references to "social justice" see *Quadragesimo Anno*, 59, 71, 74, 88, 101, 110, 126. Pope Pius calls Pope Leo's teaching a "new social philosophy" in n.14. See also nn.9-11, 17-21, 27-28, 39, 76, 96, 97, 110, 141, 147.
8. Taparelli d'Azeglio introduced the term "social justice" in a work of his that appeared in 1840. See the explanation by Ernest L. Fortin, "Natural Law and Social Justice," *The American Journal of Jurisprudence*, vol. 30 (1985):13-14.
9. See *Quadragesimo Anno*, nn.18, 101, 110.
10. See J. Brian Benestad, "The Catholic Concept of Social Justice", *Communio: International Catholic Review* 11, 4 (1984): 364-381.

    The view that by "social justice" Pope Pius XI is referring to the Thomistic notion of general or legal justice receives additional support from Pope Pius' two references to "social justice and social charity." (See *Quadragesimo Anno*, nn.88, 126.) These two references echo a point made by Thomas Aquinas about justice and charity being, each in its own way, "general" virtues: " . . . a thing is said to be general according to its efficacy; thus a universal cause is general in relation to all its effects; the sun, for instance, in relation to all bodies that are illumined or transmuted by its power; and in this sense there is no need for that which is general to be essentially the same as those things in relation to which it is general, since cause and effect are not essentially the same. Now, it is in the latter sense that, according to what has been said, *legal justice* is said to be a *general virtue*, inasmuch, to wit, as it directs the acts of the other virtues to its own end, and this is to move all the other virtues by its command; for just as *charity* may be called a *general virtue* insofar as it directs the acts of all the virtues to the divine good, so too is legal justice insofar as it directs the acts of all the virtues to the common good."
11. See Benestad.
12. See Fortin, "Natural Law," 14-15.
13. See Strauss, *Natural Right and History* (Chicago, 1953), 252-294; Bloom, "The Education of Democratic Man: *Emile*," *Daedalus* vol. 107, no. 3 Summer, 1978:135-154.
14. Bloom, 136. The phrase does not appear in this text. In one of his famous

impromptu comments, however, Bloom interjected the phrase while delivering this lecture at Harvard University on 14 March 1977.

15. Kant, *Perpetual Peace*, First Supplement, in Immanuel Kant, *On History*, ed. L. W. Beck (Indianapolis, 1963), 111-112.

16. *The Homilies of Saint John Chrysostom on Matthew*, pt. 2 (Oxford, 1844), 721.

17. See the review of this debate in M. D. Chenu, "Les signes des temps," in *L'eglise dans le monde de ce temps* ed. Yves Congar, vol. 2 (Paris: Editions de Cerf, 1967), 208-209.

18. *Gaudium et Spes*, n.89.

19. See "Reflections by Cardinal Maurice Roy on the Occasion of the Tenth Anniversary of the Encyclical 'Pacem in Terris' of Pope John XXIII," in *The Gospel of Justice and Peace* ed. Joseph Gremillion (New York, 1970), 562.

20. *Ibid.*, 561.

21. *Ibid.*, 562.

22. *Ibid.*

23. *Octogesima Adveniens*, n.4.

24. Clodovis Boff, "The Social Teaching of the Church and the Theology of Liberation: Opposing Social Practices?" *Christian Ethics: Uniformity, Universality, Pluralism* ed. Jacques Pohier and Dietmar Mieth (New York, 1981), 19.

25. *Octogesima Adveniens*, n.7.

26. *Ibid.*, n.27.

27. See *The New York Times*, Sunday, 5 February 1989, 20.

28. See Eusebius, *Laus Constantini*, I,6; III, 5-6 *et passim*; E. Cranz, "Kingdom and Polity in Eusebius of Caesarea," *Harvard Theological Review*, 45 (1952):47-66.

29. See Ernest L. Fortin, "The Trouble with Catholic Social Thought," in *Boston College Magazine* (Summer, 1988):37-42.

30. Aristotle, *Politics*, bk. 3, 1282b:20-25.

31. Chenu, "Les signes des temps," *Nouvelle Révue Théologique*, 87 (1965):32.

32. *De Doctrina Christiana*, II.28:44.

33. See Ernest L. Fortin, "Augustine's *City of God* and the Modern Historical Consciousness," *The Review of Politics*, vol. 41, no. 3 (July, 1979):323-343.

34. *Gaudium et Spes*, nn.4, 11, 22.4, 39.1.

35. See *The Pope Speaks*, 24, no. 1 (Spring, 1979):49-67.

36. For example, see *Instruction on Certain Aspects of the "Theology of Liberation"*, sec. I and II; sec. V, nn.4, 8; sec. X. Also, in *Instruction on Christian Freedom and Liberation*, in his Introduction, Cardinal Ratzinger refers to the awareness of man's freedom and dignity as one of the "major characteristics of our time" and not one of the "signs of the times." Moreover, it is clear in this second document that this major characteristic is to be understood in the light of "the truth." However, in the same document, note chap. 1, sec. 1, n.5.

37. See Leo Strauss, *The Political Philosophy of Hobbes*, trans. Elsa M. Sinclair (Chicago, 1952), xix; *idem*, "On Collingwood's Philosophy of History," *Review of Metaphysics*, 5 (June, 1952):585.

THE HARMONY OF
FAITH AND REASON:
HEGEL AND LONERGAN ON THE
ARGUMENTS FOR
THE EXISTENCE OF GOD
Anthony M. Matteo

The goal of this Centennial Symposium is to celebrate the rich history and tradition of Catholic higher education. At its best, Catholic education has stayed firmly rooted to a belief in the harmony and complementarity of faith and reason. One of the boldest and most eloquent products of this belief is the work of St. Thomas Aquinas. For the Angelic Doctor both faith and reason were pathways to God: "the ultimate end of the whole man, and of all his operations and desires, is to know the first truth, which is God."[1]

Aquinas is here enunciating the fundamental principle that inspired his daring thirteenth-century attempt to integrate what he considered the human wisdom of Aristotle and divine wisdom contained in the Catholic tradition. Like the "Philosopher," Aquinas could say that all human beings by their very nature desire to know. Furthermore, Aquinas insisted, this desire is unlimited! Although he teaches that the proper object of the human intellect in this earthly, embodied state is the abstracted essence of material things (*quidditas abstracta rerum materialium*), this does not represent, in his view, the total object of the intellect *per se*. In Aquinas' words:

> Now the intellect regards its object under the common aspect of being, since the possible intellect is that which becomes all things.

Now the first thing conceived by the intellect is being, because everything is knowable only insofar as it is in act.... Hence, being is the proper object of the intellect and it is that which is primarily intelligible, as sound is that which is primarily audible.[2]

Thus, for Aquinas, the primary movement of the intellect is toward being as such. The limitations of our senses, stemming from our embodied state, do not destroy the intellect's fundamental orientation toward being in general. To be sure, Aquinas is not here postulating some direct, suprasensible intuition of nonmaterial or transcendent being. However, the human intellect, which must begin with the data of sense experience, can proceed beyond the sensible-material realm to an indirect or analogical knowledge of transcendent realities insofar as they are manifested in material things. It is precisely the active quality of the intellect which makes this analogical procession beyond material being possible.

According to Aristotelian-Thomistic epistemology, knowledge is not achieved by a merely passive reception of information by the intellect. The active intellect (*intellectus agens*) is driven by an unrestricted desire to know which impels it to seek the intelligible element within sense images (*phantasmata*). This dynamic desire to know is not satisfied with comprehending the individual essences of material objects but strives to coordinate them in an ever expanding and unified vision that has nothing less than the totality of being or, if you will, the absolute as its ultimate *terminus ad quem*.

It is one of the major contributions of modern Transcendental Thomism to have retrieved the significance of the "dynamic" orientation of the intellect at the heart of Aquinas' theory of knowledge. The Belgian Jesuit philosopher, Joseph Maréchal affirms that in Thomistic terms the dynamic form or nature of the active intellect "is a form whose constructive capacity cannot be exhausted by a finite datum... and which, therefore, cannot find expression except in the very unlimited nature of being as such."[3] Thus the fundamental orientation of the intellect is not toward individual beings but toward being itself. This primal drive is the source of our intellectual restlessness, our need to proceed beyond partial and tentative insights in search of ever more comprehensive explanations. It is the root of that wonder and curiosity that are the distinguishing hallmarks of the species *homo sapiens*. Echoing Maréchal on this issue, Bernard Lonergan writes:

Prior to conception and to judgment, there is the dynamic orientation of intelligent and rational consciousness with its unrestricted object. This orientation is man's capacity to raise questions and thereby to generate knowledge . . . . As its objective is unrestricted, so it regards not only single compounds of essence and existence but also the universe, totality, infinity.[4]

It is a fundamental contention of Transcendental Thomists that this primal dynamism of the intellect toward the totality of being or the absolute is implicitly present in every human attempt to make sense out of reality. This they take to be the import of Aquinas' dictum: "All knowing things implicitly know God in everything they know."[5] Thus they contend that the affirmation of God's existence is linked with a proper understanding of the cognitional process by which we come to know anything at all. It is not that we can "prove" God's existence in the way, say, we might someday establish the existence of intelligent life on other planets, or in the way twentieth century physicists go about establishing the existence of subatomic particles. Rather the necessity of affirming God's existence emerges as a result of our reflecting on the "activity" of thinking that goes into any attempt at proof whatsoever.

When Aquinas' epistemology is understood in this way, we can more readily understand why he shows no fear in integrating faith and reason: God is the end toward which both are striving. Theology has nothing to fear from a philosophy that understands as its mission the quest for the absolute. In turn, theology's goal is to complete, not supplant, the rational, philosophical search for God.

This understanding of Aquinas' epistemology also aids us in properly evaluating his natural theology and the arguments for the existence of God (the famous *Quinque Viae*) that form its centerpiece. Each of these arguments reveals the mind's natural tendency to ascend toward God, the infinite and necessary being, as the sole, sufficient explanation of some finite and contingent aspect of our experience. They all give explicit expression to the implicit search for total intelligibility that underlies all cognition. Our pure desire to know can never rest satisfied in accepting the brute "givenness" of our finite, empirical experience. Its ultimate aim is to understand everything about everything. And just as every play or move in a game is subordinated to, and derives its meaning from, the ultimate aim of victory, so every cognitive act must be seen against our ultimate intellectual drive for total comprehension. As Joseph Donceel has affirmed:

> We would have no concepts, no ideas, we would be unable to think and to speak, we would have neither language nor civilization, we would be confined to the animal level of knowing, were it not for the fact that whatever we know is known by us against the Infinite Horizon of Being, of God. Hence the intending of this horizon, the (implicit) affirmation of God, is the a priori condition of the possibility of all human thought and action. It is not only psychologically necessary for humans to affirm God's existence... it is also logically necessary.[6]

It is not that we can conceptually capture God as part of our content of consciousness. As infinite being, God transcends the limited categories of genus and species by which we catalogue and comprehend the finite realities of our experience. In fact, when we seek to understand the finite entities that surround us, we are not immediately aware of God in an explicit fashion as the ultimate end of our intellectual striving. Indeed we can spend a lifetime trying to fathom the myriad finite objects that enter our experience without ever seriously scrutinizing the very activity by which "understanding" comes about. However, if we do reflect on this activity or what Lonergan calls the "cognitional" process by which we come to know anything at all, we discover that its ultimate aim—the root underlying motivation of all its particular operations — is the continual drive for total intelligibility, i.e., to understand everything about everything. What drives us intellectually—what accounts for our distinctively human sense of wonder and insatiable cognitive curiosity — is the search for the "absolute" perspective (*visio sub specie aeternitatis*). As a result, no finite or limited grasp of any aspect of the universe can still our longing for more and more comprehensive vistas. In sum, when we properly understand ourselves as "knowers," we see that our primal intellectual orientation toward absolute being gives rise to and dominates the process by which we come to know finite things. We recognize these things as "finite" and transform them into objects of our knowledge because of our pre-apprehension (which further reflection makes explicit) that the being that they possess does not embody the totality of being toward which we are tending; they represent an analogous and partial expression of that fullness of being which alone can satiate our pure desire to know. As J. Defever so delightfully puts it: "It is because we know implicitly what God is that we know what things are, and not the other way around."[7]

Commenting on Aquinas' arguments for the existence of God, Lonergan states:

> the five ways in which Aquinas proves the existence of God are so many particular cases of the general statement that the proportionate universe is incompletely intelligible and that complete intelligibility is demanded.[8]

Furthermore, Aquinas' *Quinquae Viae* can be multiplied virtually indefinitely for "there are as many other proofs of God as there are aspects of incomplete intelligibility in the universe of proportionate being."[9] In other words, *a posteriori* proofs of the existence of God are rooted in the principle of sufficient reason that demands a "total" explanation of the proportionate or finite realm of being. Such total explanation has as its *a priori* condition of possibility the assumption that being is completely intelligible. The proofs point to the fact that the complete intelligibility of being (or all that "is") rests on the existence of an infinite, necessary being (*Causa sui*) that undergirds the finite, contingent being of our experience, for as Lonergan asserts:

> every proportionate being that exists, exists conditionally; it exists inasmuch as the conditions of its existence happen to be fulfilled; and the contingence of that happening cannot be eliminated by appealing to another happening that equally is contingent.[10]

In other words, no causal chain of finite conditions — however far-reaching and complex — for any state of affairs offers an adequate response to the human mind's quest for total explanation, for the very existence of that causal chain likewise begs to be explained. To argue that any causal chain simply "exists" as a brute unanalyzable "given" is, in effect, to claim that it is irredeemably unintelligible. This in turn implies that the drive for total explanation (i.e., the pure desire to know), that is the lifeblood of all our intellectual operations, is a vain aspiration. Hence what is at issue in the "God Question" — what is really at stake in the affirmation or non-affirmation of a necessary being which alone provides a sufficient explanation for the existence of finite being — is the very integrity of our cognitive powers as such. Not to affirm the existence of God is to negate the validity of the primal drive that inspires all human attempts to understand just when it makes its most fundamental claim.

We see this same linkage of the intelligibility of the universe and the affirmation of the existence of God (the infinite and necessary Being) in Hegel's treatment of the traditional metaphysical proofs. In Hegel's view, when these proofs are *properly* understood, they reflect the mind's (spirit's) natural elevation from the finite to the infinite, from the contingent to the necessary. In Hegel's own words:

> And what men call the proofs of God's existence are seen to be ways of describing and analyzing the inward movement of the mind . . . that thinks the data of the senses. The rise of thought beyond the world of sense, its passage from the finite to the infinite, the leap into the super-sensible which it takes when it snaps asunder the links of the chain of sense, all this transition is thought and nothing but thought. Say there must be no such passage, and you say there is to be no thinking. And in sooth, animals make no such transition. They never get further than sensation and the perception of the senses, and in consequence they have no religion.[11]

Like transcendental Thomists, Hegel denies that the finite *qua* finite can be adequately understood. As a contingent reality, it is only intelligible against the background of that which is noncontingent or necessary. In other words, the intelligibility of the finite being of the universe depends, in the form of a transcendental precondition, on the existence of a necessary Being or God. In Hegel's view, we fundamentally miss the force of the proofs if we construe them as moving from some finite or contingent aspect of our experience, say, change that is intelligible in itself to the further affirmation of the existence of the infinite or God. Finite or contingent realities are merely possible: they may or may not exist. What the proofs indicate is that the sufficient condition of the existence of the finite, what alone makes them ultimately intelligible, is the existence of the infinite. As Hegel puts it:

> Not because the contingent is, but, on the contrary, because it is non-Being, merely phenomenal, because its Being is not true reality, the absolute necessity is. This latter is its Being and Truth.[12]

Hence transcendental Thomists like Lonergan are joined with

Hegel in arguing that the necessary affirmation of God's existence is revealed when we properly attend to the "activity" of thinking, to that quest for total intelligibility and understanding that is the quintessential feature of *homo sapiens*. The desire to know that underlies and motivates all our cognitive activity is grounded in the assumption that the real is the rational or that being is intelligible. This insight dawns on us when we comprehend the universe as a seamless web of interlocking realities none of which can be fully understood in isolation from the totality. Discrete particulars remain unintelligible until we find the common bond that unites them. But the human quest for intelligibility does not cease when we have uncovered the unity of species or natural kind. We then struggle to unite species into genera and so on *ad infinitum*. Hence the innate drive for intelligibility transcends any partial and relative unification we might achieve and tends toward a total and absolute vision of the unity of being as such. As a result, no finite level of unity or intelligibility can satisfy the intellect's longing for ever greater comprehension. Thus it experiences all its achievements as limited in nature. Now we can only know a limit as "limit" by being beyond it in some way. For example, we can only identify an animal as a "horse" — that is, as a particular, limited representative member of a species — if in some way we are already aware that the essence of "horseness" (of what it is to be a horse) is wider than its concretion in this individual horse under consideration. Now the "limitedness" we experience in reference to the universe cannot be spatial or physical in character. What the proofs give utterance to is our sense of the metaphysical limitedness of the universe as such: i.e., its very existence rather than non-existence begs for an explanation in terms of some higher level of being. Hence the validity of our drive for total understanding, and likewise the validity of the separate acts of understanding form the subordinate moments of this overall drive, are inextricably linked to the existence of God as necessary being. When we view the cognitive process in this way, we can truly say that only if God "is," can we be said to understand anything at all. Thus, as Quentin Lauer affirms:

> To speak, then, of "proofs" (or of a "proof") for the existence of God is not to speak of a way of arriving at God by beginning with what is not God. It is the recognition that God is present from the beginning in all true thought, in all true knowledge. But because this very recognition requires the labor of speculative thinking, it can be said

that God is "proved" if thinking is recognized for what it is. Thinking is the ineluctable logical march of the concept to objectivity, and
the ultimate objectivity short of which thought cannot stop (and still
be thought) is the reality of God.[13]

It is clear that for both Lonergan and Hegel God is the necessary
condition for the intelligibility of the universe as a whole and for
the rational coherence of our striving to understand any of its
myriad aspects. However, one might counterargue in Kantian
fashion that on theoretical grounds we still have no justification for
affirming that God in fact exists. Kant fully admits that "God" is an
idea of reason (*Vernunft*). The drive of reason to seek the uncondi-
tioned ground of our experience leads it to postulate the idea of
God as the union in one being of all perfections. It is important to
stress that for Kant the idea of God, along with the other ideas of
reason (namely, the soul as permanent ego and the world as the
totality of causal sequences) are neither innate nor gleaned from
empirical data. They stem from the natural tendency of reason to
complete the synthesizing activity of understanding. However,
their function in the cognitive process is merely heuristic in nature:
they induce us to seek an ever expanding and more comprehensive
theoretical grasp of reality. But, since they point to realities that
transcend sense experience, and since we are not privy to direct
suprasensible intuitive insight, they only possess the status of pos-
tulates which theoretical reason can neither confirm nor deny.[14] In
essence, then, we must act "as if" the universe is intelligible in our
intellectual pursuits but we have no way of theoretically justifying
that action.

One can hear the echo of Kant's voice in the following recent
argument against the theoretical convincingness of proofs for the
existence of God rooted in the principle of sufficient reason:

one's verdict on the cogency of a theistic argument depends upon
what one already believes.... If one is deeply committed to belief in
God, then a cosmological proof will be so obvious as to be redun-
dant. One may already believe in God's necessary existence, that is,
that God's non-existence is impossible. God will be clearly seen as
the ultimate explainer of everything that is. If one does not have
that commitment, then one might rest content with believing that
the universe is, at its most fundamental level, inexplicable and refuse
to press the question — the questioning process must stop somewhere, one contends, so why not here?[15]

Clark's argument rests on the contention that one's commitment to the principle of sufficient reason is not a theoretical necessity but stems from some other optional source, say, a prior faith in the intelligibility of the universe based on an adherence to the veracity of claims made to that effect in a divinely inspired scripture. Or perhaps the assertion that "being is intelligible" just happens to resonate with one's personal view of reality in some inexplicable fashion. A similar view was put forward a number of years ago by Victor Prellar in his celebrated book on Aquinas, *Divine Science And The Science of God*.[16] Prellar correctly affirms that the principle of sufficient reason or intelligibility lies at the heart of Aquinas' epistemology and motivates his enunciation of the famous *Quinque Viae*. However he is unwilling to grant that this principle enjoys more than a psychological necessity governing the way we confront reality. "It does not follow . . . that our desire to 'see the necessity' of things is more than a psychological ideal doomed to frustration by 'the way things are.'"[17] We may, of course, decide to take the natural desire of the mind, embodied in the principle of sufficient reason, as indicative of the actual nature of reality and proceed accordingly. But Prellar warns us:

> that such a "taking" is not forced on us; it would be a *decision*. We are free to argue that our natural desire to see the necessity for the existence of things is somehow indicative of how things are, but the presupposition that no natural desire is in vain is not self-evidently true. To elevate such a hypothesis to the level of a synthetic a priori of our conceptual system seems a bit rash.[18]

Prellar concludes that Aquinas — and the same critique can be extended to Lonergan and Hegel — comes to the existence of the absolute as a logically necessary condition of our intellectual activity by the injection of a prior theological commitment into a purportedly philosophical analysis. In his view, Aquinas and like-minded thinkers *know* on the basis of revelation that the created human intellect is oriented toward its creator as its final end and fulfillment. It is this prior theological assumption that leads such thinkers to construe the essentially ambiguous activity of the intellect as necessarily revealing a teleological orientation toward an actually existing absolute being. In short, Prellar is asserting that we "may" (indeed, perhaps, "must") think of the universe "as if" it were intelligible, but that does not imply that it is so. The principle of sufficient reason on which the traditional proofs rest for their cogency turns out, in Prellar's view, to be merely a heuristic device by which we make our way in the world but carries with it no apodictic certitude as to its own validity.

In responding to this critique it is important to note that neither Hegel nor Lonergan thinks of the business of philosophizing as a detached, ahistorical enterprise. Philosophy does not suddenly rise up of a piece and stand perched above the fray of other theoretical and pretheoretical ways in which human beings seek to comprehend the reality that engulfs them. The proofs were not constructed in a spiritual vacuum: a thinker like Aquinas could not expunge his prior belief in God from his mind so that vis-à-vis the God question it would be transformed into a *tabula rasa*. Belief in God does not have to wait on the composition of philosophical proofs as a necessary condition for its emergence. Hegel quips that such a view:

> would find its parallel if we said that eating was impossible before we had acquired a knowledge of the chemical, botanical, and zoological qualities of our food; and that we must delay digestion till we had finished the study of anatomy and physiology.[19]

No one approaches the God question philosophically from an utterly neutral perspective, if by that we mean untouched by prior beliefs, born of a lifetime of experience, about the existence or non-existence of God. Psychologically our beliefs about God are intimately intertwined with the self-definitions that give meaning to our lives. This is equally as true of atheists and agnostics as it is of theists. But a "critical" thinker will not give absolute priority to beliefs emanating from the will to meaning; a little reflection clearly illustrates that illusions can be powerful sources of meaning for human beings, often with devastating consequences. Hence these beliefs must be tested in the light of the pure desire to know whose sole goal is greater and greater insight into the truth. For the believers who formulate philosophical proofs, they represent exercises in "faith seeking understanding" (*fides quaerens intellectum*): i.e., assorted demonstrations that their religious belief is in accord with the pure desire to know and, hence, authentically rational, not illusory. The proofs reveal that the elevation of the mind to God expressed in pretheoretical ways (myth, ritual, art) exists in a complementary relationship with the theoretical search for truth. In fact they represent two sides of the same coin. For non-believers the proofs lay down the challenge of theoretically scrutinizing their "disbelief" to discover whether it embodies an obedience to, or an evasion of, the cognitional imperatives: be attentive, intelligent, reasonable and responsible. As Hegel comments on the issue, the proofs are an attempt to see:

> if thought, which in the process of reasoning proceeds in a formal and methodical way, rightly conceives of and expresses the course followed in the elevation of the soul to God.... Conversely ... we have to find out whether those thoughts and the connection between them can be shown to be justified, and have their reality proved, by an examination of the thoughts in themselves, for it is only in this way that the elevation of the soul to God really ceases to be a supposition, and the unstable element in any right conception of it disappears.[20]

Thus antecedent belief or disbelief does not predetermine one's response to the proofs as both Clark and Prellar contend. For both believer and nonbeliever it is a question of confronting their prior positions with the maximal level of openness and honesty that the pure desire to know demands. What, then, of their second contention: that there is no logical necessity to adhere to the principle of sufficient reason? This claim rests on the assumption that some aspect of "being" may in principle be unintelligible. Furthermore, since we do not now comprehend the totality of being (the universe in all its complexities), we cannot a priori discount the possibility that it is per se unintelligible. Let us submit this line of thought to further scrutiny.

Hegel proclaims that the "real" and the "rational" are coterminous. Hence that which is irrational or unintelligible cannot exist. In like manner, Lonergan asserts:

> being is intelligible. It is neither beyond nor apart nor different from the intelligible. It is what is to be known by intelligent grasp and reasonable affirmation. It is the objective of the detached and disinterested desire to inquire intelligently and to reflect critically; and that desire is unrestricted. On the other hand, what is apart from being is nothing. If existence is mere matter of fact, it is nothing. It follows that to talk about mere matters of fact that admit no explanation is to talk about nothing.[21]

We can perhaps best grasp Hegel and Lonergan on this issue by asking ourselves what we mean by a "universe?" It can signify nothing other than an organic whole in which each individual element exists in a complex yet intimate interrelationship with all other elements. From this understanding flow two important corollaries: 1) there can be no isolated elements in the universe; 2) no element of the universe can be completely understood unless viewed against the background of the totality. Hence there can be no mere "matters of fact" or "brute givens" if by that one means elements of the universe whose sufficient explanation is not inextricably intertwined with the evolution of the totality. Consequently one can only speak of the possible existence of elements of the universe that are in principle unintelligible if one's reckonings are beclouded by a faulty grasp of the nature of things. As David Bohm asserts, in a manner reminiscent of Hegel:

> Wholeness is what is real and . . . fragmentation is the response of this whole to man's action, guided by illusory perception, which is shaped by fragmentary thought. . . . So what is needed is for man to give attention to his habit of fragmentary thought, to be aware of it, and thus bring it to an end.[22]

However can we still sensibly view the universe as such as a mere matter of fact, i.e., as a reality whose existence rather than non-existence simply defies explanation? Here we must be clear on the distinction between finite and infinite being or what Lonergan calls proportionate and transcendent being. The mark of finite or proportionate being is that its existence is merely "contingent" or "possible." That which is contingent or possible can never *on its own* become actual. To assert that it can bespeaks a fundamental misunderstanding of the very meaning of contingency and possibility. It is to claim that the contingent is the necessary and that the possible is the actual. In short, the series of finite elements that make up the universe cannot be the ground or sufficient condition of its being or existence. Hence to speak of the finite without simultaneously recognizing the existence of the infinite as its necessary correlate or pre-condition is to talk literal nonsense.

To what, then, can we attribute the persistence of this kind of talk? As in others of investigation, so in this one, moral and psychological factors emanating from the will to meaning can encumber the pure desire to know and obscure the clarity of our analysis. However it would appear that both Lonergan and Hegel see the fundamental difficulty as rooted in an inadequate appraisal of "thinking" itself or cognitional process. The remedy lies in intellectual conversion: an authentic self-appropriation of what our "thinking" and "knowing" actually are. In Lonergan's view, we achieve knowledge by being attentive, intelligent, and reasonable in our perceptual and intellectual operations. it is not merely a matter of sensing or intuiting reality in some unmediated fashion. Instead knowing is the result of thinking, namely, that ongoing process of asking questions, gaining insights, making judgments and, when necessary, effecting revisions, whose end is the achievement of ever more comprehensive answers. At the heart of the questioning process itself is the question of God, the question of the one, necessary being which alone provides an ultimate explanation for the multiple, contingent beings that we indubitably experience. The proofs indicate that the value and validity of the questioning process, which is rooted in the assumption that the universe is in principle intelligible, depends on an affirmation of God's existence as infinite or necessary being. Furthermore, reflection reveals that one cannot question (call into doubt) the "questioning process" itself without in so doing tacitly assuming its validity and, thereby, falling into a performative contradiction. The point is that the intelligibility of being cannot be coherently doubted, and if being is ineluctably intelligible, then God exists. As Lonergan expresses the matter syllogistically: "If the real is completely intelligible, God exists. But the real is completely intelligible. Therefore, God exists."[23]

From Hegel's perspective it is vital not to divorce our abstract capacity of thought (*Verstand*), by which we define and distinguish one thing from another, from the speculative exercise of thought (*Vernunft*) "which gives due expression to the process-nature in things, as a unity of differences and contrasts."[24] If we mistakenly restrict our concept of thinking to *Verstand*, we will be deluded into granting the finite particulars of our experience an independent status and fail to realize how the existence of the finite necessarily implies the existence of the infinite. In Hegel's own words:

> The demonstration of reason [*Vernunft*] no doubt starts from something which is not God. But, as it advances, it does not leave the starting-point a mere unexplained fact, which is what it was. On the contrary it exhibits that point as derivative and called into being, and then God is seen to be primary, truly immediate and self-subsisting, with the means of derivation wrapped up and absorbed in himself.[25]

In summary then, neither Hegel nor Lonergan claims that the proofs of God's existence are necessary conditions of belief in God. The origin of belief or non-belief in each individual is enmeshed in a complex web of spiritual and psycho-social factors. Theologically one might want to speak of the prevenient grace of God enabling the individual to surmount personal and cultural obstacles to belief. However what the proofs do provide is a means for those who have achieved a theoretical impetus and criterion of all intellectual activity: the pure desire to know. They challenge non-believers by pointing to the theoretical incoherence of their position and may actualize within them at least the initial movement toward a theistic perspective on reality.

NOTES

1. *Summa Contra Gentiles* III, I, 25, 10. We are employing the translation by Vernon J. Bourke (New York: Doubleday, 1956).
2. *Summa Theologica* I, 79, 7, and I, 5, 2.
3. *Le Point de Départ de la Métaphysique* (Paris: Désclee, 1964); 119.
4. *Insight* (New York: Longmans, 1957); 370.
5. *De Veritate* 22, 2, ad 1.
6. *The Searching Mind* (Notre Dame: University of Notre Dame Press, 1979); 82.
7. As quoted in *The Searching Mind*; 125.
8. *Insight*; 678.
9. *Ibid.*
10. *Ibid.*, 654.
11. *Logic* 50.
12. "Lectures on the Proofs of the Existence of God" in *Lectures on the Philosophy of Religion* III (New York: Humanities Press, 1968); 285.
13. *Essays In Hegelian Dialectic* (New York: Fordham Press, 1977); 134-35.
14. For Kant's treatment of this matter, see the "Transcendental Dialectic" in the *Critique of Pure Reason*.
15. Kelley James Clark, "Proofs of God's Existence," JOR (69): 1, 67.
16. Princeton: Princeton University Press, 1967.
17. *Ibid.*, 171.
18. *Ibid.*, 164.
19. *Logic*, Introduction 2.
20. "Lectures," 270.
21. *Insight*; 652.
22. *Wholeness and the Implicate Order* (Boston: Routledge, 1980); 7.
23. *Insight*; 672.
24. William Wallace, "Prolegomena," in *The Logic of Hegel* (Oxford: Clarendon Press, 1874), clxxxiii.
25. *Logic*, 36.